Words of the

Real People

Words of

Alaska Native Literature
in Translation

the
Real People

Contributions by

Howard Amos

Herbert Anungazuk

Robert Drozda

Esther Arnaq Ilutsik

Deanna Paniataaq Kingston

Tom Lowenstein

Elsie Mather

Marie Meade

Vera Metcalf

Phyllis Morrow

Cathy Moses

Tadataka Nagai

Carol Tukummiq Omnik

Patricia Partnow

Alice Rearden

Willem de Reuse

Sophie Shield

Susie Silook

Edited by

Ann Fienup-Riordan and Lawrence D. Kaplan

UNIVERSITY OF ALASKA PRESS — FAIRBANKS

© 2007 University of Alaska Press
P.O. Box 756240
Fairbanks, AK 99775-6240

Library of Congress Cataloging-in-Publication Data

Words of the real people : Alaska native literature in translation / edited by Ann
Fienup-Riordan, Lawrence D. Kaplan.
   p. cm.
Includes bibliographical references and index.
ISBN 978-1-60223-004-0 (pbk. : alk. paper) — ISBN 978-1-60223-005-7 (alk. paper)
1. Eskimos—Alaska—Folklore. 2. Yupik Eskimos—Alaska—Folklore. 3. Tales—
Alaska. 4. Eskimo literature—Translations into English. I. Fienup-Riordan, Ann.
II. Kaplan, Lawrence D.
E99.E7F2465 2007
398.2089'971—dc22   2006103101

This publication was printed on paper that meets the minimum requirements for
ANSI/NISO Z39.48–1992 (Permanence of Paper).

Cover and interior design: Dixon J. Jones, Rasmuson Library Graphics

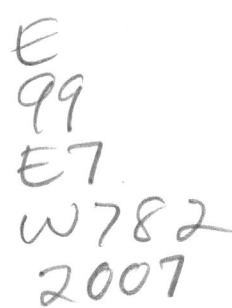

E
99
E7
W782
2007

Contents

vii   *Contributors*

xi   *Preface and Acknowledgments: Smoked Fish and Jars of Jam*

xvii   *Introduction: Yupik and Iñupiaq Literature in Translation*
Ann Fienup-Riordan

1   **PART I—Central Yup'ik and Cup'ig Narratives**

1   Introduction to Central Yup'ik and Cup'ig Narratives
Ann Fienup-Riordan

7   Yaqutgiarcankut / Yaqutgiarcaq and Her Family
Natalia White, Elsie Mather, and Phyllis Morrow

30   One Who Didn't Think Much of a Man's Stomach
Paul John and Sophie Shield

41   Quliraq
Frances Usugan and Cathy Moses

64   Aanakallii Ner'aqallii / I Have Eaten My Mother
Frank Andrew and Alice Rearden

84   The Five Sisters
Lena Atkiq Ilutsik, Virginia Ilutsik Andrew, and Esther Arnaq Ilutsik

89   Atkuut Tengaurturalriit / A Flying Parka
Paul John and Marie Meade

102   Uraqural ͨrig / Sibling Brothers
Nuratar Andrew Noatak, Nakaar Howard Amos, and Robert Drozda

122   Notes

124   Works Cited and Suggested Reading

127   **PART II—Iñupiaq Narratives**

127   Introduction to Iñupiaq Narratives
Lawrence D. Kaplan with Deanna Paniataaq Kingston

133 Uvaŋa Atiġa Aliitchak / My Name Is Aliitchak
Minnie Gray, Tadataka Nagai, and Lawrence D. Kaplan

146 A Long Unipkaaq
Jimmie Killigivuk, Carol Tukummiq Omnik, Tom Lowenstein

169 The Story of the King Island Wolf Dance
Lucy Tanaqiq Koyuk, Earl Aisana Mayac, and Deanna Paniataaq Kingston

180 King Island Iñupiaq Stories
Frank Ellanna, Bernadette Alvanna-Stimpfle, and Lawrence D. Kaplan

188 An Unwritten Law of the Sea
Herbert O. Anungazuk

200 Notes

200 Works Cited and Suggested Reading

203 PART III—St. Lawrence Island / Siberian Yupik Narratives

203 Introduction to St. Lawrence Island / Siberian Yupik Narratives
Lawrence D. Kaplan

207 Yuuk Neqenyuqaq / The Good Hunter
Vera Metcalf and Theodore Kingiikaq

211 Three Generations of St. Lawrence Island Writers:
The Work of Paul Silook, Roger Silook, and Susie Silook
Susie Silook

220 Qati Hik: A St. Lawrence Island Yupik Tale
Della Waghiyi and Willem J. de Reuse

234 Works Cited and Suggested Reading

237 PART IV—Alutiiq Narratives

237 Introduction to Alutiiq Narratives
Patricia Partnow

243 The Power of Story: Arnaq Taqukaraam Pillra / The Woman Who
Was Gotten by the Bear
Ignatius Kosbruk, Patricia Partnow, and Jeff Leer

259 Notes

260 Works Cited and Suggested Reading

263 Index

Contributors

Virginia Ilutsik Andrew was born in Kanakanak in 1961 and attended the University of Alaska Fairbanks, where she studied the Yup'ik language under Steve Jacobson. She subsequently worked for Southwest Regional Schools as a bilingual/bicultural teacher in Aleknagik, where she was honored for her service. While raising her family she worked as a translator with the Bristol Bay Campus/Ciulistet Research Association. At the time of her death in 2001 she was continuing to transcribe and translate elders' knowledge.

Nakaar Howard Amos, a Cup'ig Eskimo from Mekoryuk on Nunivak Island, is an advocate for and practitioner of the traditional knowledge, skills, and values of his elders, as well as a subsistence user and commercial Bering Sea fisher. As director of Nuniwarmiut Piciryarraata Tamaryalkut'i (Nunivak Cultural Programs) he is a rigorous promoter of the revitalization of his Native Cup'ig language, music, and dance. He is co-compiler, along with his wife, Muriel Amos, of the *Cup'ig Eskimo Dictionary*, published by Alaska Native Language Center in 2003.

Herbert O. Anungazuk is originally from Wales, Alaska, on the western shore of Bering Strait. He is a cultural anthropologist with the National Park Service in Anchorage, where he is part of a team of anthropologists in the Division of Cultural Resources working with researchers from universities in the United States and abroad. He acknowledges his work with elders as "feeding his soul."

Robert Drozda currently manages a portion of the ANCSA Historical Places and Cemetery Sites collection at the Rasmuson Library archives at the University of Alaska Fairbanks. He also works as a consultant to the Mekoryuk cultural programs office (Nuniwarmiut Piciryarraata Tamaryalkut'i), which he helped to establish along with Howard Amos in 1998.

Ann Fienup-Riordan is a cultural anthropologist who has lived and worked in Alaska since 1973. Her books include *The Nelson Island Eskimo* (1983), *Eskimo Essays* (1990), *Boundaries and Passages* (1994), *The Living Tradition of Yup'ik Masks* (1996), and *Wise Words of the Yup'ik People: We Talk to You because We Love You* (2005). In 2000, she received the Alaska Federation of Natives President's Award for her work with Alaska Natives. At present she works with the Calista Elders Council, mentoring Yup'ik men and women in documenting traditional knowledge.

Esther Arnaq Ilutsik was born and raised in the Bristol Bay region. She received a master's degree in education administration from the University of Alaska Fairbanks in 1990. That year she began work with Yup'ik elders inquiring about traditional knowledge as a founding member of the Ciulistet Research Group, which has since inspired educators throughout the state to create similar programs.

Lawrence D. Kaplan is director of the Alaska Native Language Center and professor of linguistics at the University of Alaska Fairbanks. He has worked with the Alaskan Iñupiaq language, particularly in northwestern Alaska, and is a co-author of the *Comparative Eskimo Dictionary*.

Deanna Paniataaq Kingston is associate professor of anthropology at Oregon State University. She has a King Island Iñupiaq background and conducts much of her research on King Island. She currently directs a major project to document traditional culture, science, and perspectives on land and land use.

Jeff Leer is a linguist and teacher at the Alaska Native Language Center, University of Alaska Fairbanks. He works primarily on the Tlingit and Alutiiq languages, as well as on comparative Athabascan-Eyak-Tlingit.

Tom Lowenstein teaches at Chelsea School of Art and Design in London. He is the author of two books on Tikigaq narrative and ritual: *Ancient Land, Sacred Whale* and *The Things That Were Said of Them: Shaman Stories and Oral Histories of the Tikigaq People*.

Elsie Mather is a Yup'ik Eskimo raised in Kwigillingok. She lived in Bethel from 1959 to 2005, when she moved to Anchorage. She is the author of *Cauyarnariuq (A Time for Drumming)*, a description of Yup'ik ceremonialism.

She also has worked with linguist Osahito Miyaoka, written on Yup'ik oral tradition, and continues to work on translations of Yup'ik traditional tales.

Marie Meade was raised in Nunapitchuk, Alaska, and has worked as a translator and Yup'ik language specialist for more than thirty years. Since 1993 her translations have been the foundation of a number of bilingual books, including *Agayuliyararput / Our Way of Making Prayer* and *Ciuliamta Akluit / Things of Our Ancestors.* Marie presently teaches Yup'ik language and culture at the University of Alaska Anchorage.

Vera K. Metcalf was born and raised in Savoonga on St. Lawrence Island and now lives in Nome, where she is the executive director of the Eskimo Walrus Commission at Kawerak, Inc. She has given numerous presentations nationally and internationally on cultural awareness, multicultural orientation, and cultural heritage.

Phyllis Morrow is a cultural anthropologist at the University of Alaska Fairbanks. From 1979 through 1981 she directed the Yup'ik Language Center of Kuskokwim College in Bethel and developed bilingual / bicultural curricula for the Lower Kuskokwim School District until 1987. She co-edited (with William Schneider) *When Our Words Return: Writing, Hearing, and Remembering Oral Traditions of Alaska and the Yukon.*

Cathy Moses was born in Kotlik at the mouth of the Yukon. She attended St. Mary's High School where she met Charlie Moses, and after graduation the couple returned to Charlie's home in Toksook Bay on Nelson Island. In the 1980s both Cathy and Charlie earned degrees in education at the University of Alaska Fairbanks. Cathy now teaches in the Yup'ik immersion program at the Toksook Bay School.

Tadataka Nagai is a Japanese doctoral student in linguistics and Alaska Native languages at the University of Alaska Fairbanks. He has done linguistic fieldwork on Iñupiaq in Ambler on the Kobuk River, collecting oral narratives and studying Iñupiaq verb categories.

Carol Tukummiq Omnik was a bilingual Iñupiaq elder from Point Hope. Between 1975 and 1977, she used her language skills and traditional knowledge to translate for Jimmie Killigivuk and Tom Lowenstein, when they collected and worked on Jimmie's stories. In her later years she taught Iñupiaq in the Point Hope school.

Patricia Partnow is an Anchorage anthropologist who has worked in multi-cultural education and studied oral tradition in Alaska for thirty-five years. She is an independent consultant who works with museums, universities, and school districts to design culture-based materials and programs. She is the author of *Making History: Alutiiq/Sugpiaq Life on the Alaska Peninsula* (University of Alaska Press, 2002).

Alice Aluskak Rearden from Napakiak is a recent graduate in anthropology and history from the University of Alaska Fairbanks. Since 2000 she has worked with the Calista Elders Council. She is a fluent Yup'ik speaker committed to working with regional tradition bearers to gather, translate, and share their knowledge. Her first bilingual book, on family values, is *Yupiit Qanruyutait: Yup'ik Words of Wisdom* (2005).

Willem J. de Reuse is assistant professor at the Department of English at the University of North Texas, Denton. He has worked on St. Lawrence Island Yupik and is the author of *Siberian Yupik Eskimo: The Language and its Contacts with Chukchi*. He is currently working on Western Apache grammar, lexicography, and discourse and on Han Athabascan.

Sophie Shield was raised in Tuntutuliak. She began work with linguist Irene Reed in the 1970s. In the 1990s she translated the narratives of Nelson Island elder Paul John, published as *Qulirat Qanemcit-llu Kinguvarcimalriit / Stories for Future Generations: The Oratory of Yup'ik Eskimo Elder Paul John*. Between 1996 and 2004 she worked for the Lower Kuskokwim School District's bilingual program. Sophie passed away in 2004.

Susie Silook was born and raised in Gambell on St. Lawrence Island. As a child she starred in Walt Disney's *Two Against the Arctic*. Today she is known internationally as a visual artist whose distinctive ivory carvings have been exhibited throughout Alaska and the United States. Her poetry has been published in the prestigious *Alaska Quarterly Review* special issue on Alaska Native writers, storytellers, and orators.

Smoked Fish and Jars of Jam

Preface and Acknowledgments

> Some...are concerned that the stories...survive. The ideal vehicle for survival is stewardship and natural transmission within the community, but this is no longer possible in many places in the indigenous language, although it may be possible in English. It's the difference between the salmon run and smoked fish; the berry patch and jars of jam.
>
> —Nora and Richard Dauenhauer,
> "The Paradox of Talking on the Page," p. 27

WHAT FOLLOWS WILL BE A FEAST for anyone hungry for the rich narratives that Native and non-Native contributors to this book have prepared. As our hosts, these men and women have set the table with their stories so that readers may see, hear, smell, even taste the texture of their diverse narrative and scholarly traditions. Most Yupik and Iñupiaq contributors are fluent in their Native languages, and they were privileged to hear stories from their parents and grandparents as part of an oral tradition thousands of years old. Tlingit scholars Nora and Richard Dauenhauer aptly compare this vibrant narrative tradition to the salmon running upriver and berries growing on the tundra—an abundance with the power to sustain us. But those who do not live by rivers and tundra are hungry, too. This book is for them.

"Much of great importance is lost and added in translation," A. L. Becker (2000:90) reminds us. The truth of his words captures both this book's weaknesses and strengths. Each translated text is at once less than the original telling—devoid of the shapes and sounds of the narrator's voice—and more. Through the double process of translation from an Alaska Native language to English and from oral to written form, readers gain access to a body of northern literature as compelling as any Western or Eastern classic.

This anthology of Iñupiaq, Siberian Yupik, Yup'ik, Cup'ig, and Alutiiq literature in translation includes contributions from both scholars and Alaska Natives actively recording and writing in their languages. The range of material is wide, including translations of traditional tales, historical and personal narratives, and creative writing. Some contributions include minimal interpretation, while others include more extended commentary. Some appear in both the original Native language and English translation, while other Alaska Native writers chose to use English. All translations reflect both the literary qualities of the original texts as well as the continued vitality of narrative traditions in contemporary Yupik and Iñupiaq communities. Together they show the diversity of storytelling in Alaska today.

We began work on this book in 1997 at the suggestion of Brian Swann, and we are grateful for his inspiration and encouragement. The original idea was to create an Alaska version of his groundbreaking *Coming to Light: Contemporary Translations of the Native Literature of North America* (1994), with short introductions followed by detailed texts in translation. Swann sought contributions for the volume he edited by sending letters to scholars and translators, and Larry Kaplan and I initiated this project in the same way. Because we live in Alaska, we could meet with Native and non-Native scholars and translators—many of whom we know well—and the narrative artists themselves to talk about the form and content an anthology of Alaska Native literature might take. We also worked with Native authors and contemporary storytellers.

Early in our collaboration, we decided to focus on narrative traditions of speakers of the Eskimo-Aleut family of languages. We believed that there was more than enough material to merit such a specialized collection. Other excellent anthologies already present the full range of Alaska Native writers and storytellers, such as Jeane Breinig and Patricia Partnow's *Alaska Native Writers, Storytellers and Orators: The Expanded Edition*. We wanted *Words of the Real People* to present the breadth and depth of approaches that have been applied to issues of translation and presentation of oral traditions within a single extended language group.

Three major gatherings contributed to this book, including workshops in February 1998 and February 1999 at the annual statewide Bilingual Multicultural Education Conference in Anchorage and at an invited session at the American Folklore Society's annual meeting in Anchorage in October 2001. We are grateful to both organizations for giving us these opportunities, and to the National Science Foundation, which helped to fund contributors' travel to the folklore meeting.

At our first workshop, we introduced the project to Iñupiaq and Yupik educators and translators who had traveled to Anchorage for the bilingual meetings. These men and women work with elderly tradition-bearers in their communities and teach Native students in their own languages. Many were enthusiastic about the creation of an anthology showcasing their literature in translation. They were quick to point out, however, the importance of protecting the rights of the men and women who might contribute stories, as well as insuring that they benefit fully from their contributions. They reminded us that free, democratic access to information should not be assumed.

Many Native elders view knowledge as something to be earned. Although sharing knowledge is highly valued, responsibilities attend the process. Stories are not objects to be collected, classified, paginated, and sold for personal profit, and writing them down does not confer ownership. Participants also reminded us that words are inherently powerful, having the capacity to create that which they describe. Words have never been used lightly within Yupik and Iñupiaq oral tradition, and participants took seriously the challenge of how best to translate and share their oral traditions in written form.

Fifteen contributors and interested observers met again to discuss our progress at the 1999 meeting. Gathered in a circle, each in turn presented selections from translation work in progress, including Sophie Shield, Marie Meade, Phyllis Morrow, Esther Ilutsik, and Pat Partnow. Others offered comments and suggestions on the difficult but rewarding task of turning oral literature into written texts.

Discussion focused on how much interpretation should be included with the translations. All recognized that the context of a story was essential to grasping its meaning and that many non-Native and younger Native readers would require some cultural and linguistic information to fully appreciate the texts. Our Yup'ik contributors, however, were especially reluctant to assign a "moral" to stories. When asked if questions were appropriate in a storytelling context, many said no, that stories were "just told" and that asking questions destroyed them. We lose something when stories are explained, they reminded us. Successive hearings or readings reveal different meanings, depending on the experience the listener brings. This depth of meaning, many pointed out, is the mark of great literature worldwide. Yup'ik scholar Elsie Mather compared analysis of oral literature to "opening up stories with a can opener," causing listeners to lose their sense of awe. Another participant compared analysis to rotten meat, warning us, "Be very careful of analysis as it can poison you." Elsie and others emphasized that much more is lost than gained by the scholarly tendency to overanalyze and explain.

We held our last and perhaps most celebratory gathering at the annual meeting of the American Folklore Society in October 2001. Most contributors to this book had been invited to present their work to fellow Alaska Natives as well as to an international audience of non-Native scholars. Many in the audience were visiting Alaska for the first time and were eager to hear from Alaska Natives themselves. They were a microcosm of the audience for whom this volume is intended, including all those Natives and non-Natives in and outside Alaska interested in both past and present Yupik and Iñupiaq narrative traditions and the unique view of the world they embody.

This volume, like the gatherings from which it grew, has been shaped by the concerns and choices of individual contributors. Many contributions grow from longtime scholarly collaborations, such as that between Elsie Mather and cultural anthropologist Phyllis Morrow. Others reflect long-standing relationships between particular narrative artists and their translators, such as Sophie Shield's work with Yup'ik elder Paul John and Alice Rearden's work with Frank Andrew. Others, like Vera Metcalf and Esther Ilutsik, chose to share in written form the stories their parents passed on to them. Still others, such as Susie Silook and Herb Anungazuk, provide contemporary accounts rooted in their personal experiences of what it means to be twenty-first-century Yupik and Iñupiaq women and men. The creative power of their writing attests to their desire to move their storytelling onto the printed page (Ruppert and Bernet 2001:2). Their contributions embody the richness and variety of Iñupiaq and Yupik narrative tradition as practiced by gifted verbal artists today. They speak for themselves, giving readers the opportunity to learn about the diversity of contemporary Yupik and Iñupiaq literary expression as well as the variety of ways "traditional" stories can be presented.

Our biggest debt is to the narrative artists themselves, including Frank Andrew, Frank Ellanna, Minnie Gray, Lena Ilutsik, Paul John, Ignatius Kosbruk, Jimmie Killigivuk, Theodore Kingiikaq, Lucy Koyuk, Earl Mayac, Andrew

Noatak, Frances Usugan, Della Waghiyi, and Natalia White. These men and women are each recognized and respected masters of the oral literatures of their people. Their engaging contributions make the point more eloquently than any scholarly explication that so-called "traditional" narratives are never anonymous. They are the authors of this volume, and as editors our role has been to present the literary performances they have chosen to share.

Nothing in these pages can adequately convey the compassionate and loving spirit that shaped their stories. Paul John once told me that children should never be talked to harshly, as it blocks their minds and prevents them from learning: "If those who are giving them advice speak with compassion, it would be like giving them strong, healing medicine and would help bring them to happiness." We are deeply grateful for the gifts these orators have given us and their trust that we treat these gifts responsibly and respectfully and share them in our turn.

Contributors to this volume are not just trying to *say*, but to *do* something. They know they possess a narrative tradition second to none, and they want others to recognize its eloquence and give it the respect it deserves. The image of the igloo-dwelling Eskimo still smiles out from many a gift shop window in Alaska. Though few contributors directly confront this simple-minded and insidious stereotype, they sense that this display of narrative artistry strikes its foundations, destabilizes it, and sends it crumbling down. Contributors' contemporary narrative references to the past are active efforts to shape the future—a future in which storytellers, translators, and authors believe that Alaska Native distinctiveness should be recognized and valued.

In recognition of the importance of continuing to work with speakers of the indigenous languages of Alaska to gain both recognition for and understanding of their narrative traditions, all royalties from sales of this book will go to the Alaska Native Language Center at the University of Alaska Fairbanks, an organization dedicated to documenting and perpetuating Alaska Native languages. This anthology is just one story among many: the beginning of understanding, not the end. Cup'ig narrators sometimes say at the close of a story, "Things that I missed, may they get into their places resounding," implying their desire that in future tellings their omissions will be heard and mistakes set right. Our hope is the same.

—AFR

Introduction: Yupik and Iñupiaq Literature in Translation

Ann Fienup-Riordan

Linguistic Traditions

The literary traditions presented in the following pages are rooted in a family of closely related languages referred to as Eskimo-Aleut, including Inuit/ Iñupiaq, Siberian Yupik, Central Alaskan Yup'ik and Cup'ig, and Alutiiq. These languages are not mutually intelligible. The ancestors of contemporary Yupik and Iñupiaq speakers are believed to have arrived in the New World between two and four thousand years ago, traveling across the Bering Land Bridge from Siberia to settle along Alaska's Pacific coast as far south as Prince William Sound. Historically all indigenous coastal dwellers in northern and western Alaska spoke one or more of these languages.

Before 2,400 years ago the ancestors of modern Yupik and Iñupiaq speakers were probably present in small numbers at prime coastal locations. At that time the number of large coastal villages increased, triggered by the adoption of net-fishing technology and the shift toward salmon, which allowed use of previously marginal locations. South of Norton Sound, Yup'ik dependence on sea mammals decreased and was replaced by the mixed reliance on salmon, migratory waterfowl, caribou, and small game that characterizes the region to this day. As coastal populations increased, the individualistic character of relatively isolated groups lessened (Shaw 1998:242). Gradual encroachment eastward, at the expense of interior residents, occurred into historic times along large river and lake systems, at which point they came into contact with Athabascan people speaking one of a number of Dene languages.

Inuit/Iñupiaq is spoken along the Arctic coast of Alaska, northern Canada, and Greenland. Iñupiaq speakers in Alaska live from Norton Sound throughout the Seward Peninsula and on the islands of Bering Strait, northward through Kotzebue Sound, and eastward across the North Slope and Brooks Range.

Yupik is closely related to the Inuit/Iñupiaq branch of the Eskimo-Aleut language family. There are four Yupik Eskimo languages: Pacific Yupik (also called Alutiiq or Sugpiaq), spoken around Prince William Sound, the tip of the Kenai Peninsula, Kodiak Island, and part of the Alaska Peninsula; Naukan, originally of East Cape Siberia; Central Siberian Yupik, spoken on St. Lawrence Island in Alaska and across the Bering Strait in Siberia; and Central Alaskan Yup'ik, spoken on the Bering Sea coast from Norton Sound to the Alaska Peninsula as well as along the lower Yukon, Kuskokwim, and Nushagak rivers. Within Central Alaskan Yup'ik are four dialects: Norton Sound, Hooper Bay/ Chevak, Nunivak, and General Central Yup'ik. All are mutually intelligible with some phonological and vocabulary differences (Jacobson 1984:28–37;

The major Eskimo-Aleut linguistic divisions in Alaska.

Words of the Real People

Woodbury 1984a:49–63). The Nunivak dialect—Cup'ig—is the most divergent and is written with a special adaptation of the standard Central Yup'ik orthography, and some have maintained that it is a separate language (Amos and Amos 2003). With the exception of Cup'ig elder Andrew Noatak, all of the Yup'ik narrators in this book speak General Central Yup'ik. Note that no apostrophe is used when speaking of the Yupik languages or of Siberian Yupik, but an apostrophe is used for Central Alaskan Yup'ik (called simply Yup'ik here), including dialects such as Cup'ig and General Central Yup'ik.

Genres of Oral Narrative

Iñupiaq and Yupik narrators traditionally told stories in homes, campsites, and public places like the communal men's house (*qargi* in Iñupiaq and *qasgi* in Yup'ik, *kiiyar* in Cup'ig) for the enjoyment and edification of adults as well as any young people present. Parents were admonished to share their knowledge broadly within the community. Yup'ik elders still say that if people are stingy with their knowledge, their minds will rot. The written narratives and essays gathered below descend directly from this time-honored oral tradition.

Yupik and Iñupiaq people distinguish between two broad, overlapping narrative types (Fortescue and Kaplan 1989; Jacobson 1984; Morrow 1994; Woodbury and Moses 1994). The first includes legends or tales told by distant ancestors and passed down from generation to generation—what James Ruppert and John Bernet aptly call distant-time stories (Ruppert and Bernet 2001:9). These include origin stories and tales of the time when the earth was thin and humans interacted freely with animals and other nonhuman persons. Such legends are designated *unipkaaq* (singular) among the Iñupiat of north Alaska, *ungipaghaan* among the Siberian Yupik of St. Lawrence Island, and *unigkuat* among the Alutiiq. Cup'ig orators on nearby Nunivak as well as Central Yup'ik speakers from the Yukon area and Norton Sound sometimes use the expression *univkar* or *univkaraq* (from *unite–*, "to leave behind," plus *–vkar*, "to allow to," literally "that which is left behind") for a legend or traditional tale. Most Central Alaskan Yup'ik speakers use the alternate form *quli'ir* or *quliraq* (*qulirer* in Cup'ig) to refer to legends.

The second broad story category consists of historical narratives related by known persons, labeled *quliaqtuaq* in North Slope Iñupiaq, *quliapyuk* in

King Island Iñupiaq, *ungipamsuk* in Siberian Yupik, *qanemciq* among Central Yup'ik speakers, *qanengssi* among Cup'ig speakers, and *quli'anguaq* in Alutiiq. The words *qalamciq* and *qalangssak* (from *qalarte–*, "to talk, to speak") also mean "story" for Yup'ik speakers living in the Bristol Bay area, where *qanengssak* (from *qaneq*, "mouth," or *qaner–*, "to speak," the same base as *qanemciq*) is used to designate stories from distant times. Historical narratives include stories of bow-and-arrow warfare, encounters with ghosts or other-than-human persons, past events involving named and known people, and personal experiences.

The Alaska Native distinction between legend and historical narrative is sometimes equated with the Western distinction between fanciful myths or fairy tales and factual history. In fact, legends and historical accounts are considered equally reliable sources of information, simply referring to different time periods—the distant past and recent times. As such, legends and historical accounts exist along a continuum and are not mutually exclusive. At the beginning of one legend, for example, Paul John said, "This *qanemciq* I'm going to tell is a *quliraq*," using the word *qanemciq* to designate a general story category. At the close of another legend he used the formulaic ending, *"Tuaten tua-i taktaluku qanemciuguq man'a"* ("That is how long this story is").

Yupik and Iñupiaq stories are neither owned nor inherited, and any knowledgeable man or woman can recount them. When telling a story, however, it is common to this day for narrators to frame their accounts by acknowledging their sources—where and from whom they learned the story—and in other ways establish the truth of their narration, as Nunivak elder Andrew Noatak does in his contribution to this volume. Narrators may also apologize for the limits of their knowledge, commenting like Vera Metcalf in this volume that they fell asleep before the story's end. These disclaimers reflect modesty rather than lack of competence (Orr and Orr 1995:371).

What follows these acknowledgments and disclaimers is not a verbatim repetition of a memorized text, but an artful elaboration specific to the narrator's experience and the audience addressed. Yupik and Iñupiaq storytellers have considerable leeway in the phrasing they choose to elaborate events. In Iñupiaq as well as all four Yupik languages the same noun and verb bases can be ordered differently or combined with different postbases to produce varying rhetorical effects, depending on the narrator's audience and the storytelling context. Although accomplished narrators do not have the freedom to change the sequence of events, they can embellish this sequence with considerable effect. Alaska narrative is far from rigid repetition, and no two tellings of the same story, even by the same narrator, are ever exactly alike.

Anthony Woodbury notes that despite careful transmission, no immutable legend canon exists: "Repertoires and stories vary, not only from region to region but among storytellers in the same village." What varies less often, Woodbury continues, are standard themes, settings, and characters: "It is these characteristics, as much as the individual stories, that constitute the inherited tradition" and shape the listeners' understandings of the stories (Woodbury and Moses 1994:18).

Origin and animal stories, including creation accounts involving Raven, are well represented in the literature (Fienup-Riordan 2000:29–33, 48, 50–53; Nelson 1899:452–467; Tennant and Bitar 1981:149–153). Some describe humans encountering animal persons and learning from them or being cared for by them. In her study of Eskimo personality and Nunivak mythology, Margaret Lantis (1953) remarks on major themes in Cup'ig mythology, including the poor boy, the deceitful husband, and the haughty girl. She notes that in Alaska Eskimo mythology generally, about a third of traditional tales concern heroes, and half of these are "poor boys" (usually orphans). These stories describe the self-reliant individual who overcomes adversity to ultimately succeed. Another common theme is the selfish or overbearing hunter or shaman whose cruelty and disregard for others ultimately results in his undoing. Murderous and vengeful episodes during the bow-and-arrow wars that occurred in Alaska into the nineteenth century are another common story theme.

Stories touch on every aspect of human interaction, including the consequences of both appropriate and inappropriate conduct between husband and wife, father and son, mother and child, grandparent and grandchild, and brother and sister. The relationship between the sexes was, in fact, ambiguous in real life. Although men and women depended on one another, they also circumscribed their interpersonal relations so that animals would continue to find them attractive and willingly approach them.

Many narratives, both distant-time stories and historical and personal accounts, contain explicit moral direction and vividly describe the consequences of inappropriate actions. For example, in Frank Andrew's story of the child who ate his mother, the young woman brought on her own demise by failing to follow advice she was given—not to be ashamed of her deformed child but to show him to the people. Taken together, these stories provide a veritable manual for the properly lived life.

Yet a story's meaning was also far from fixed. As Julie Cruikshank and others working with contemporary oral tradition have made clear, storytelling has always been a social activity in which narrators tailor their stories to suit their listeners. Storytelling remains a relationship between people, and a story's meaning is always established in context.

Storytelling was a ubiquitous part of community life in the past. In the 1870s Edward Nelson observed long storytelling sessions in the *qasgit* (communal men's houses) of western Alaska, where a single story was told over a period of days. He also observed how two men would work together telling a tale—one man speaking while the other kept track of the story line by placing pieces of wood on the ground to mark his progress (Nelson 1899:451). Elders still enjoy telling stories among peers, both in formal elders' conferences and informally around the table after a meal. Younger men and women today are also active tellers of tales, both orally and in written form.

Contemporary young people often have limited opportunities to listen to accomplished storytellers, but in the past listeners included even the very young. Ruppert and Bernet (2001:3) noted that bad luck was said to befall the Koyukon listener who fell asleep during a storytelling session. In contrast, many Iñupiaq and Yupik men and women recall falling asleep listening to stories as children. Johnny Thompson (February 27, 1994) of St. Marys remembered, "I'm the kind of person who doesn't really know about *qulirat* because I slept too much when they told them. Sleep robbed me of that knowledge. I can't tell you a *quliraq* from the beginning to the end." Sleep was not the only factor. Kwigillingok elder Frank Andrew, a man with an exceptional memory for traditional technology and vocabulary, sadly remarked that his story repertoire was limited because he was often running errands and doing chores for others in the *qasgi* during storytelling sessions when he was young.

Much has been written about the role of observation and practice in learning the techniques necessary to survive in Alaska. Less well known was the importance placed on verbal instruction. The narrative repertoire, including both stories and detailed rules for living, was vast, and children could only master it through attentive and repeated listening. Among Yup'ik and Cup'ig people, the ideal was that elders speak and young people listen. Elders who did not speak publicly but shared knowledge only with their own children were considered selfish or "jealous." Conversely children who "failed to pay attention to the speaker's mouth" or left the room before the speaker was done were admonished that they would someday be found dead in the wilderness "with their teeth gleaming at the end of a snowdrift." With this constant speaking, listeners likely heard a number of versions of the same or related stories (Fienup-Riordan 2005).

Yup'ik elder Paul John described the narrative tradition in which he was raised:

> Nowadays there are people who are chosen to speak at meetings and conferences. When one was picked to speak, he would prepare himself mentally and think about the words he would say. In the past the older folks seemed to be prepared for this job at all times.
>
> When some problem arose in the *qasgi*, that single incident would prompt a designated elder to begin speaking to everyone there. If one man's actions weren't acceptable to the elders, he would speak to everyone present. He would speak, making sure that young and old alike understood what he had to say.
>
> And back in those days when we were young boys, they would include every kind of information when they spoke. They would not hold back information because of the presence of the young boys. They would speak to everyone in the *qasgi*, and their message would come right to the basics.

Narrators were taught from youth to carefully attend to the words of their parents and grandparents and never to repeat what they did not know from their own observation or experience. Many elders today still claim only to speak for themselves. They do not tell stories that they do not know in detail, nor do they describe past patterns of life, ceremonies, or subsistence pursuits in general. Instead, they consistently give information in the form of first-person narratives describing their own experiences. Listeners who recall alternate versions or parts of a story are encouraged to add what they know to increase understanding (see Morrow 1995).

How Stories Are Told

> The most respected conveyers of Yup'ik knowledge are those who express things that listeners already know in artful or different ways, offering new expressions of the same.
>
> —Elsie Mather, "With a Vision," p. 32

In the stories that follow one can admire not only what the narrative artists have to say, but the creative and precise ways in which they say it. Titles are not a traditional feature of Yupik and Iñupiaq oral literature, although narrators sometimes refer to a story by the action described. In their written form contributors have used key phrases or the names of protagonists as titles for the different tales. Some Yup'ik narrators use common opening phrases, including, "There was a couple living all by themselves right along the river" or, less frequently, "A long time ago." Legends are characterized by a variety of formulaic opening phrases, marking these performances as formal retellings of old, often well-known tales.

As with the stylized beginnings, narrators often close their tales with phrases such as, "This is the length of my story," "That's where the story ends," or the more elegant, "This is how long this legend is. And the parts that I missed have situated themselves in their proper places." Stylized endings differ from place to place and person to person, depending on who tells the story. For instance, narrators on the lower Kuskokwim sometimes end their stories, "It is going forward on its path, getting better and better." Such endings are used less frequently today, but they are far from extinct.

Yupik and Iñupiaq narratives resemble European fables or Biblical parables but with important differences. One message—to live life attentively according to the rules—was often indirectly stated at the beginning of the story and at the end through detailed accounts of the successful completion of the annual cycle. These detailed accounts both frame the story as a formal telling of an old tale and reflect an intense interest in recreating that which they describe. Convinced of the power of their words to affect the future, narrators may have routinely framed these exceptional events in ideal descriptions of life as they believed it should be.

Just as touch and sight were potentially powerful senses, restricted in some contexts and extended in others, the spoken word had the power to evoke that which it described. In many tales, the protagonist sings songs that produce hoped-for results, and the stories themselves had the potential to influence events. Storytelling provided both enjoyable recreation and instruction; it was also an activity fraught with the potential to affect the narrators' and listeners' futures. The reader should not assume that because everyone already knew the sequences described, the "reported facts were unimportant." On the contrary, Yupik and Iñupiaq narratives remain to this day powerful vehicles that promote a successful future as they recall in detail the past cycle of activities (Fienup-Riordan 1996:168–171, 2000:23; Lantis 1953:163).

Margaret Lantis (1953:19) aptly points out the emotional content of Cup'ig narrative: "Eskimo technology shows intelligence, stories their feelings." Undoubtedly listeners could empathize with the predicament of the abandoned wife or the isolation of the poor boy. Typically protagonists experience a range of emotions, from feelings of fear and rage to satisfaction and relief. The verbal artists and authors in this anthology are not reciting mathematical formulas. Rather they are sharing history, teaching about their past with their eyes firmly on the future. By sharing their words we hope to amplify their voices and extend these lessons one step farther.

Translation

In *Beyond Translation*, philologist A. L. Becker cites Jose Ortega y Gasset's description of the paradox involved in all speech—that every utterance is simultaneously deficient and exuberant. Each is deficient because it says less than it wishes but exuberant in that it transmits more than planned. When translating from one language to another, we are always confronted with these "exuberances" and "deficiencies"—things said in the translation but not in the original and things said in the original but not in translation (Becker 2000:5, 73; Ortega 1959).

Becker (2000:6) goes on to describe the enormous challenges of translation. Again he cites Ortega's insight that speech consists above all of silences:

> A being who could not renounce saying many things would be incapable of speaking. And each language represents a different equation between manifestations and silences. Each people leaves some things unsaid *in order* to be able to say others. Because

everything would be unsayable. Hence the immense difficulty of translation: translation is a matter of saying in a language precisely what that language tends to pass over in silence.

An example of such a "silence" is gender, which is not grammatically expressed in either Yupik or Iñupiaq. Becker (2000:6) eschews the explanation that gender is "understood" or "implied" in these languages: "It is simply not there." He also notes that in our daily life we routinely fill in the silences of speech based on context and past experience. When a parent yells, "Stop," or a friend whispers, "Thanks," much is implied. Filling in silences across languages, however, is more complicated "where the silences may well have new meanings, involving new distinctions that are silent in English" (Becker 2000:7).

Becker is not the only one to describe the deficiencies and "silences" across languages. James Clifford remarked, "The good translation gets you far enough into the other world to begin to see what you are missing. You take your translation device...and watch it run out of meaning" (Cruikshank 1998:98). Swann (1994:xxxv) cites Mikhail Bakhtin's profound recognition of the differences across languages:

> Language...lies on the borderline between oneself and the other. The word in language is half someone else's.... The word does not exist in a neutral or impersonal language...but rather exists in other people's mouths, in other peoples' contexts, serving other peoples' intentions: it is from there that one must take the word and make it one's own.

Swann (1994:xxxv) writes that one important message of his anthology of Native American literature in translation is the degree to which many Native American texts "almost successfully resist assimilation.... As William Bevis has written, 'We won't get Indian culture as cheaply as we got Manhattan.'" The deficiencies and exuberances of indigenous languages and English are not congruent, and recognition of the silences across languages is essential to mutual understanding.

Linguist Gregory Shreve (2002:7) describes the paradox of translation. Languages themselves can never be translated, he notes, but only the "sociocultural containers of social meaning and communicative value" called texts. He concludes:

> One could claim that all of translation is patently impossible, but because we so much desire to read, in our own language, what others have written in theirs, about their experiences…we do it anyway. We must accept translation's inherent faults, or rather faulting…in the geological sense. The translation…slips away from the source along the fault line of sociocultural difference.…The translation is like the Phoenix, it rises from the ashes of the old text, its parent, but it is a new being, alive in its own right, alive in its own writing.

All translators in this volume have confronted the enormous challenges Becker, Shreve, and others describe and offer strategies for bridging differences between languages without erasing them. For most, the goal has been a "natural sounding," free translation, as opposed to either literal translation (at one extreme) or paraphrasing (at the other). Paraphrasing may communicate some of the sense of the original, but such interpretive translations modify the original to the point where the speaker's voice is erased or transformed. Literal, word-for-word translation also falls short. At best it is awkward, and at worst it makes no sense. The narrator's choice of words is respected in this book, although word order and sentence structure may be modified slightly to communicate original meaning within a different linguistic framework.

Because their primary goal is communication, no translation in this book mechanically follows the structure of the indigenous language. For example, Yupik and Iñupiaq word order is "English turned on its head," in which suffixes indicating tense, person, case, and other units of meaning are appended to verb and noun bases. Thus, the English phrase "my little boat" corresponds to the single Yup'ik word *angyacuarqa*, which consists of *angya–* "boat," plus *–cuar–* "little," plus *–qa* "my," so that the order of the parts within the Yup'ik word is "boat, little, my." In discourse the object also typically precedes the verb in these languages. A literal translation might read "bucket/new one to make." A more natural translation would employ typical English word order, that is, verb followed by object, and would read "to make/the new bucket." Thus translation involves a continuous process of reordering (Meade

1999:273; Morrow and Mather 1994; Orr and Orr 1995:xxvii; Woodbury 1984a, 1984b).

Other "exuberances" in the indigenous languages have been carefully retained. For example, redundancies and repetitions were commonly edited out of translated texts in the past, but today many translators recognize them as integral to narrative structure and meaning. Use of repetition gives Yupik and Iñupiaq texts a denser texture than typical English phrasings, which careful attention in the translation can retain.

Narrators included frequent repetitions in their storytelling. Structured repetitions are characteristic of Yupik and Iñupiaq narrative art and vital to its structural integrity. To smooth them over or omit them would impoverish the translations. Repetitive phrasings enhance memory and add emphasis and depth. As Paul John reminded his listeners, "These Yup'ik people don't write things down on a piece of paper so that they can look at it. Starting from way back, the paper they had was in their heads. When they say something to us, their young, they would say it without making a mistake." In 1977 Paul said of himself, "I used to learn them and apparently not forget again after hearing them just one time."

As we ponder both the limitations and power of translation to communicate meaning across cultural and linguistic boundaries, it is useful to return to Becker (2000:18) and his recognition that translation is but the beginning of understanding. We invite the reader to engage the diverse narratives gathered here and use them as starting points. The profound differences between literary traditions, in turn, make it possible for us to recognize our own exuberant selves.

Good translation involves more than a technical process—it is a moral act involving responsibility and respect. A Malay friend once told Becker that he hoped Becker would not translate a Malay classic into English, because then no one would read the original. Yupik and Iñupiaq people face the same dilemma. Translators' efforts to understand and provide access to texts and stories are not neutral acts but are "necessarily full of politics and semi-intended errors" (2000:19). Becker (2000:19) concludes:

> Translation fidelity itself demands reciprocity, a sorting out of
> exuberances and deficiencies, a confession of failures and sleights

of hand. It is the only way I know of by which to make restitution to those who, in old Malay, "wrought the words and in that sense own them."

Transcription

As if translation from one language to another were not challenging enough, this book involves the movement from oral to written language. Most contributions in this volume begin with the verbal artistry of individual storytellers. Critical to understanding each performance is the transcription of the orator's voice onto the page.

Through the 1970s translators routinely ignored the dynamics and dramatic techniques of the performance, including the speakers' shifts in tone and rhythm. The oral origins of the texts were obscured from view. Paragraph form ruled, as if the paragraph were the "natural" form of all speech. Linguist Dell Hymes (2002:23) recently noted:

> So far as I know, no one has encountered among Native Americans or others recently nonliterate a local term equivalent to 'paragraph.' It is as if paragraphs were as inevitable and natural as containers for water. During the last 40 years or so, some of us have come to realize that paragraphs are about as natural a unit in telling stories as high heels are in swimming.

In the 1980s many basic tenets of anthropology were scrutinized, including the ubiquitous paragraph. Rather than assume a prose format in their transcriptions of Native American texts, Hymes and fellow linguist Dennis Tedlock experimented with verse forms that might more accurately reflect both the structure and dynamics of the original performances. As Tedlock pointed out, oral storytelling is a kind of measured poetry (Hymes 1981; Tedlock 1983).

Hymes focused primarily on the structure of Native American texts, and his concerns were fundamentally formal. Tedlock, on the other hand, worked with recent recordings of narrative performances to develop a transcription style that reflected the dynamics of oral performance. Both used broken lines, spacing, and small and large type to reflect voice quality, pause length, and other speech patterns. The length of the pause in a speaker's delivery was the determining factor in where lines and stanzas should end.

Tedlock and Hymes inspired a generation of linguists and anthropologists to adopt and adapt their transcription insights, igniting a veritable renaissance in translation of Native American literature (Swann 1994:xxviii). Most contributors to this volume have been either directly or indirectly influenced by these developments. Some, such as Phyllis Morrow, Elsie Mather, and Cathy Moses, employ a "short line" or "line pause" format to recapture the emphasis and cadence of the actual performance. In this format a new line marks a noticeable pause in delivery, which may or may not correspond to the end of a sentence or clause. Although pause length often corresponds to grammatical units, it may also "run on" in oral delivery to heighten dramatic effect. This verse format allows the reader to more accurately "hear" the speaker's voice. Moreover, translators such as Howard Amos, Marie Meade, and Alice Rearden, who continue to use a prose format, do so with a new sensitivity. Paragraphs in this volume evolved from the original texts and are distinguished by prominent line-initial particles, like *tua-i-llu* (so then), by cohesion between contiguous lines, and by pauses between units. The addition of a blank line denotes longer pauses or topic changes.

Editing and Annotation

Along with paying close attention to the written form in which the oral narratives are presented, contributors to this volume have sought to communicate the narrators' meanings and intentions. For Alaska Native readers and other "cultural insiders" familiar with Yupik and Iñupiaq narrative traditions, little explanation may be necessary. Yet regardless of how knowledgeable the listener and skillful the translator, written texts do not unambiguously speak for themselves (Cruikshank 1990:ix). Nora and Richard Dauenhauer (1999:21) point out that oral performances tend to be highly contextualized, which in translation creates a "laconic and confusing text."

Each contribution begins with introductory remarks intended to give readers a better understanding of the speakers', translators', and authors' varied backgrounds and intentions without explaining the stories away or tying them down to single interpretations. Storytellers assume that listeners possess basic linguistic and cultural information, and we have tried to provide this to readers without such knowledge.

Readers will encounter stories from different parts of Alaska and learn about some of the many ways in which these stories can be approached. We have organized the narratives by language groups, each proceeded by a brief historical introduction to the people and their narrative traditions. Comments on the narrator, performance context, rhetorical style, and any additional information necessary to fully appreciate the piece introduce each story.

Many of the translations in this book emerged from dialogue between a Native elder and a younger community member and between non-Native and Native scholars. These highly specific interpersonal relations between oral storytellers and the men and women who render their spoken words in written form are essential to understanding why narrators told particular stories and why translators chose to share them in the ways they have. As Cruikshank (1990:x) points out, oral narratives are too often written as though the storyteller were addressing the impersonal universe, but storytelling actually takes place in very specific cultural contexts. Introductions and notes allow contributors to visit this dialogue, so important in the process of intercultural translation, and carefully explain the nature of their collaboration with particular narrators.

Some judge written accounts as no better than a chunk of ice compared to the ever-changing rivers and streams of oral tradition. Translation and transcription transform the active storytelling process into a static, objectified text. Others contend that the so-called "frozen" story text still gets read and retold in myriad ways. A different dynamic emerges as the written text is reintroduced to younger generations, recirculated, and retold in new and previously unimagined ways. As anthropologist Greg Sarris (1993:4) notes, written words are not just a representation of past interaction, but also occasion interaction in the future.

As editors, Larry Kaplan and I encouraged submissions, but the selection of what to share was left to contributors. Rich and diverse, their choices include traditional tales, personal reminiscences, historical accounts, even songs. Some stories are presented only in English and some in both English and the original Native language. This variety is a virtue, giving readers an opportunity to sample some of the many ways stories can be presented. The storytellers are the authors and original editors in deciding what to share. Translators help them communicate with a wider audience. Together they are the hosts of this verbal feast, and readers are the guests at the table.

Why Stories Are Told

In her *Social Life of Stories*, Julie Cruikshank (1998:71) points out that if we do not know why a story was told, we will understand very little about it. Storytellers in this book spoke for a variety of reasons. Many, like Yup'ik elders Paul John and Frank Andrew, were motivated by the belief that Native young people need to hear these stories to guide their future lives. Paul John compares the healing quality of such "speaking out" to medicine:

> This usual method of speaking, the method of giving guidance to someone, apparently is like medicine which can heal a person's body and mind....This method of giving advice and guidance is unquestionably the right way (Shield and Fienup-Riordan 2003:325).

These elders know that writing the stories, both in Yup'ik and in English, extends their reach. They recognize that many Native young people are hungry for their history, and they are concerned that they be fed.

Many storytellers and authors in this volume seek to integrate difference and construct coherent Native identities in a rapidly changing world. They do so with reference to values already firmly in place. Accomplished storytellers use stories to blend new experiences with old values. They and their contemporaries still routinely tell tales of the personhood of living things and the importance of compassion and restraint in human relations. These stories can explain a dearth of fish as the fishes' reaction to inappropriate treatment and a poor berry harvest as the berries' withholding themselves when people do not share food. This is why many continue to "speak their past"—not to recite dead facts, but to provide tools for understanding the present. Their narratives help to explain contemporary events with reference to the past and to claim their legitimacy as alternatives to Western interpretations.

Along with recognition of profound and meaningful points of difference between Native and non-Native history and tradition, contributors also celebrate important ways in which all people are the same. They enable their readers to simultaneously recognize their shared humanity and reevaluate their special place in history. They emphasize similarities between Native and non-Native worlds in order to explain them, validate them, and put them on an equal footing.

Storytellers share stories with listeners and readers as undeniable acts of compassion. Elsie Mather noted that she grew up listening to stories that she really did not understand. The value of the stories, she said, was in hearing them. That her parents and other village elders cared enough to tell her stories was more important than any particular moral or meaning the story might possess. In sharing their stories here, both the storytellers and their translators insist that we not cease listening to stories that can allow us to be real people. As one narrator noted, these are stories to grow on. Ironically, sharing the stories, giving them away, enables us to keep them. This has always been true of oral traditions, and in this book narrators, authors, and translators see this sharing continuing in new ways.

The storytellers expected us to present their remembrances with dignity, respect, and as accurately as we could so that their stories survive on a level with other great traditions. These stories are not mere texts but loving and healing acts. Their potency recalls the power of words in Alaska Native oral tradition to constitute that which they signify. These stories have come across language and time, from oral to written form, from people living off the land to those living in urban centers. The fact that such meanings survive is testament to their power.

This collection offers readers a gesture of compassion and respect. The storytellers and their translators are providing entertainment, advice, and knowledge, some seeking to correct false images of Native peoples as those without literature. Among Yup'ik people, elders correct only those they care about, giving them advice that they hope will help them later in life. Readers should take this as a high compliment and cherish the gift they have been given. Someday, perhaps, one of these stories may come to mind, guiding wise choices to live life well.

Works Cited and Suggested Reading

Amos, Muriel M. and Howard T. Amos. 2003. *Cup'ig Eskimo Dictionary.* Fairbanks: Alaska Native Language Center, University of Alaska Fairbanks.

Becker, Alton L. 2000. *Beyond Translation: Essays toward a Modern Philology.* Ann Arbor: University of Michigan Press.

Cruikshank, Julie. 1990. *Life Lived Like a Story.* Lincoln: University of Nebraska Press.
 1995. "'Pete's Song': Establishing Meanings through Story and Song," in *When Our Words Return: Writing, Hearing, and Remembering Oral Traditions of Alaska and the Yukon.* Phyllis Morrow and William Schneider, eds., pp. 53–75. Logan, UT: Utah State University Press.
 1998. *The Social Life of Stories: Narrative and Knowledge in the Yukon Territory.* Lincoln: University of Nebraska Press.

Dauenhauer, Nora Marks and Richard Dauenhauer. 1999. "The Paradox of Talking on the Page: Some Aspects of the Tlingit and Haida Experience," in *Talking on the Page: Editing Aboriginal Oral Texts.* Laura Murray and Keren Rice, eds., pp. 3–42. Toronto: University of Toronto Press.

Fienup-Riordan, Ann. 1996. *The Living Tradition of Yup'ik Masks: Agayuliyararput / Our Way of Making Prayer.* Seattle: University of Washington Press.
 (ed.) 2000. *Where the Echo Began and Other Oral Traditions from Southwestern Alaska Recorded by Hans Himmelheber.* Fairbanks: University of Alaska Press.
 2005. *Wise Words of the Yup'ik People: We Talk to You because We Love You.* Lincoln: University of Nebraska Press.

Fortescue, Michael and Lawrence D. Kaplan. 1989. *Comparative Eskimo Dictionary.* Fairbanks: Alaska Native Language Center, University of Alaska Fairbanks.

Hymes, Dell. 1981. *"In Vain I Tried to Tell You": Essays in Native American Ethnopoetics.* Philadelphia: University of Pennsylvania Press.
 2002. "Translation of Oral Narratives," *Anthropology News* 43(5):23.

Jacobson, Steven A. 1984. *Yup'ik Eskimo Dictionary.* Fairbanks: Alaska Native Language Center, University of Alaska.

Lantis, Margaret. 1953. "Nunivak Eskimo Personality as Revealed in the Mythology," *Anthropological Papers of the University of Alaska* 2(11):109–174.

Mather, Elsie. 1995. "With a Vision beyond Our Immediate Needs: Oral Traditions in an Age of Literacy," in *When Our Words Return: Writing, Hearing, and Remembering Oral Traditions of Alaska and the Yukon.* Phyllis Morrow and William Schneider, eds., pp. 12–26. Logan, UT: Utah State University Press.

Meade, Marie. 1999. "Translation Issues," in *Alaska Native Writers, Storytellers, and Orators*, special issue of *Alaska Quarterly Review* 4(3–4):271–273.

Morrow, Phyllis. 1994. "Oral Literature of the Alaskan Arctic," in *Dictionary of Native American Literature*. Andrew Wiget, ed., pp. 19–26. New York: Garland Publishing.
　1995. "On Shaky Ground: Folklore, Collaboration, and Problematic Outcomes," in *When Our Words Return: Writing, Hearing, and Remembering Oral Traditions of Alaska and the Yukon*. Phyllis Morrow and William Schneider, eds., pp. 27–51. Logan, UT: Utah State University Press.

Morrow, Phyllis and William Schneider, eds. 1995. *When Our Words Return: Writing, Hearing, and Remembering Oral Traditions of Alaska and the Yukon*. Logan, UT: Utah State University Press.

Morrow, Phyllis and Elsie Mather. 1994. "Two Tellings of the Story of Uterneq: The Woman Who Returned from the Dead," in *Coming to Light: Contemporary Translations of the Native Literatures of North America*. Brian Swann, ed., pp. 37–56. New York: Random House.

Nelson, Edward William. 1899. *The Eskimo about Bering Strait*. Bureau of American Ethnology Annual Report for 1896–1897, vol. 18, pt. I. Washington, DC: Smithsonian Institution Press (reprinted 1983).

Orr, Eliza Cingarkaq and Ben Orr. 1995. *Qanemcikarluni Tekitnarqelartuq / One Must Arrive with a Story to Tell: Traditional Narratives by the Elders of Tununak, Alaska*. Fairbanks: Alaska Native Language Center, University of Alaska.

Ortega y Gasset, José. 1959. "The Difficulty of Reading," *Diogenes* 28:1–17.

Ruppert, James and John W. Bernet. 2001. *Our Voices: Native Stories of Alaska and the Yukon*. Lincoln: University of Nebraska Press.

Sarris, Greg. 1993. *Keeping Slug Woman Alive: A Holistic Approach to American Indian Texts*. Berkeley: University of California Press.

Shaw, Robert D. 1998. "An Archaeology of the Central Yupik: A Regional Overview for the Yukon–Kuskokwim Delta, Northern Bristol Bay, and Nunivak Island," *Arctic Anthropology* 35(1):234–246.

Shield, Sophie and Ann Fienup-Riordan. 2003. *Qulirat Qanemcit-llu Kinguvarcimalriit / Stories for Future Generations: The Oratory of Yup'ik Eskimo Elder Paul John*. Seattle: University of Washington Press.

Shreve, Gregory. 2002. "Translation, Fidelity, and Other Mythical Beasts I Have Sited," *Anthropology News* 43(7):7.

Swann, Brian, ed. 1994. *Coming to Light: Contemporary Translations of the Native Literatures of North America*. New York: Random House.

2004. *Voices from Four Directions: Contemporary Translations of the Native Literatures of North America*. Lincoln: University of Nebraska Press.

Tedlock, Dennis. 1983. *The Spoken Word and the Work of Interpretation*. Philadelphia: University of Pennsylvania Press.

Tennant, Edward A. and Joseph N. Bitar, eds. 1981. *Yupik Lore: Oral Traditions of an Eskimo People*. Bethel, AK: Lower Kuskokwim School District Bilingual/ Bicultural Department.

Woodbury, Anthony C. 1984a. "Eskimo and Aleut Languages," in *Arctic*, vol. 5, *Handbook of North American Indians*. David Damas, ed., pp. 49–63. Washington, DC: Smithsonian Institution Press.

1984b. *Cev'armiut Qanemciit Qulirait-llu / Eskimo Narratives and Tales from Chevak, Alaska*. Fairbanks: Alaska Native Language Center, University of Alaska.

Woodbury, Anthony C. and Leo Moses. 1994. "Mary Kokrak: Five Brothers and Their Younger Sister," in *Coming to Light: Contemporary Translations of the Native Literatures of North America*. Brian Swann, ed., pp. 15–36. New York: Random House.

PART I

Central Yup'ik and Cup'ig Narratives

THE HISTORIC AND CONTEMPORARY HOME of Alaska's Yup'ik Eskimos has at its heart the broad low-lying delta of the Yukon and Kuskokwim rivers. This vast delta region is bordered by mountains and uplands that separate it from the Nushagak drainage and Bristol Bay to the south and Norton Sound and Seward Peninsula to the north. The region's current population of more than thirty thousand (the largest Native population in Alaska) lives scattered in seventy villages of between two hundred and one thousand persons and in larger regional centers in Bethel and Dillingham. Today this huge region is cross-cut by historical and administrative differences, including three dialect groups, three major Christian denominations, six school districts, two census areas, and three regional corporations established by the Alaska Native Claims Settlement Act (ANCSA) in 1971 (see Fienup-Riordan 2000a:3–28).

The Bering Sea coast supports abundant resources, including sea and land mammals, waterfowl, and fish. Men hunt for walrus and bearded, spotted, and ringed seals from the shorefast ice, beginning in March or early April. By May geese and ducks crowd the flyways, returning to their summer nesting grounds. In June many families move to fish camps, where men set nets for herring, salmon, and flounder that women dry for winter use. Children fill baskets with kelp laden with herring eggs and the tiny capelin that wash up during high tides. Women gather greens close to home or camp on the tundra for days at a time with their families to gather eggs and berries. Fishing and trapping continue into late fall, when people return to their winter villages where harvesting activities are more circumscribed. Prehistorically this abundance supported the development and spread of Inuit culture; some scholars have called the Bering Sea coast the "cradle of Eskimo civilization."

Although rich in subsistence resources, the lack of commercial resources—whales, furbearers, mineral deposits—made the region less attractive to a resident non-Native population compared to other parts of Alaska. Following initial contact in the 1840s, waves of epidemics (influenza, diphtheria, tuberculosis)

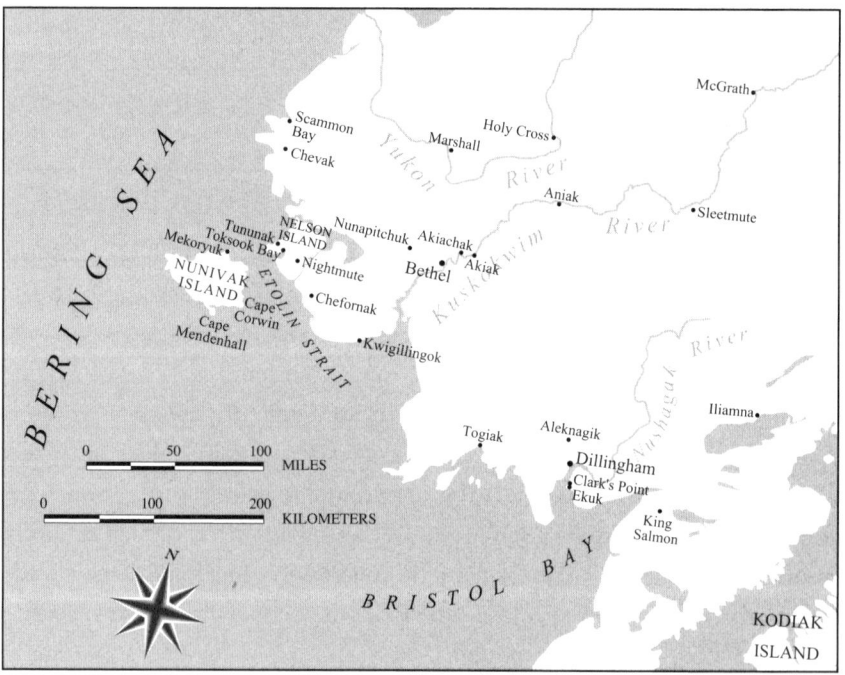

Nunivak Island and the Yukon–Kuskokwim Delta.

decimated the Native population. Whole villages disappeared and families were devastated, yet they endured. The first non-Natives to settle in significant numbers were Christian missionaries, beginning in the late 1800s. Elders living in the region today were born into a world very much like that of their forebears, especially in their reliance on the harvest of fish and game. Most were raised in small settlements residentially divided between a communal men's house (*qasgi*) and separate sod homes for women and children.

Rapid change has since come to coastal and riverine communities. Social reforms of the 1960s, passage of ANCSA in the 1970s, and the Alaska oil boom supported the establishment of modern villages, each with its own formal city government, high school, corporation store, daily air service to the regional center of Bethel, electricity, television and telephone service, and, in some cases, indoor plumbing. Despite these changes, both late contact and lack of commercial resources have meant that the Yup'ik region has retained many social patterns that have been lost in other parts of Alaska, and many traditions—especially dancing and elaborate community gift-giving—remain living links to the past.

The Central Yup'ik language is the second most commonly spoken Native language in the United States and the third most common in North America north of Mexico after Navajo and Inuktitut (spoken among Canadian Inuit). More than half the Native residents of southwest Alaska speak Yup'ik as their first language. In a quarter of the villages Yup'ik is spoken by everyone from the eldest to the youngest. This continued cultural and linguistic vitality has contributed to the position of the Yup'ik people as among the most traditional Native American groups, actively working both to retain the best of their past and carry still-vital traditions into the future.

Explorers and missionaries were among the first to document Yup'ik and Cup'ig oratory and to translate what they recorded into English. Stationed at St. Michael from 1877 to 1881, naturalist Edward Nelson recorded several dozen Yup'ik and Iñupiaq tales, which he published in his classic *Eskimo about Bering Strait* in 1899. Living in Bethel and traveling widely throughout the region in the 1880s and 1890s, Moravian missionary John Kilbuck documented Yup'ik life in his "Something about the Inuit" (Fienup-Riordan 1988). Edward S. Curtis (1930) visited Nunivak Island in 1927 and published a handful of traditional tales that he gathered during his trip. He was followed by the German folklorist Hans Himmelheber, who traveled down the Kuskokwim in fall 1936 and spent the following winter on Nunivak Island, where he recorded a number of tales and stories (Fienup-Riordan 2000b).

Anthropologists also largely ignored southwest Alaska until well into the twentieth century. Margaret Lantis, who lived on Nunivak in 1939, was among the first to work in the region. Her *Social Culture of the Nunivak Eskimo* includes forty-one translated tales as well as the Cup'ig transcriptions and translations of four stories. In the 1960s Wendell Oswalt in Napaskiak and Lynn Ager in Tununak documented the unique Yup'ik pastime of recreational storytelling known as "storyknifing." Unlike the long *qulirat* (tales) and *qanemcit* (stories) told by men in the *qasgi*, they observed and described small groups of young women and girls telling each other stories that they illustrated by drawing pictures in the mud or snow with ivory storyknives (Ager 1971; Oswalt 1964).

Although Yup'ik men and women continued to tell each other stories in their own language, through the 1960s it was primarily non-Natives who recorded and wrote them down—almost all in English with no Yup'ik transcription. This began to change with the establishment of the Eskimo Language Workshop at the University of Alaska Fairbanks in 1967, which moved to Bethel in 1974 to become the Yup'ik Language Center. Supported and inspired by Alaska Native Language Center's Michael Krauss, linguists Irene Reed and Steven Jacobson worked with Yup'ik speakers, including Paschal Afcan, Martha Teeluk, and many others, to develop a standardized orthography for the Yup'ik language. Working together at the Yup'ik Language Center from 1979 through 1981, Elsie Mather, Phyllis Morrow, and others began to use this new orthography to record, transcribe, and translate Yup'ik traditional tales and stories.

From these beginnings came a burst of recording, much of it by Yup'ik and Cup'ig speakers. Although rarely turned into written form, the Bethel radio-television station KYUK documented and broadcast countless hours of Yup'ik oratory and traditional tales. Yup'ik students at Bethel Regional High School launched an oral history project and recorded hundreds of hours of interviews with elders. Although some tapes are technically flawed, many contain fine examples of Yup'ik oratory. Likewise ANCSA historical place and cemetery site investigations by the Bureau of Indian Affairs beginning in the 1970s yielded more than a thousand taped interviews with Yup'ik and Cup'ig elders.

Through the 1980s, transcriptions and translations by Yup'ik and Cup'ig men and women appeared in many publications, including Bethel Regional High School's *Kalikaq Yugnek / Book for the People*; Edward Tennant and Joseph Bitar's *Yup'ik Lore: Oral Traditions of an Eskimo People*; Anthony Woodbury's *Cev'armiut Qanemciit Qulirait-llu / Eskimo Narratives and Tales from Chevak*; and Elsie Mather's groundbreaking book on traditional Yup'ik ceremonies, *Cauyarnariuq / A Time for Drumming*. Bilingual publications continued in the 1990s, including Eliza and Ben Orr's *Qanemcikarluni Tekitnarqelartuq / One Must Arrive With a Story to Tell*; Marie Meade and Ann Fienup-Riordan's *Agayuliyararput / Our Way of Making Prayer*; and *Ellangellemni / When I Became Aware* by the Orrs in collaboration with Victor Kanrilak and Andy Charlie. Elsie Mather and Phyllis Morrow have published a number of excellent English translations of traditional Yup'ik tales. The twenty-first century has already seen the publication of three new bilingual publications: *Qulirat Qanemcit-llu Kinguvarcimalriit / Stories for Future Generations: The Oratory of Yup'ik Eskimo Elder Paul John* by Sophie Shield and Ann Fienup-Riordan; *Ciuliamta Akluit / Things of Our Ancestors* by Marie Meade and Ann Fienup-Riordan; and *Yupiit Qanruyutait / Yup'ik Words of Wisdom* by Alice Rearden, Marie Meade, and Ann Fienup-Riordan.

A written Yup'ik and Cup'ig literature is also emerging, including works by Anna Jacobson, Mary Jane Mann, and Alice Fredson. Today, taped source material continues to be transcribed and translated by a number of dedicated men and women with years of experience working with their language, including Howard and Muriel Amos, Oscar Alexie, Sophie Barnes, David Chanar, Anna Jacobson, Elsie Mather, Marie Meade, Eliza Orr, and Alice Rearden.

The six Yup'ik stories and one Cup'ig story that follow have much in common. Each was told in Yup'ik or Cup'ig by a respected elder, born in the late 1800s and early 1900s after change had come to the region but while stories were still regularly told in *qasgit* and homes. All the contributors except Paul John told stories expressly so that they could be recorded, transcribed, and translated. Nonetheless, each story was an intimate gift given to friends and close relatives—Lena Ilutsik speaking to her daughters, Frances Usugan to her daughter-in-law, Frank Andrew to his son, and Paul John to his many nieces and nephews. In most cases a non-Native listener was also present at the telling, but never as the primary audience.

Each story was carefully transcribed into Yup'ik or Cup'ig and translated into English. Readers will notice the greatest variation in the forms of the finished translations. Two tales—Natalia White's "Yaqutgiarcankut" and Frances Usugan's "Quliraq"—are rendered in line-verse format instead of paragraphs. Three contributors chose to include Native language transcriptions of the stories—two Yup'ik and one Cup'ig—along with their translations. This is a real gift, especially to Native speakers who can enjoy the dynamics of the elders' original performances in their language.

Yup'ik and Cup'ig storytelling remains very much an oral tradition. The written stories that follow descend directly from that tradition in their richness and variety.

—AFR

Introduction
Yaqutgiarcankut / Yaqutgiarcaq and Her Family

Told by Natalia White

Transcribed by Elsie Mather

Translated by Elsie Mather and Phyllis Morrow

Natalia White of Nunapitchuk told this story to Karen Michel and Elsie Mather in 1980, when Natalia was sixty-four years old. Karen was recording the story under a National Endowment for the Arts grant for a public radio series that was never, in the end, broadcast. At the time, Elsie and I worked at the Yup'ik Language Center (YLC) in Bethel; Karen came to YLC with the idea of collaborating with us on the project. Marie Meade and Joan Neck, who also worked at YLC, were both from Nunapitchuk and recommended Natalia as a storyteller. I had lived in Nunapitchuk myself in 1977 and remembered her as a wonderful and expressive person.

Natalia recalled hearing this and many other stories when she was a girl. Her mother passed away when she was a child, and her father was the family storyteller. Speaking in Yup'ik, she reminisced:

> My father must have really loved me. Since I was very young, every time we went to bed I would ask for stories. I have forgotten many of them. These two stories, though [*Yaqutgiarcankut* and a Raven story that she also told] I never forgot them, while the rest, I don't remember. I would always ask to be told the *Yaqutgiarcankut* story since I really enjoyed it.

While Karen, who did not understand Yup'ik, could only listen respectfully, Elsie enjoyed Natalia's imitations of the old woman's voice as she lured the girls into her house and then became increasingly frustrated with them.

Although Elsie had never heard this story before, she recalls a variant in which the old woman was called Kaaguagacungaq. In Elsie's mother's version, Kaaguagacungaq was big, fat, and mean. She caught up with some children, took off her bloomers, put the children inside them, and tied the openings shut. Then she went off to fetch her *uluaq* (woman's knife). While she was gone, the children untied the knots, got out, and filled the bloomers with rocks. They escaped, crossing a river on the crane's legs. When the fat woman returned, she plunged her *uluaq* into the bloomers, blunting the blade flat on the rocks. The crane also stretched out his legs to let her cross the river, but she was so fat that he pulled his legs back when she was halfway across and she drowned. A very similar story, told by Olinka Michael, became the basis for a children's book published in Yup'ik for the Bilingual Education Program in the early 1980s. In this adapted version, the (male) giant's name was Akaguagaankaaq (McGill n.d.).

In the following transcription, Elsie Mather used line breaks to indicate groupings that link grammatical structure, intonation contour, content, and pause phrasing to reflect the narrator's delivery. Double spacing between lines indicates a larger content grouping, and triple spacing corresponds to a topic shift. When the narrator emphasized an entire line or phrase, it is preceded by an exclamation point in the Yup'ik. Words in brackets have been added when a minor clarification of the original is needed (for example, to indicate who is speaking). The one English word, "gray," that Natalia White used is in italics in the Yup'ik transcript. To the extent possible, the English translation that follows parallels the Yup'ik transcription.

Our thanks to Natalia White and to Karen Michel for permission to retranscribe, retranslate, and publish this story.

THE ELDEST DAUGHTER'S NAME, Yaqutgiarcaq, suggests the Yup'ik word for "bird," presaging her final transformation. In an earlier translation, we gave her a roughly equivalent English name, "Birdie," to suggest this resemblance, but we eventually decided to keep her less transparent Yup'ik name. The story begins with the parents and children moving to a new location in late summer, which would not have been unusual in the days before permanent settlements, because people relocated frequently in family groups to take advantage of different resources in season. With tundra berries ripe for the picking, children (now as then) are apt to wander off from their parents when they are out of the boat, so there may be a cautionary element to this tale. In any case, the older sister fails to respond to her younger sister's warnings, and her heedlessness causes the two to be left behind.

Aspects of the narrative style, setting, characters, and dialogue in the story of Yaqutgiarcaq and her family are reminiscent of storyknife tales, which used to be very popular. When women told storyknife tales to girls, or girls told them to each other, they used bone or ivory storyknives (and later, table knives) to illustrate stylized characters and settings, often house interiors from above, as if viewed through a sod house smoke hole. The storytellers stored up their saliva (often stimulated by a wad of chewing tobacco or tobacco-fungus mixture [*iqmik*]) so that they could periodically spit in the mud to moisten it for illustration. As they held back a mouthful of saliva, their stories were punctuated by small slurping sounds. This sound became habitual in the narrative style of many women. In fact, storyknifing was such a habit among women from earlier generations that I can remember sitting on the boardwalk in Nunapitchuk with a friend, Jeannie Tobeluk, absent-mindedly drawing on my arm—and "slurping"—as she told me stories about what she had been doing earlier that day. On the audiotape, Natalia White can be heard making this quiet noise, although she did not illustrate this story.

Storyknife tales often centered around young female characters who disobeyed their elders to explore forbidden places, particularly hills, which commonly turned out to be sod houses inhabited by supernatural beings (sometimes, as in this story, old women) from whom they had to escape (see Oswalt 1964:334). Lynn Ager (1971:78) also notes that hills were associated with burials, hence spirits. One story Wendell Oswalt recorded from Napaskiak features an almost identical exchange as that which takes place in Natalia White's narrative. In the Napaskiak storyknife tale, two grandchildren and their grandmother go to a forbidden hill and enter the house of an old woman. The old woman wants them to look for lice in her hair. The children want to urinate, and the old woman tells them to do so on [her] hands. Their grandmother says not to urinate on the old woman's hands. The old woman yells [as the girls are leaving] to come back and look for more lice (Oswalt 1964:320; brackets original). In another story recorded by Oswalt (1964:317), a girl is unable to escape a grandmother's house under the pretext of having to "go toilet" and is told instead, "No, use your pot."

Marie Meade, Natalia White's niece, is among the contributors to this volume who participated in a discussion of this story in Anchorage in 1999. She had never heard her aunt's story in its entirety before that reading. However, Marie had written a children's book, *Cetugpak* ("Big Nails"), based on elements from storyknife tales that she remembered from childhood. She incorporated some motifs common to *Yaqutgiarcankut* in that book. Ina Carpenter, also present at the Anchorage reading, recalled a story in which a number of people tried to cross a river on a crane's outstretched legs. In that version, the good people crossed safely, and the bad ones fell in.

The grandmother–grandchild relationship also figures strongly in both storyknife tales and other traditional Yup'ik tales (*qulirat*). The grandparent–grandchild pair is referred to by single words that signal closeness, such as *tutgara'urluqellriik* (a grandchild-related pair) or *maurluqellriik* (a grandmother-related pair). Because of the extension of kin terms to people other than biological relatives, it is not unusual to find out about such a relationship only when an elder explains it. So the old woman's attempt to endear herself to the girls, saying that she is their grandmother, would not have been improbable.

Of course, the old woman turns out to be something not quite human. At first, she behaves normally, asking the girls to clean the lice from her hair. In the days when lice were a ubiquitous plague, it was an affectionate duty to pick them out for someone (and to eat them). But something strange starts to happen when the lice and nits turn out to be mice and voles. Here, Yaqutgiarcankut recalls the widespread Inuit story of Sedna, which is reported only in fragmentary versions in western Alaska (Sonne 1990). Some inland variations of the motifs found in the coastal Sedna complex appear in this story set in the "tundra marsh" region where Natalia White lives.

In the eastern Arctic, Sedna is the mother of sea beasts. When sea mammals were scarce, the shaman would travel to the sea bottom to coax Sedna to release them. He would do this by picking lice from her hair, which she could not do because she lacked fingers. She lost them when she made an inappropriate marriage to a dog or a sea bird (fulmar). Her father, outraged, threw her from a boat, cutting off her fingers when she tried to cling to the side. Her finger joints were transformed into seals, whales, and walruses, rising to the ocean surface as Sedna sank.

Natalia White's story contains several similar motifs in a tundra/riverine setting. For example, the old woman's "louse nits" (small tundra animals) boil to the surface of the river and scurry to land as she sinks, in a way reminiscent of the origin of sea mammals in the Sedna story. Although a more tenuous point of comparison, it is interesting that Sedna is connected with the fulmar, a sea bird, and Yaqutgiarcankut with common tundra birds (cranes, ptarmigans, and hawk owls).

The origin of the crane's coloration in this story recalls other tales detailing how birds (for example, Loon and Raven) got their markings when humans or other animals painted them, sometimes in revenge, other times in gratitude. Dialogues with objects such as the berry bucket, roasting stick, and tree stumps are also found in other Yup'ik stories, where objects as well as animals speak and interact with people. Compare for example the dialogue between a fish-skin mitten and a grass bag in a story told by Mary Worm (1986:46).

In the last part of the story, the girls make it safely to their family's new home, only to find that their foolish parents insist that they have died. As was customary, they avoided mentioning the names of the dead, which carried a person's essence (namesoul). But they also ignored good evidence that the girls had returned safely. In this way, they failed to act like sensible human beings. And then they turned into birds, fluttering up in a noisy panic, as ptarmigan are wont to do.

Describing the parents' "flighty" behavior at the end, Natalia White could barely contain her laughter, and when she finished, she went on laughing for a long time. Elsie thinks that Natalia's laughter was partly out of embarrassment. Telling this story in the presence of Karen, the white stranger with the tape recorder, was a reminder that an unseen radio audience unfamiliar with historic Yup'ik life might be offended by references to lice and urination—but we are confident that all audiences will enjoy this story.

—Phyllis Morrow

Yaqutgiarcankut

Told by Natalia White of Nunapitchuk

Yaqutgiarcankut ukut upalriit.

Angyarrlugluteng.

Aatiit ukamarluni.
Yaqutgiarcankuk-wa.
Alqaat Yaqutgiarcamek aterluni.

Yaqutgiarcankuk-wa kinguqlini-ll' cavelriik
aaniit-wa aqutellria.
Kinguqliak-wa kan'a.

Tua-i tamaaggun kuigkun ayagluteng.

Tua-i-ll' kaingameng arulairluteng nerqataameng
Yaqutgiarcankuk kinguqlini-ll' iqvarlutek kavirlinek ayagarrlutek
angayuqatek nerellratni.

Tua-i-ll' iqvainanragni qayagpaganglukek cama-i atraasqellukek,
    ayakatarniluteng.

Kinguqlian Yaqutgiarcam pia,
"Alqallraa, ayakatartut-gguq
atrarnaurtukuk."
Alqallriin-am pia, "Atatatata, ukut wani kavirlirugaat
    iqvalaaggaarluki."

Aren tua-i iqvarluki.

"Ampi-gguq. Ayakatartut-gguq!"

Yaqutgiarcaq and Her Family

Yaqutgiarcaq and her family were moving to a new place.

They were traveling in a skin boat.

The father was on the shore pulling the boat along.
Yaqutgiarcaq and the other one.
The oldest sister was called Yaqutgiarcaq.

Yaqutgiarcaq and her younger sister were rowing
while their mother was paddling in the back
and their brother was down there [in between].

They were traveling on that river.

So then, since they were hungry they stopped and were about to eat when
Yaqutgiarcaq and her younger sister scrambled off to pick cranberries
while their parents were eating.

So then, while they were picking, their family started shouting to them to
    come back, saying they were ready to leave.

The younger sister said to Yaqutgiarcaq,
"Older sister, they're saying they're ready to leave.
Let's go back down."
The older sister replied, "Wait, wait! After we quickly pick this bunch of
    cranberries."

And so they picked them.

[Younger sister] "They're telling us to come now. They say they're leaving!"

"Atata, tang ukut amllellriit!"

Tua-i-am atataangekili.

Tua-ll'-am Yaqutgiarcam pia,
"Qayagaunritut. Atam taiqaa qaltama epuan kangia
    qalrialartuq.
Atam niicugniqerru."

Ullagluku niicugnia,
qalriagurlun'. Anuqem.

Tua-i-ll' iqvarlutek.
Muiriamek-llu tuay atrarlutek.
Atraryaaquk imkut ilakek tayim'.
Unillukek-am ayallinilriit.

Ukuk-wa cung'ulquk,
enerrluyagaam cung'ulquk
kenillrem caniani, una-w' atiignek maniarutellra.

Tua-i-ll' taukuk cung'ulquk avv'arrlukek,
akmatkuigteka'arrlukek nerlukek.

Nererraarlukek-llu iqvamegnek nerevsiarraarlutek.
Yaqutgiarcam aptaa tauna pi,
atami maniarutellra,
"Usuuq maniarutellruaraaq natmun ilapuk ayagtat?"
Taum-am maniarutellrem kiugaa,
"Ing'um ing'um cingiim amatiinun qip'arcenartut."

Kitak-gguq yaavet pilliniut.

Tua-i-ll' kuigem ceniikun ayaglutek.

Ayaglutek.
Ayainanermegni, canegpaungan,
can'get akuliitni
tuar tang pam(na) aruvak.

[Yaqutgiarcaq] "Later. There are so many berries here!"

She kept on saying "later."

Then Yaqutgiarcaq said to her sister,
"They are not calling. Come here. There is a noise coming from the handle
     of my berry pail.
Listen to it."

She came over and listened.
Sure enough, it was making noise, from the wind blowing on it.

And so they picked.
When they filled up their pails, they headed down.
When they got down there their family was gone.
They had gone ahead without them.

There they found a fishhead,
a head part of a fish skeleton,
by the remains of a campfire, and a roasting stick their father had used.

So the girls separated the head in two,
each eating a half.

And after eating that and after eating some of their berries,
Yaqutgiarcaq asked that object,
her father's roasting stick,
"You there, roasting stick, where did our family go?"
And then that roasting stick replied,
"Over there, over there, they went around the other side of that point."

Well then, they had gone over there.

So they went on along the river.

They went on.
As they went along and since there was tall grass there,
they thought they saw smoke back there
through the grass.

Tua-ll' arulairlutek piuk,
pamna tang aruvagnauluni ellma aruvkallutellria.
Tayima-ll' tang.
"Tang paqteqernaurpuk. Pamna tang yugtangqerrsugnarqell'."
Alqallriin-am pia.

Tua-i-ll' taglutek.
Tekitaak enecualler una amiiga ikingqaluni.
Tua-i nauluku can'get
qanganaruat-llu naumaluku.

Tua-i-ll' mayurlutek egalranun uyangtuk,
arnassagall'er kan'a,
tua-i amia agaluni ugaan arnaurtem.
Kankuk-wa tang kenillrani kangipluaraak,
cupuraraqlukek.

Cupurarqaku aruvanga'artelallinilria.

Tua-i-ll' uyangqaqanragen'gun
tauna tang tangenrrilngermikek arnassagall'er qanertuq ciuggluni,
"Kitak aren tutgara'urluugmaa,
kitek iterlutek kumakirtegnga.
Tangerrluku ungiliq'ngelrianga."
Tua-i kinguqlia alingluni.

Aren alqallriin-am,
"Usuuq alingnaituq. Tang maurluqlinikvuk,
ullagluku iterlunuk kumakirraarluk' aneniartukuk."

Tua-i-ll' iqvatek taukut unilluki keggavet iterlutek.

Itramek akiqliqlutek kumakirluku.

Tauna tang kinguqliurlua piqertuq
nuyain akuliitni man' !angyayagaq.
"Ila-i tang man' angyayagaq!"
"Aulluggai taisgu ingqiqaqa!"

So they stopped and looked.
Sure enough there seemed to be smoke back there, a small waft of smoke.
And then it was gone.
"Let's go see what it is. There must be someone back there,"
the older sister said.

So they went back there.
When they got there they came to a poor old [sod] house with its door open.
There was grass
and even wormwood plants [artemesia] growing all over it.

And then they climbed up to the top and looked in through the window
and saw an ugly old woman down there.
She was so old her skin was hanging on her.
They also saw two pieces of charred wood in her firepit
and she would blow on them.

They saw that whenever she blew [on the firepit] it would start smoking.

They had been looking in a short time
when the old woman, even before she saw them, put her head back and said,
"Well then, my two dear grandchildren,
come in and look for lice on my head.
My head has gotten itchy."
The younger sister was scared.

The older sister said,
"Look, she is no one to be afraid of. See, she says she is our grandmother.
Let's go in and then leave after we look for her head lice."

And so they left their berries outside and went in.

When they entered they settled across from each other and looked for lice.

That poor younger sister then saw
a vole in the old woman's hair!
"Oh! Look! There is a vole!"
"Be careful! Give it to me! It is my louse nit!"

Taum tang tunngaku
!teguqerluk' nerkiliu.

Tuamtell' alqaa,
"Ila-i man'a tang avelngaq!"
"Taisgu nerestekaqa!"
!Neraa-am.

Alay! Tua-i kinguqliurlua taun' alinglun' piuq,
"Tua-i tang wii nakacingelrianga yuqerceskuk."

(Tua-ll', aren), "Kanavet qurrutellramnun qurritek."

Tuall'-am Yaqutgiarcaq,
"Yuut qurrutaitnun qurrsuitaqukuk!"
"Wall'uq' yaavet enem ingluanun yuqertek."
"Enet iluitnun yuqercuitaqukuk!"

"Wall'uq' tumiigemnun?"
"Yuut tumaitnun qurrsuitaqukuk!"
Alqallraan-am kiugurluku.

"Wall'uq' ciutegemnun?"
"Yuut ciutaitnun qurrsuitaqukuk!"
"Wall'uq' qanemnun? Aitarrnaurtua."
"Yuut qanritnun qurrsuitaqukuk!"

"Eqnaqvagtak ukuk!
Wall'u-qaa qaugna tapengyak taitegu,
qukatek qillerrluki yuqercetnaamtek ayagyuartutek."
"Ayagngaitukuk, iterciqukuk!"

Tua-i-ll'-am qillercatek anlutek.

Aren qamiqunanek ima tanem kanani ketvaarni tangellrulriik,
nunamun-llu waten ingluit pulaluteng.

Tua-i-ll' ayaglutek
taukut qamiqunat tungiitnun.
Qam'um nuqtaqlukek yaaqvanun pisqevkenakek.

When the girl gave the vole to the old woman
she grabbed it and ate it!

And then her older sister cried,
"Oh look! Here is a mouse!"
"Give it to me! It is my louse!"
And she ate that, too!

That poor younger sister was horrified and said,
"I need to pee. Let us go outside to pee."

(And then [the old woman said]), "Use my old urine bucket."

And Yaqutgiarcaq spoke up,
"We never pee into other people's urine buckets!"
"Then go over there to the edge of the house."
"We never pee inside houses!"

"How about into the palm of my hands?"
"We do not pee into anyone's hands!"
That older sister kept on with her answers.

"How about into my ears?"
"We never pee into people's ears!"
"Into my mouth, then. I'll open it."
"We never pee into people's mouths!"

"Oh! How infuriating you two are!
Bring me that leather rope then.
Just in case you take off, I'll tie it to your waist and then let you out to pee."
"We won't go anywhere. We'll come back in."

So, when she tied the rope on them they went out.

Oh! Earlier they had seen some old roots down toward the river,
some half-buried in the ground.

And so they went
toward the stumps.
That one inside would pull the rope and tell them not to go far.

"Ii-i, canimaarmun anayuitut."

Tua-i-ll' qamiqunat,
angilluku tuaten,
tekicamegneki taukunun qillerquqaarluku taman' tapengyak,
!ayagarrlutek.
!Kuigem ceniikun aqvaqurlutek.

Ip'arrlutek
igvaartuk
ikegkuk qucillgaak.

Tua-ll'-am alqallriin,
"Kitaki ikegkuucungaak
ceturrlutek iruvtegen'gun qerarcecikuk.
Mingugniamcetek kavirrlutek qaisek-llu mingugluku."

Cetu'urcagnek-am qer'aqertuk!
Tua-i-ll' qung'arrlutek.

Imna-am akemna kingunrak qayagaunguq.
Qayagauryaaqvigminek tamana imna tapengyak, kiuyunrilagni.

Aren! Taukut ima tanem qamiqunat alerquqai Yaqutgiarcam,
"Qayagauraqaci waten pikici,
'Qurrsuiqsaitukuk, anaqsuiqsaitukuk!'"

Aren, tua-i-ll'
qenngami arnassagaam
cayugareskiini tang cakem' amigmun migpak!

Aren maaten tang im' anelrartuq
qamiqunat ukut amiigani keviusngalriit!
"Eqnarivakar caqtaaqtartak!
Unguvarpetek tua taqciqamtek!"

Tukerluki tua aug'angnaqluki augaata,
tumkegen'gun cetamanek ipilirlun' !kingunragen'gun.

"No [we won't go far]. But people don't defecate by the houses!"

And those stumps....
They untied the rope on the way
and after tying it to those stumps when they reached them
they took off!
They ran along the river!

In a bit they were out of sight
and suddenly saw
two cranes across the river!

Then the older sister called,
"You, dear ones across there,
spread out your legs and let us cross.
We will decorate you with ochre and paint your bodies."

So when the cranes stretched out their legs they scrambled across!
And then the cranes pulled their legs back.

And then that one across there started calling to them.
Finally she gave up calling them since they didn't answer. And that rope....

Oh! Yaqutgiarcaq had instructed those tree stumps,
"Whenever she calls, say,
'We haven't finished peeing, we haven't finished going!'"

So then,
the old woman got angry
and yanked on the rope. And there was a loud thump out in her entryway!

When she went out there
there were those stumps stuck in her doorway!
"How maddening those two are to do this!
I won't be finished with you two until you're dead!"

She pushed, trying to dislodge the stumps. And when they were free
she followed their trail and took off after [the girls] on all fours!

Tua-i-ll' ika-i kana'arrluni!

Ika-i, "Qaill' pilutek qerarcetek?"
Aren, imkuk-wa qucillgaagnek ilalutek.

Tua-ll'-am alqallraan pia,
"Uiluaraak ituarrlukek!"

Agaa-i-am uilunek yuangarrluni,
uiluq-am qupraarluku
!tucaaqekiini kill'uni.

"Naw'un qerarcetek?"
"Qeltengulluaraak ituarrlukek!"

Agaa-i-am qeltengullugculaagluni,
qeltengulluugnek-am itullukek
!tucaaqekiitek kill'uni.

"Naw'un picetek? Qanrutegnga!"
"Can'guar qup'arrluku."
Tua-i-am qupraarluku tucaaqekiini kill'uni!
"Eqnaqvagtak ikegkuk! Naw'un waniw' qerarcetek?"

Tua-ll' Yaqutgiarcam piak taukuk imkuk yaqulgek,
"Qanrullauk atak iruvtegen'gun qerarnilunuk.
Ceturrlutek qerarcetniartek.
Qukaqan'gu-ll' tuay kuik qukaqaku
cayugarrluk' irutek!"

Tua-i-ll' agaa-i aqvaquallrani,
"Qucillgaak irukegen'gun!"

"Kitak qucillgacungaak, irutek ceturteki qerarnaurtua!"

Tua-i-ll' ceturrlutek.

Ceturcagnek
cetamanek ipilirluni

And then there she was at the river's edge!

Then she called, "How did you get across?"
Oh! The two cranes were with the girls.

Then the older sister said,
"We put two clam shells together!"

The one across there scrambled around looking for clam shells,
opened one,
stepped into it, and fell into the water.

"How did you get across?"
"By putting two pieces of wood bark side by side."

The one across there scurried around for pieces of bark,
put two together and stepped on them,
but fell in!

"How did you get across? Tell me!"
"We split a piece of grass in half."
And she split a piece of grass, stepped in, and fell in again!
"How infuriating those two are! Now how did you two get across?!"

So then, Yaqutgiarcaq said to the two birds,
"Should we tell her we came across on your legs?
Then you stretch out your legs and let her cross.
And when she is halfway across, when she gets to the middle,
quickly pull your legs back!"

So, as she was scurrying around across there, [Yaqutgiarcaq said]
"We came across on the crane's legs!"

"Well then, you two dear cranes, stretch out your legs so I can cross!"

So they stretched their legs out.

When their legs were stretched across,
she started coming over

ayapertuarturluni uka-i agiirrluni.

Tua-i-ll' kuik qukaan irutek
!yuuniapaglutek cayugarrlukek.

Cayugarcanki-ll' tuay im' arnassagall'er kill'uni!

Aren tayima-ll' tang tuay 'leryirrluni kic'an
!avelngaat angyayagaat-llu kuimelriit,
!tagelriit nunamun.
!Tua-i angyayagaulun' un' avelngaulun' tagluteng nunamun.

Nutaan imkuk taukuk qucillgaak
kitugglukek,
irukek-llu minguglukek tungulriamek
qaurakek-llu kavirutmek.
Qaikek-ll' avisgarmek minguglukek.

Qaqitenqegcaaraamegenki tuay quyalutek pia,
"Nani waniw' imkut ilapuk uitaat?"
Taukuk qucillgaak piak,
"Ama-i nunalillruut yaavet yaantut cingiim mat'um yaatiini."

Tua-i-ll' ayaglutek
tengengagnek taukuk.

Aren tua-i-gguq imna qucillgaam ukua
kavircetellria
Yaqutgiarcankuk mingullrak.

Tamana-ll' qaingak *gray*-aaq mingullrak,
unkuk-llu iruk tungurpiik.

Tua-i-ll' tekilluk',
ena igvarluku.
Ik'ik' enekegtaar una nutaraq.
Marayaq.

crawling on all four limbs!

And then when she was halfway across the river
the cranes gave a loud groan and quickly pulled their legs back!

When they pulled their legs back that old woman fell in!

And when she sank, making all that gurgling sound,
there appeared all those voles and mice!
swimming up to the riverbank!
There was nothing but voles and mice in the river scrambling toward the land!

Then finally they [the girls]
fixed up those two cranes.
They painted their legs black
and colored their foreheads with red ochre.
And they painted their bodies with blue clay.

Only after they completely finished with them they said thankfully,
"Where, then, would our family be?"
And the two cranes said,
"Over there. They made a place there beyond this point."

And so they left
after the cranes flew off.

They say that the crane's forehead,
which is red,
was painted by Yaqutgiarcaq and her sister.

They also painted their bodies gray
and their legs black.

And so they came
to the house their family had built.
It was a fine new house.
Of sod.

Elaturraanun iterlutek
evcuksugtellragni
kinguqlipataariik.
Qamna yuk anqerrluni igvaartuq im' kinguqlipataariik!
Tangvakarraarlukek-llu tayim' itqerrluni.

Itqerrlun' qama-i,
"Aan, tang alqallraagka tekitellinilriik!"

Qamkut tang qalrillagtut!

"Aren alqallraagken apqaunrituk,
ak'a tayim' tuqullruuk."
Tua-i.
"Atam uantuk!"
Tayim' anqerrluni-am qama'i itqe'rcan.

Anqe'rcan-am Yaqutgiarcam aqlitmi ingluanek cikiqaani
     tayim' itqerrlun',
"Tang waniw' aqlitii alqallrama."
qalrillagluteng!

"Aren eqnarqut qamkut!"

An'aqan tuay aqlitmegnek cikiryaaqaqluku
qalrillagnaurtut tuqullrunilukek tayima.

Tua-i-ll' Yaqutgiarcaq piuq,
"Eqnarqut qamkut!
Qaill' atak qamkut piqerlapuk?
!Aarpagaluki taugaam itqerreskumegnuk.
Anrraartelluku imna."

Tua-i-ll'-am anngan
nangnermek aqlitiin aipaan, aipaminek cikiqaaku
tayim' itqe'rcan,
qama-i-am qalrilliita,
!aarpagalutek itqerrlutek.

They came into the porch
and while they were brushing themselves off
their little brother.
Someone in there scrambled out—and there was their little brother!
He looked at them for a moment and rushed back inside.

They heard him rush in,
"Mom! My older sisters are here!"

Suddenly, they heard everyone crying inside there!

"Oh! Your sisters must never be mentioned.
They are dead now."
Then.
"Look! They're out there!"
He rushed out and back in again.

When he came out again, Yaqutgiarcaq gave him one of her earrings and he
        scrambled back in,
"See, here is my sister's earring!"
They started bawling again!

"Oh! How stupid they are!"

Whenever the little brother came out they would give him an earring,
but those inside would burst out wailing, saying the two had died.

So then, Yaqutgiarcaq said,
"They are so stupid!
What shall we do with them?!
We should scream and holler at them and barge in
after he comes back out."

And when the brother came out again,
and when Yaqutgiarcaq's sister gave him the last earring,
after he went back in,
When they started to wail again
the girls hollered and screamed as they ran inside!

!Itqercagnek imna enem ilua
!tem'illagluni im',
!qangqiirnek muiqerrluni.
Qangqiiruluteng tengvallakilit.

Egalerkun-ll' anqercata
elkek nacaqerlutek tengvallagtuk
!eskaviarulutek.

!Malirqeraluki tamakut qangqiiret,
!qecugmiarluki allgurluki.
Qenarqellruata unitellruicetek-llu.
!Allgurluki caunrirluki.

Tua-i-w' nangelria.

When they ran into the house
there was a thundering sound!!
It was suddenly full of ptarmigan!
They had turned into ptarmigan and were fluttering out.

As they flew out through the smoke hole
the two sisters pulled on their hoods and flew out
as hawk owls!

They went after the ptarmigan,
clawing them, tearing them up!
Because they had been so foolish and they had left them behind!
They tore them up into nothing!

That is all.

Introduction
One Who Didn't Think Much of a Man's Stomach

Told by Paul John

Transcribed and translated by Sophie Shield

Kangrilnguq (Paul John) was born in 1928 in Cevv'arneq, the original site of the modern village of Chefornak, fifteen miles south of Qaluyaaq (Nelson Island). The much-loved only child of John Kungurkaq and Anna Angayiq, Paul lived with his mother and aunts in a sod house until age five, then moved into the *qasgi* with his father and uncles. There he spent countless hours listening to their stories and advice. Schools had not yet been established in most coastal communities. The first resident missionary settled on Nelson Island after Paul was born. Paul recalled:

> When I became aware, people I saw survived only through hunting and gathering. And I personally never ate *kass'aq* [non-Native] food besides a little bit of flour and sugar.... That was the way I saw it, even though I am not very old. These *kass'at* didn't come to the coast right away. A school was not built in my village for many years. That is why I saw that way of life, the way our ancestors lived.... And when I was seven years old, the priest [Father Deschout] finally arrived. I became aware of my surroundings before the ways of the authentic Yup'ik people changed.

Paul grew to manhood following the seasonal round of his forebears, moving between spring and fall camping places and their permanent winter settlement in Chefornak. In 1952 he married Martina Usugan and moved to Nightmute to live with her family. The young couple continued to move seasonally until 1960, when they settled in Nightmute so that their eldest son, Mark, could attend the new school.

In 1964, to avoid the arduous annual move between the winter village of Nightmute and spring camp at Umkumiut, Paul led a number of families to found the village of Toksook Bay. Paul's leadership is recognized both locally and regionally, and he continues to serve his people in numerous capacities.

His vision extended to sharing traditional knowledge for documentation, convinced that Yup'ik young people will be better prepared for the future if they understand their past.

Paul John told the following story, along with many others, to Toksook high school students during a two-week period in February 1977. I was working as a substitute there and was invited to record what Paul said. Paul was directing his talks to Yup'ik young people to help them understand their history, but what I learned enriched my understanding of Yup'ik oral traditions one-hundredfold.

In 1992 Sophie Manutuli Shield began to transcribe and translate everything Paul had shared. Sophie was born and raised in Tuntutuliak. She was an expert transcriber and translator who began her linguistic work with Irene Reed in the 1970s. Until she passed away in 2004, she worked for the Bilingual Program of the Lower Kuskokwim School District. Her work with Paul was published in 2003 as *Qulirat Qanemcit-llu Kinguvarcimalriit / Stories for Future Generations: The Oratory of Yup'ik Eskimo Elder Paul John*. At the American Folklore Society meetings in October 2001, Sophie described that work:

> My mother used to say all the time, "The legends are our ancestors."
> About eight years ago I had the privilege of being asked to translate
> Paul John's work. He's an elder from Toksook Bay and this [book]
> is all of his work, including lots and lots of information. Whenever
> I hear him speak out, I'm always impressed with how much knowl-
> edge he has, and I'd like to read a quote. This is what Paul said: "I was
> just thinking now about these papers, and it seems that I am passing
> them on to all of my children's children, and I am also thinking about
> my great grandchildren. It seems that when I die, I will pass this on
> to them and to all of the world's inhabitants."

Throughout his weeks speaking in the high school, Paul took his role as educator very seriously, giving young people advice on how to live life that many might not otherwise have received. He told many stories, including both *qulirat* and *qanemcit*. Most of these narratives either directly or indirectly concern how people should act toward one another and the consequences if they failed to follow traditional instructions guiding interpersonal behavior. Paul often followed his accounts with advice on how people should live their lives. The story we have chosen to include here is a fine example of this interplay between story and instruction. "One Who Didn't Think Much of a Man's Stomach" is a cautionary tale, portraying the consequences of a wife's selfishness. At the end of the story Paul discusses how couples ideally should act toward each other.

Although speaking of his past, Paul also clearly communicates something of the present and the future. Here, as elsewhere, he introduces and explains words that students might not understand, using his stories as an opportunity to expand their knowledge. The story also reveals a high degree of interaction between Paul and his young audience, connecting the abstract lessons of ancient tales with contemporary lives, and Sophie's translation retains direct evidence of his narrative's important communicative function.

Sophie chose to render Paul's words in paragraph form. These paragraphs are not arbitrary groupings but are distinguished by the cohesion between contiguous lines and her perception that lines go together. This is often associated with a change in pitch. Groups of lines also often begin with line-initial particles such as *tua-i-llu* (so then), clearly indicating a shift in narrative action.

—AFR

One Who Didn't Think Much of a Man's Stomach

Told by Paul John of Toksook Bay

I AM GOING TO TELL YOU A *QANEMCIQ* that is almost like the one I told the [students in the class] just before you.

In the old days when *kass'aq* food was not available, our ancestors left their villages to hunt, just so they could find more food from other places. Some people weren't lucky when they went, and some were lucky.

In those days, a married couple went fall camping to fish because they thought that they might be a little luckier if they went to a place away from their village. They were a couple without children. And there was no one else living in their fall camp, they lived there alone.

(You young women, think of the times that you will not choose to prepare food for your husbands when you marry when I come to the part where they were hungry.)

When those two went out to fall camp, they stayed even though winter came while they were there. When winter came, they spent the winter there. Their parents were down in their village. They both had parents. This was in the days when people didn't die young. You probably heard that people in the old days lived for a long time, that they didn't die so young. In those days when people didn't die so young, people had many children while their parents were still alive. Young couples would have many children while their parents were living.

So then, since those two were the only ones who spent the winter there, even though her husband tried to hunt, and because they probably didn't bring much food when they left the village, they eventually ran out of food. Their food supply dwindled. Even though her man took off in the winter to hunt, the weather was always bad. He wasn't very successful at hunting. He would catch some, but not enough.

When the food they brought with them dwindled, his wife hid what remained so her husband would not see where they were. Then she told her husband that they had run out of food. When she wanted to eat and since she had hidden some food, she would wait for her husband to leave for the wilderness and eat. That poor husband of hers thought they really ran out of food. When he left, that poor thing would try to hunt without eating anything. His wife never lost any weight, even though her husband lost weight.

One day he came home when his wife had just finished eating. The odor of food is probably very strong when one is starving. Well, one day when he came home just after she had eaten, when he entered their home it had a very strong fish smell. They say his wife had hidden some smoked fish. She lied to her husband that they ran out of food.

He asked her, "Oh my, where is the smell of fish coming from inside our house?"

His wife took hold of the hem of her parka and shook it, "The smell is probably coming from my old parka. You know how I wore it last summer when I worked on fish."

Her poor husband believed that he probably smelled some fish odor from her parka.

Well, her man became thin, but his wife's weight never changed. After trying a number of times, her man gave up and stopped going anywhere. His wife was even running low on food.

Considering what she had left, his wife began to realize that she was not going to have food left. Her husband was getting very weak and couldn't travel very far. She said to her husband, "Gee, I should go down to our village and tell them to come and get you. I am definitely stronger than you are."

Well, her husband was grateful because he knew that there was no way he could survive.

When his wife left him there, she traveled to her village with provisions since her food was almost gone, and she soon arrived. When she got to the village to ask them to retrieve him, [instead] she told her relatives that her husband had gotten ill and become very skinny and died. She said she left him in the house they had been living in and did not take him out. (As she was leaving, it was actually [her husband] whom she had told that she would send someone to get him. This was because he really looked as though he was going to starve to death when she left him, and he didn't have any food at all.)

After she left he kept himself busy inside their house. While keeping himself busy, he dug underneath the grass bedding to pile them together and found a small piece of smoked fish underneath the old mat they used. It turned out that his wife had hidden her supply of food underneath her side of the bedding. She had forgotten that one. The poor thing found a small piece of fish that she hadn't seen. So he started eating that. He would eat a pinch [of fish] when it was time to eat. He would chew that bit of fish until it was very fine and then swallow it. As time passed, his strength that had been declining began to return, he began to revive.

When was that person who was to fetch him going to come? He never arrived. No one came to get him.

So his food was gone. He ran out of food. Soon he noticed a mouse coming in through the door, and it proceeded to come in on the other side of the house. As the mouse walked in, he thought, "Gee, what a waste, you are indeed plenty of food!"

They say their small supply of grass was in the corner across there. [The mouse] got to that grass and started making a nest. It started to chew on them to make them soft. He was very envious knowing that the little mouse was something to eat.

Well, the mouse went back out when it was tired of scurrying around. When it went out, since he probably had materials to make one, he made what they call a trap, a small trap for it. He didn't have any other weapons handy to catch it with.

Well, when the mouse came back in again, and his trap ensnared it and killed it, that poor thing gratefully ran over to it, grabbed it, and skinned it. After skinning it he went out, since he was able to walk around now. Since he knew where the tundra area was, he went to it and started digging for what they call "reindeer food," which are lichens. He went out to the tundra area outside their house and started digging, since he knew their location. When the [lichens] started appearing, he took some and went back in. When he went back in, he took some of the roof boards [for fuel], put some lichens in the pot, cut the mouse into small pieces, and started cooking that mouse. Soon the house was filled with the delicious aroma of the mouse. After it was completely cooked, he ate it sparingly and had it for food for a long time. It was getting to be spring around that time.

They said he also had a small *qasgi* right near the river, close to the river. The vent for the firepit opened right onto the river's edge because it was right along the river. He had a small *qasgi*. And in his *qasgi* was a bunch of wheat grass for matting.

He was getting stronger. He started going outside. Soon the water along the sides of the river down there started to raise because it was starting to get warm outside. He, too, was getting stronger after nearly starving.

He finished the small amount of mouse he had, even though he ate very sparingly from it. When it was gone, when the sides of the river had plenty of water, he went out in the evening and sat down on the lee side of his house, and something appeared swimming along the side of the river. When it got closer, he noticed that it was a muskrat. Oh goodness, this time he really craved it, and even though he was alone that poor thing said that it sure was plenty of food because he had run out of food.

While he kept a close eye on it, it dove in right next to his *qasgi*. It dove in and didn't come back up. Then he quickly thought, "Gee, I wonder if it went into my *qasgi* through its vent to eat! I know that there are mats that muskrats eat, wheat grass matting." [The muskrat] was gone for a while. He was keeping an eye on it, and when it appeared from that spot, it swam upriver.

When it took off and was some distance away, he went down to check his small *qasgi* (probably because he was able to go down and was curious). He peeked into his small steam house and saw that the inside was filled with water. There was a pile of food in the spot where [the muskrat] ate its food. [That muskrat] had been eating some of his matting there and had been using them for a perch near the stove.

Well, when he went back to his house, he took one of his roofing boards that was strong and pliable and made a bow and arrow.

Muskrats get hungry in the evening just before dark. They start going to their eating areas when they come out of their sleeping places.

When evening came and he finished constructing his bow and arrow, he went down to his small steam house to wait for it. He stayed there, and when the right time came, the water that filled the area where his fire pit was started to rise slightly, and in a second the muskrat appeared right through there. He, too, didn't make a move suddenly and stayed still. When the muskrat appeared, it didn't pay any attention and quickly perched right near the fire pit. It didn't pay any attention and started to shake the water off. The muskrat turned its back on him and started eating. Only then did he prepare his bow and arrow and shoot. It died when he shot it with his bow and arrow since it was at close range.

Well, having hit it, he grabbed it and took it up to his house and skinned it. (He didn't have a kayak either.) That one gave him plenty to eat.

They say that he had parents and a younger sister back in his village.

Wow! That muskrat provided him with a large food supply. He cooked it like the previous one, but he didn't cook it all at once like the mouse. He cooked it with lichen and reindeer moss.

Soon the river that he was on started breaking up. Summer was arriving before someone came to get him. Here his wife had said that she would have someone fetch him.

Soon, the river that he was on started breaking up. One evening, he thought, "Gee, I've been in the house all winter long!" The weather was starting to get beautiful and was getting warmer. "I think it would be a good idea for me to leave my little house that I have been sick in and make another little house over yonder and move there." (Apparently [he had building materials] because there were bushes in that area.)

He went out and, since there were some bushes, made what they called a shelter, a small house. Then he started living there.

Whenever birds passed, he would covet them, but he couldn't catch them since he didn't have any proper weapons. Also, since he didn't have any sealskin boots he never went anywhere, although he wanted to, but just stayed there. That muskrat saved his life, providing him food for a long time.

One morning, there came the sound of a boat. It was definitely a boat splashing against water. Sometimes it would make a racket like the noise a boat makes. This was when the weather was always calm. He waited for it to come into view. Soon it came into view, and three people were in it. When they got close enough to recognize and were right below him, he saw that they were his parents and his younger sister. When they arrived, they disembarked and went into the house together. After going in, they came out.

Because he was a man, he was embarrassed to be seen in such a weak condition even by his parents, and he didn't make himself known as they passed. He just watched them until they reached his house.

After being inside for some time, they came out of the house and started circling the house, "Gee, where in the world did she place him? I thought she said she left him inside."

Well, when they started circling, he thought they were looking for him, so he went out of his little shelter and squatted down beside it.

At that moment his younger sister started coming toward him and then squatted down to urinate not too far from him, not paying attention to her older brother. While urinating, she started looking around and saw her older brother. When she saw him, she quickly stood and ran to her parents. When she got to them, she seemed to have spoken to them, and in a minute they started asking her where he was. Their daughter came in his direction, and they all started coming toward him.

Well, when they reached him, they all stood still. They just looked at each other without saying a word. His mother said, "Gee, are we imagining things?"

Finally their son said to them, "Of what?"

"Gee, I thought your wife said you got sick and got very skinny, and she left you when you died. She said you got sick, got thin, and died, so she left you."

He told them that he hadn't died.

"Gee, I thought your wife said she left you because you got sick and died. And we came here to bury your bones properly because she said she left you in the house."

Well, he said that he hadn't died.

His wife hid some food from him and said that they ran out of food, and she also told him that she would have someone fetch him. When she went down, she lied and told them she left him because he died from sickness. It was because he looked like he would surely die of starvation. She lied about him because she thought that he would die when she left him.

So, he accompanied his parents downriver [to their village]. When the fish arrived, he fished vigorously, thinking about the time he had gone hungry. When he arrived and started fishing, his wife went to them and helped them cut and dry their fish. Her husband never complained about his wife; he wasn't angry at her, even though she had lied about him. His wife cut the fish; she was helping his mother, her husband's mother. Her husband didn't pay any attention to her, and he wasn't angry with her, even though she was cleaning and drying fish for them. During that time he didn't hate her nor was he angry with her.

Since he fished vigorously, only when the fish finally dried did he say to his mother, "Let's give my wife some of our fish since she has worked on some of our fish, and send her home to her parents. Even though I am not angry with her, I just don't want her as my companion. Let's give her some food and let her return to her parents."

His mother followed their son's request and gave her some of the fish they harvested and had her return to her parents, terminating their marriage. Their son then acquired a wife of his own choosing. They had his previous wife go back to her parents after giving her some fish, providing for her what they called *avvuyutaq* [a sign of separation or something divided between two parties], because she had helped them work on the fish. That aforementioned one got another wife and started to make a living just like the others.

Because food was their only means of survival and because of that story, they used to tell young women like you to first think of the stomachs of the ones who are traveling around for their sakes, not to think of themselves first because they are women. Some reminded them of that story, the one who pretended to run out of fish and told her husband that they ran out of food and caused him to get very thin while she never lost any weight. They admonished them, using that as an example. They told them to always think of those who are traveling for their sakes, even if they are running low on food, because women didn't go to the wilderness and suffer hardship. They told them to make a special effort to provide food for the ones who traveled for their sakes because they go through hardship while doing so.

They told women not to sit around, but to quickly prepare provisions for them to take if they have some when the men said they were going to hunt in the wilderness. They asked them to think like this, "My spouse is going to try to provide food for me. I am preparing some things for him so that he will not have any problems in the wilderness."

They used to advise young women who hadn't gotten spouses that they should prepare food the same way for their older brothers, if they had older brothers, just before they left. They told them to put everything they could remember, even though he hadn't mentioned them, into his backpack or his grub box, trying not to forget anything. That was what they advised them to do.

Some women criticized other women for not paying attention to their husbands, saying that she put herself above her husband. They criticized those people.

They also advised men never to belittle their wives because they would be like a father and mother to each other, even though they have parents. The wife will be like a mother to him, and the husband will be like a father to her. They told them never to belittle one another because they have formed that relationship.

They said to them, "Being poor doesn't kill people. If a couple lives harmoniously together, they will be like rich people."

Then they said that if a couple had some children and they were poor, and their children always wore torn or old clothes because they didn't have any others, their rich reward would come later when their children grew older. It is said that even though a child grows up in poverty, it is not going to weaken him if they respect the children while they raise them. It will be as though they are surpassing the rich ones, even though in those days they were hardly making it. Their son will hunt for them and provide some food for them. After acquiring a husband, their daughter will bring them some food that her husband has caught. That will be the time when that couple will be wealthy. This is if they have lived in harmony among themselves while they had children and taken care of their children, even though they were going through hardship. It is depressing to live in a broken family.

It is true what people say, that a couple will start depending on each other. They will be like a mother or a father to each other. I am beginning to understand that it's really like that. I do have a mother, although I have lost my father. Whenever my spouse is not in our house, my mind is worried, not knowing what to do. I feel as if I don't really have a mother, even though my mother is in the house with me. Spouses are mothers and the men are fathers. It is true.

Introduction
Quliraq

Told by Frances Usugan
Transcribed and translated by Cathy Moses

In July 1985 Piiyuuk (Frances Usugan) told this moving *quliraq* to Cathy Moses and me while we visited in her home one sunny afternoon. Cathy and I were working together with elders from Toksook Bay on a Nelson Island Oral History Project. We had already visited a number of elders, including Frances. She was always lively and enthusiastic and gladly welcomed us into her home. She was particularly happy to share this story with Cathy, who was the wife of her brother's eldest son. Cathy was raised in Kotlik, at the mouth of the Yukon, and Frances wanted to share with her the history and stories of Nelson Island. To this end she explained things in great detail.

In June 1915 Frances was born at Up'nerkillermiut, a spring camp about six miles west of Toksook Bay. She was the eldest daughter of Angalgaq and Nalugaralria Moses. The family moved between spring and fall camps when Frances was young, wintering in the village of Nightmute. When Nightmute residents established Toksook Bay in spring 1964, her family moved with them. Her eldest brother, Cyril, died in 1977, but her two brothers Teddy and Philip and younger sister Stella, along with many of their children and grandchildren, still lived at Toksook when Frances told this story. Frances passed away peacefully at age ninety at her son's home in Chefornak in May 2005.

Cathy Moses transcribed and translated this *quliraq* the year after Frances told it, writing it out by hand in the days before computers. In 1983 and 1984 Cathy had worked as a translator when archaeologists with the Bureau of Indian Affairs had interviewed Nelson Island elders on historic sites. She subsequently earned her degree in education from the University of Alaska Fairbanks. Today she teaches in the Yup'ik immersion school in Toksook Bay, where she lives with her husband, Charlie, and seven children.

Linguistic theory did not directly influence Cathy's choice of a verse format for Frances's *quliraq*, rather, her sense of the story's rhythm. When asked to contribute a translation for this book, she immediately chose this tale, as it is among her favorites. Like the narrator, she was moved by pity and compassion for the woman in the story.

Frances peppered her delivery with numerous asides to her listeners. She noted her own sympathy for the story's central character. She also made a number of references to features of the story that were characteristic of *qulirat* in general to enhance her listeners' understanding of what she said. For example, when the woman encounters a stranger who turns out to be a young man, Frances noted parenthetically: "This is also common in *qulirat*."

Indeed, the story is recognizable as a *quliraq* in many respects. It tells the story of a woman living peacefully with a man so full of pride for his firstborn son that he carves a wooden bowl for the baby before the child is able to eat on his own. But the man soon loses interest in his wife and child. The poor woman leaves home in distress and overcomes great hardships before finding a new home. Years later she returns to her faithless husband, confronts him with his actions, and departs, leaving behind the bowl, the object of his pride, which magically destroys the entire community. The themes of abandonment and retribution are common in *qulirat*, and this is a particularly poignant rendering.

This story is exceptional not only in what it says but in how it is told. Frances's narration is wonderfully expressive. In a number of places she slowed her speech for dramatic emphasis. Cathy has indicated this with dashes in her translation. For example, as the abandoned wife journeyed away from her village, Frances intoned: "She tra-vel-ed and tra-vel-ed." Frances also made use of terracing for additional dramatic effect, repeating a phrase or word to allow the listener to linger in that moment. For example, when the abandoned wife confronts her husband after many years, Frances says:

> As she entered the *qasgi*, she noticed
> her husband, the one across there, lying comfortably....
> She and her husband who were once young,
> in the past,
> the two who were once young.

Some translations might erase this lengthening, while in Cathy's work this and much else are beautifully rendered.

—AFR

Quliraq

Told by Frances Usugan of Toksook Bay

There was once this village which was situated
along a river.

Well, villages are always near a river as one knows
but the rivers all have openings
that flow out into the ocean.

It is said that village had a *nukalpiartaq* [accomplished hunter].

It also had big families.
(You know, big families are as one sees them even today.
These here,
I am imagining a large family
all closely related.
It had big families. It included big families
in that village.)

And so
one day their *nukalpiartaq*
acquired as a wife
one of the women.

(I really sympathized with that man's wife.)

He acquired a wife,
and eventually his wife became pregnant.

Today, when a woman becomes pregnant,
when she becomes pregnant, like they do,
they prepare to go for a checkup at the hospital.

But in past generations, when a woman was pregnant

they used to examine her by hand.

And one who is an expert
and who is not a young lady examines the woman
trying to find the embryo at its early stage.

And so that woman told her husband
that she was pregnant.

Her husband, because he was a *nukalpiaq*, was very happy.
He then said, "Okay,
go to the mother of the big family."
Then she could examine her to find the embryo.

(A ringed seal.
You know the ringed seals which are inflated?
And also, they never used to do away with bearded seals' stomachs.
The stomachs,
the Yup'ik people always used to inflate bearded seals' stomachs
and fill them with seal oil.
When they did not have plastic containers
the stomachs,
a ringed seal's stomach
they always used to inflate them.)

And so,
the seal's stomach
they used to call them *maklinraat*.

(Today even the intestines are called *maklinraat*.

Well, the stomachs used to look like so
the so-called pointed object.
And they were like so
inside the container or through the esophagus
filled with as much seal oil
as possible.)

She took the inflated ringed seal's stomach and flattened it
with the bearded seal skin.

She put a bearded seal skin over it
and went over to the mother of the big family.

(This story is a real *quliraq*.)

And so, as she entered, she told the mother she had come to see her.
This is as though she had gone to see the doctors,
she said she came to see her for the examination.

(For the examination, they used to lie down on their backs with the knees
    bent.
They used to lie down
with the knees up
not really flattening them.)

And so, with that
while she examined her
she told her that she had found it
and said,
"True, it appears in a boy's usual place."

(Those people, in those days, were very skilled
when they lived as they did.
And the elders spoke in truth.)

This is how, after she found the embryo, as small as it was,
the mother of the big family,
who probably was an old woman then,
had told the woman,
"It appears where a boy's [embryo] usually is."

(Because I have no other story to tell, this story
over the years—I have learned.
Even though I have forgotten many stories, I never forget this story because
    I sympathized with the woman.)
And so
she went home.
At home she told her husband
that the mother found the embryo.

She said, "It appears where a boy's [embryo] usually is."

How they know, I don't know.
The woman told her husband.

And so, she carried through the pregnancy.
And when the time came, it came out a baby boy.

They took the child as their own
and raised him. The baby grew,
probably as big as [Ann's]
baby is now [six months old].
After fall time,
it was winter.

And so the person
because he was proud of the birth,
the father
made a small bowl for him,
even though the baby could not eat for himself yet.
He made a small circular bowl.
The so-called *uivluar*—a circular wooden bowl.
Because of his pride
he made a small bowl
even though his son could not eat on his own.

The father made a wooden bowl despite the fact that his son was a baby,
even though he was still very young.

And so, they say, this one, over the winter
the husband hardly entered anymore
since they had a child
that one
the father.

(And in this way
the houses in those days had wooden beds,
those houses which were genuine houses.

The soil down there was supported by wooden posts,
like the kind used for drying racks.)
All those houses had beds.

Sometimes, they say, when he entered
he would sit on the bed for a moment and then leave.

He never actually sat next
to his wife.
Her husband would always leave.

And soon, they say,
when he entered,
down there on the floor,
he would pace on it for a second, similar to walking around,
and then leave.

Well, the man's poor wife
became puzzled on account of her husband's actions.
She became lonely because of the way he was.

And because the poor woman was breast-feeding,
she did not confide in anybody.

(A long time ago, they took good care of their babies when they were
    breast-feeding.
Also, for a baby boy
they sacrificed their sleep over them.
They never seemed to sleep.
When taking care of babies, the mothers in those days really put a lot of strain
    on themselves while caring for them.

They would also wear their parkas with nothing underneath.
They never breast-fed with a covering on themselves.
They always took their parkas off,
because they wanted their sons to become successful
hunters.

Even though they breast-fed with their body showing,
people did not mind them.

One who breast-fed for the first time always took her parka off,
even though there were other men present.

Also, during the night, they never breast-fed with the baby lying
next to them.
They always got up with the baby.
They always got up to breast-feed.)

And so
one day, one of the people told her
that her husband
was having an *ingulaq* with the younger sister of the big family.

(Well, this dance ceremony—*ingulaq*—
is also one that
is similar to a wedding ceremony.
You know how *kass'at* have dances
sometimes.
The ceremony is a dance.
At the present time we do not celebrate this dance.
They do not celebrate *ingulaq* anymore.
They performed the dance with slower motions and used different dance
    motions.
They would have big feasts during the ceremony.)[1]

They said, he was holding a ceremony with the big family's younger sister,
    her husband.
Well, it is like
her husband became a spouse for the other woman.

He held a feast
and probably
used food from their underground cache
whatever they stored, he probably used.

And so, when she heard,
the poor woman became very lonely. No wonder.
No wonder he had become as he was.
This happened during the winter quite close to spring.

And then,
since he was like that
she slowly made preparations.

She made a pair of rain boots because she had the material,
for her husband was a *nukalpiaq*.
(They used only sealskin oil containers to make rain boots.
When the containers were empty, they would hang them so the remaining
   oil would drip out.
In urine
they would wash them.
And then they would take the fur off the skin.
After they took the fur off, they would inflate the skin.
That is how they prepared the skin for rain boots.)

She made rain boots in preparation
and the grass pack basket,
because she was not lacking food,
she carefully packed the basket with food.

And the
little bowl,
the circular bowl,
she slipped it in,
thinking to use it for her seal oil.

(Also, they used to use small [seal] stomachs for dripping in seal oil, after
   making sure
that it was strong enough to hold seal oil.)

And then
one night
when the people were not walking around,
the sled,
her husband's sled.

With a reindeer skin,
because she was not in need of one as her husband was a *nukalpiaq*,

with a reindeer skin
because they had nothing else for a covering,
she used the reindeer skin to cover her child,
she secured the skin around the child with a rope.
And as her staff she used his *negcik* [gaff], which people used while out on
  the ocean.

(*Negcit* were gaffs
of wood
and the tip was a spike.
They used them as ice picks
for *qayat*.

Well, like this out in the ocean
he would use it to push away [from the ice or land].
It has many uses out on the ocean, when they used to go out on the ocean.
And also
they would use the walking stick by jabbing
on the ice,
The dangerous thin ice would quickly shatter.
That's how they used it.)

With that kind
his poor wife, using a *negcik* for a walking stick
when people were retiring
she left by the river.

She tra-vel-ed and tra-vel-ed
all-night-long-she-tra-vel-ed.

Finally, just at daybreak
the poor dear one over there
the one she was pulling, started to cry.

When he started crying,
she stopped
and breast-fed him.

(Well, like this
by pulling up their parkas halfway when it is cold
by placing them right here [on their laps]
some of them, like so,
used to breast-feed.)

Oh dear, while she was breast-feeding, this one fell asleep

Oh dear!

And then, she woke up
and realized she had suffocated her child
with her breast.

She-had-suffocated-him
because she had not slept.

And oh,
after she felt a great regret and sorrow
because she didn't know what else to do
the poor one started to bury him
because they were out in the wilderness,
She used that [reindeer skin], she wrapped him using what strength she
    could.
The poor one buried him.
She placed the sled on top
and the *negcik*
she stuck it in the ground.[2]

And so
she went on her way after packing her food supply on her back.

When-ever-she-got hungry
the poor one would stop
and take it out,
the circular bowl,
she did not throw it away because he had never used it.

She took out the circular bowl
whenever she got hungry.

She would squeeze out a little oil from the small stomach
and use the bowl for her seal oil dip.

She would eat by using it for her seal oil dip.

(*Aling, akleng* [Oh my, poor thing!]. That one sure traveled for a long time.)

And eventually, they say
she began rationing her food.

And finally when she reached the mouth of their river
along its shore, she traveled.
When she came across a river, she continued her journey up the river
along its shore.

Pretty soon,
eventually, they say,
the ice started to break up
on the river.

She was starting to ration her food supply.

She was losing weight.
The woman was becoming thin because she ate only a little
during her journey.

And then one day
she reached an area where there was a mountain a ways from the river.

While she was eating,
out of nowhere,
these two young men appeared standing
before her.

And they said, "We came to get you."
Out of nowhere, they appeared.

Oh! How scared the poor one was.
The poor woman kept on eating and here, they say, the way she was chewing,
    up there in her mouth, was very dry.

"Well,"
she said in vain, "Maybe you're not here to get me all right."
Even though she was desperate,
she did not immediately jump with joy.
The two, they say, were very attentive,
those two men.

The river, down there, was breaking up, turning into water.

And so
[the poor one] told them,
"Okay, let's go down to the riverbank.
I won't leave.
I won't do anything.
Down there, by the river
let me look at you."

The container there
after licking it carefully
because she was limited on food now
when they went down by the riverbank
that circular bowl, she carefully placed it on the water.

And when she put it there
she did this [made a circular motion with her hand].

Aren [Oh!],
the circular bowl, they say, when it began turning around
turned-around-and-around.

These-two-they say, the two men stared-and-stared.

They gazed while standing by the riverbank.

The two stared so hard.
The water started to twirl into a whirlpool.
You know, when the water became tight, and became deeper and deeper.
And the shore there
became threatening.

The bowl twirled until there was a lot of water surrounding it.

The two, as they were gazing
the water
went in their direction, you know
this big thing in action,
went in their direction and snatched them.

So it was that in the whirling water,
the two men
were suddenly taken away until they could not be seen.

And so after that happened
the aforementioned whirlpool began to weaken.
It-weakened-and-weakened.

(I used to really pity this one.)

When the whirling slowed down and weakened
the bowl surfaced in the water.

And when it appeared, she took it and stored it away.

Well, gone were the two who were snatched away.

And now after packing her bag on her back,
she left again and continued along the river toward its beginning.

And then, on her way
she saw a house over there.
A cache was situated next to it.

(*Qulirat* commonly have fish caches on stilts.
Their fish storehouses were referred to as *mayurrviit* [literally, "places with
    ladders"].
It is because the storehouses had poles and were high above ground,
where the food was stored.)

And because she was desperate
she became unafraid
because she was desperate.

She had arrived
she had looked around.
No-one-seemed-to-be-there.

So the atmosphere around her showed no sign of people.
The house there seemed empty and deserted.

And so she cautiously began to enter and went in the porch.
She listened
and heard nothing.

She entered the house and noticed
signs that someone lived there.
It certainly showed signs of people living in it and it had things in it.

So, she looked around for food
and the fish cache
and from the fish cache
she took a piece of food and ate it.

And then after she ate a little
she could not eat much because she was skinny.

(People in those days were wise
and knew when not to eat too much.)[3]

While she was sitting by the wall,
she heard sudden human sounds outside.

Oh my! When the sudden human sound occurred
even though she felt something big [like fright],
she stayed put.

Oh,
right out there.

(And the storytellers knew what would happen next.)

And when he came in, the person turned out to be a young man.

After doing his own thing, he inevitably noticed her.

(Also this is common for *qulirat*.)

When he saw her he noticed
the poor woman who was very dark in color.
Her poor parka designs, it is said,
were once of reindeer skin.
Her poor hanging decorations were worn out.
In other words they were shedding.

He noticed the woman there, it is said, was dark and skinny.
As one knows, during springtime
the weather causes one to become tanned.

And so when he suddenly noticed her, he said to her,
"Hello,
is it a living person?"

And so the person spoken to answered, "Yes,
I certainly wish that
this poor woman, who is so desperate,
has entered the house upon arrival."

Oh my, that person, it is said, the man had no immediate reactions.
He said he could not do anything to her,
that it was fine with him.
He told her to stay here and regain her health.

And then he told her, it is said,
that when she regained her health,
that he will take her for his wife.

And then, it is said,
she regained her health, for she was only very skinny.
The man who became her husband said,
"Let me tell you
the people of that village over there will come fetch me when they are
    about to do something.

But before they come for me, well, even these reindeer sinews,
maybe you can take good care of them."

So it was falltime and they had spent all summer.

Anything he caught like reindeer, she would stretch the skin to dry it.
Whatever animal sinews they had, she took care of them.

And then one day,
because this occurred when they had no telephones,
one day, a dogsled arrived.
Someone came to get him,
saying he had come to get him once again before they had a celebration.

Oh, taking a wife, that woman, he left with all
their belongings.

She-had-arrived-to-find-this-village.
Right outside the *qasgi* were houses.

And then the people celebrated Nakaciuryaraq [the Bladder Festival][4]
during the time, they brought all the things they included during the
    festival.
The food and skins the man had caught.

And when the time came for the woman to become pregnant,
she was pregnant and it turned out to be a boy.
Then again,
when the time came, he had a younger sibling
which turned out to be a boy.
No others were added, I guess. One doesn't know.

Meanwhile, the two young boys.
(This *quliraq* is like the movies where time goes fast.
Because it is a story it probably used to go on for a long time.)

The day came when the two children became teenagers.

And then,
when the two reached their teen years
once again, it is said,
she began thinking of the people she left.

Oh, how she wished she could see them.

Because her sons were teenagers now.

And because it had been so long
meanwhile, it is said, she said,
"My, my, I wish
the people from my past
could only see them."

Even though she had endured a long journey,
she had only said what she had.

When she said that, her in-law told her, "Okay,
go along with your two sons.
If you want to see them
you may go and see them.

Now, if you go, the mountain, up there
you will keep climbing it.
When you get to the top of it, you will see it.
You will see your hometown."
Oh how emotionally painful.

Packing away the circular bowl,
she left on her way, along with her two sons,
just as her in-law had advised.

When they reached the top of the mountain,
they saw a village down there.

(Oh my! Probably like the mountain up there
where we can see Tununak.)[5]

(Oh my, one that traveled a long distance!)[6]

Down-they-went. Down-they-went.
And when they arrived, she probably stopped at someone's place
that she used to know.
After which, she asked about her former husband.

Having asked, they said he was fine and was then at the *qasgi*.

"Okay," she had told her two sons,
"Okay, let's go to the *qasgi*."

She was probably an old woman by now.
She entered and noticed
her husband had been promoted to sitting on the side of the *qasgi*.

(The people of the *qasgi* never positioned themselves just anywhere.
The elders sat to the side of the wall [where the door is situated].
The young boys sat along the north, east, and west walls,
the boys who were near marrying age.
Those who had reached middle age sat on the second row
on the east and west sides.
What they reach, I don't know.
Those who are going in the direction of old age,
qakliskait—this is a word they use to refer to them.

This is what a person who saw a man used to say:
"Well, he has reached his middle age."
That is how they used to refer to them.

In one's life, after being young comes middle age.
He has reached
his middle age, they say. He has reached it.)

As she entered the *qasgi*, she noticed
her husband, the one across there, lying comfortably.
He had reached this part of the *qasgi* referred to as *nakirneq*.
She and her husband who were once young,
in the past,
the two who were once young.

And up above him were two people
two young boys were sitting there.
One, they say,
had on a mink hat and the other
a weasel hat.

They were both about the same age as her two sons.

Oh my,
as she entered she looked around for him and when they told her where he was
she went over to him.

When she did so,
she faced him, kneeling precisely.
She faced him squarely.

This was how she was going to tell him.

She said,
since she had come to this day and age
and since her two sons had grown
because she could not stop thinking of this place
she had come to see them.

"Let me tell you of the past."
She began reminding him of what happened in the past, about the past
she had to endure during that time.

She reminded him of how happy they were before they had their child.
Also,
of how he had sent her for an examination
with the bearded seal's stomach.
She mentioned it.
Also, of how over the winter
during the winter, how he hardly came in anymore.

"You used to come in
but pretty soon, you came less often
and soon you started to just sit for a moment
on the bedding."

It was like this one in front of her was feeling very uncomfortable.

"Pretty soon
you would step in for a minute and then leave.
You went out hunting a lot. And you have probably seen the one
you so much wanted for a child.

You do go out hunting and you have probably seen your sled
and also your *negcik* when you go out hunting."

Nakleng! [Poor thing!]
Since she had brought along her bag,
she took [the bowl] out from it
and said,
"But this one here,
this is the bowl you made."

And then after that
however he felt, this man of hers
said, "My sons,
don't let your visitors alone, do entertain them."
In a sense, he was trying to change the subject.
Those around him, his two sons, he had called them.

(They also called their sons *avaqutaat*.)

"My two sons, do entertain your visitors down there."
That is what he said.
The other brother
took off his mink hat and threw it, it became a mink
and went running and falling backwards
making the sound of a mink.

And the one in front caught it,
the older brother caught it
(How.)
He caught it and put it on.

And then the younger brother
when he took his hat off and threw it also with a swinging motion
the weasel, with it's own sound, flew and he caught it as a hat and put it
    back on.

And so she said, "So here it is,"
after the two were done.
"Here it is, the aforementioned [bowl]."

She put it on the floor.
"This here, the little bowl you made. To this day, I have kept it stored away.
I have never taken it out."

And so
she moved it like so [twirling it]
and when she did that,
it made a clattering noise on the floor.
(You know how something makes a clattering noise when we do something
    to it.)
It had turned around very fast with a sound like hail,
the little bowl.
And when it stopped
she took it, put it away, and they left.

When they were outside
she told her two sons, "Okay, let's go on home."
Perhaps
they probably went home that same day
after seeing what she came to see.

Up-they-climbed-going-home. Up they climbed.
And when
they reached the top of the mountain,
when they finally reached the top, they sat down.
They looked back down at the village.
The village down there was-turning-around,
it-was-turning-around-and-around
oh my!

Just-like-the-one-before,
just-like-the-one-before
when it happened at the water.
Soon, the village there
was no longer a village.

Aling [Oh my!]

They went on home and arrived.

And then when [the story] is over,

they say, they have nothing else to say.

And then, they say, they probably live on when the story ends,

those who kept on living

the ones I did not mention in the story

may they land with a loud sound in their appropriate places in the story.

Because of the long story

while telling the *quliraq*

at the ending, that is what they do.

"The ones I did not mention, may they land with a loud noise in their
appropriate places in the story."

And so the story is over.

Introduction
Aanakallii Ner'aqallii / I Have Eaten My Mother

Told by Frank Andrew

Transcribed and translated by Alice Rearden

During two frosty weeks in October 2001, Kwigillingok elder Miisaq (Frank Andrew) and his son Noah worked with Alice Rearden and me documenting the oral traditions of coastal Yup'ik people as part of our work for the Calista Elders Council. Frank and Noah Andrew had come to Anchorage to be with Frank's wife, Cecelia, who was there for medical treatment, and when time permitted I brought them up to my house where we could all work together. Frank Andrew is recognized as among the most knowledgeable and articulate elders in the region with clear memories of past practices and an active interest in sharing them.

Frank was born in Kwigillingok in February 1917. His father was originally from Qinaq and his mother from Kangirnaarmiut. The family moved to fish camp on the Kuskokwim every June and July, where they lived near relatives in Tuntutuliak. Frank recalled that from late summer to freeze-up in November they were constantly moving and fishing until they returned to Kwigillingok for the winter. There, Frank spent hours in the *qasgi* listening to his father and other village elders; he has never forgotten what he learned. Frank married in the 1940s, and he and his wife raised six children, all of whom now have families of their own.

The first days Frank spent with Alice and me were full of questions, as we sought information on family values and Yup'ik relational terms. As we got to know each other better and our sessions lengthened and relaxed, even I ran out of questions and Frank began to tell stories. *Aanakallii Ner'aqallii* was among the most memorable.

Frank began the story quietly after we had all enjoyed a good lunch, and we immediately recognized the well-known tale of the monster child who devoured his mother and caused an entire community to flee for their lives. This story continues to be told throughout southwest Alaska, and several versions have been published (Lantis 1946:273–276; Vick 1983:320–327; Fienup-Riordan 1983:441–442; Shield and Fienup-Riordan 2003:264–269). Frank's rendition, however, describes events that subsequently befell community members after some made a new home at Petmigtalegmiut on the Yukon River and others returned to their original home, Qageryalqurmiut, just below present-day Akiachak on the Kuskokwim River.

Time slipped by, as Frank shared one of the longest and most detailed Yup'ik stories ever recorded, including at least four sequences of events that other contemporary storytellers narrate as separate tales. For instance, Paul John told a variation of the same story divided into three separate tales: "I have eaten my mother," "The ones who grew," and "The big man" (Shield and Fienup-Riordan 2003:132–135, 264–269, 274–285). Stringing them together with artful connections, Frank eloquently exemplified traditional Yup'ik storytelling where, it was said, stories went on and on without stopping. Such stories were aimed at a mixed audience going in and out of the *qasgi*, rather than a stationary group of listeners anticipating a narrative of Aristotelian design. Instead of building to a climax and conclusion like Western dramas, the structure of these long narrations resembled pearls on a string.

Nineteenth-century naturalist Edward Nelson (1899:451) wrote that long stories were told over successive evenings. He also noted that some important tales were presented by two men sitting facing each other. While one man narrated the tale, the other held a bundle of sticks, placing them on the floor one at a time at certain points in the story, "forming a sort of chapter mark." Until now we had no contemporary Yup'ik examples of such extended storytelling. Frank Andrew not only shared a particular story, but provides a window on the shape of traditional Yup'ik storytelling more generally. As he noted at the outset, "Some stories they told were long."

Frank Andrew began with the story of the baby who ate his mother. Although advised by a shaman not to be ashamed of her deformed child, the mother hid him from the people, and he subsequently killed her. This disaster was a direct result of the young mother ignoring the shaman's advice to show her child regardless of its appearance. Margaret Lantis (1990:169–189). points out that in other versions of the story, the tragedy is set in motion when the girl's father fails to follow traditional abstinence practices to restrict his activity following his daughter's first menstruation. In a version of the story Lantis recorded on Nunivak, the child killed and ate his grandparents. In Frank Andrew's story the grandparents and villagers fled together, pursued by the monster child. One young man walked in the tracks of caribou to confuse the cannibalistic child, who soon died of exposure.

The story's second "chapter" describes the people's journey down the Yukon to found a new village. There they lived in peace and plenty until a woman died, leaving behind her infant child. The woman haunts her husband, begging for the child, but he refuses. After repeated hauntings a village elder advises the husband that the loss of an adult is more painful than the loss of a child and that he should give his dead wife what she wants lest he or other community members come to harm. The man does as told, but the woman continues to appear, walking with the child on her back. The villagers once again flee and return only after a shaman visiting the village provides the woman with a pinch of food which she receives as a large supply.

The third story describes the arrival of strange people who turn out to be *qununit*—seals that turn into human beings. Five *qununit* initially appear as humans wearing seal-gut rain garments dripping with water, even in the cold winter weather. This is the first indication of their other-than-human nature. Second, they refuse the food their hosts' wives offer them, perceiving it as mixed with children's saliva and urine, both substances that women were admonished never to handle lest they offend their husband's prey. Only when served food in urine buckets do they eat with relish, revealing a "reverse" perception of reality also characteristic of extraordinary persons. Unlike human hunters, the five hunted by jumping into the water and emerging with fish that they ate raw.

The final indication of their other-than-human nature comes when they suddenly depart, saying that their way home is about to be obstructed. Shortly after they leave, a woman in the village has a miscarriage, and the people understand that that was the "obstruction" referred to by the *qununit*. Traditionally a miscarriage was surrounded by strict abstinence practices, and the woman's husband was prohibited from going down to the ocean or hunting for the same reason—his presence would scare away the animals and hinder their approach. For other descriptions of *qununit*, see Paul John's accounts (Shield and Fienup-Riordan 2003:159).

The story's final "chapter" describes the arrival of small people, who come to live with a couple unable to have a child. Nelson (1899:480–481) also recorded a version of this story in which a dwarf couple comes to live in Pikmiktalik and, after the death of their tiny son, introduce people to the making of grave boxes and the custom of mourning the dead. In Frank's story the two couples exchange spouses, a practice he later described:

> A long time ago they used to trade wives, and those two would become *qat'ngutek* [dual, spouse-exchange partners] in that way. They did not practice this in just any manner. Both wives would be considered wives, and both husbands would be considered husbands, and they would all be in agreement. Their children would be related like one family. They said that it is a tradition starting from long ago, but it stopped being practiced just as I was becoming aware of my surroundings. I once saw a man from Qinaq who had two wives, but that was the last one.

During their stay the tiny man impregnates his host's childless wife, and the son she bears shares characteristics of both his human and nonhuman parents. Their relationship is ruptured by the accidental death of the tiny couple's small son. The couple then returns to their original home but leaves behind an *iinruq* (amulet) for their human son, who later uses it to overcome his adversary.

Following Frank Andrew's storytelling, Alice Rearden carefully transcribed and translated his full account. She then worked closely with language expert Marie Meade to refine the final translation. The result is Yup'ik storytelling at its finest.

—AFR

Aanakallii Ner'aqallii / I Have Eaten My Mother

Told by Frank Andrew of Kwigillingok

THERE ARE MANY STORIES; SOME ARE LONG. I am going to tell you about that baby who ate his mother, one who killed and ate his mother. It is long and I will tell it even though I don't finish it. Some stories they told were long.

Long ago, shamans used their powers to work on the fetus inside the womb during the first stages of pregnancy before the baby came out. That is what they apparently did long ago.

There was a village on a tributary of the Kuskokwim River right above Bethel. That river near Bethel was called Kuik [River]. There was a village there with many residents before Akiachak and Akiak became villages long ago. I forgot the name of that village.

Because a couple's daughter could not have children, they summoned the shaman who worked on her with his power. When he was done, he told the mother-to-be that he might have done a little too much, not to be embarrassed by the baby or hide him no matter what he looked like when he was born. He told her that he would become normal when he got older, and he told her not to be ashamed of him. He told her not to hide and be embarrassed by him even if he looked different. He advised her to let people see him, that he would become normal when he got older.

He also advised her to inform him when she started to feel contractions, that he would deliver the baby himself. When her contractions started, the couple invited him to their home and he delivered the baby. When he delivered the baby, he said, "I have overdone it just like I thought. Raise this child by following the instructions I gave you even though he looks like this, and do not hide him and be ashamed of him, he will become normal when he gets older. He will look like a regular person." He gave her those instructions.

Though [the shaman] had instructed her, she was embarrassed when she saw her baby and did not let her parents see him. She put a partition around her bed, not wanting others to see her child. She did not follow the shaman's instructions. That small baby had a mouth that reached his ears and had teeth like a dog. She was ashamed of how he looked. Though the shaman told her that he would become normal, his mother did not follow his instructions.

One night in early winter just when there was snow on the ground, [the baby's mother] went out to urinate, and right as she left, [the grandmother] went across and peeked in through the partition and saw what he looked like. That baby looked up right at her, and here he was just an infant. After peeking in, she closed it and walked back across to her bed. When she sat next to her husband she said, "His mother has not let us see him because he looks like this."

When she came inside, after looking at her mother a while, she asked, "Did you look at him?" She replied, "I didn't look at him because you have asked me not to." Her daughter sensed that she had. They went to bed when it was time. As [the grandmother] was sleeping, when the rapid beating of her heart woke her, she sat up suddenly and heard crackling from somewhere. She sat up and listened and realized the crackling noise was coming from behind the partition.

Lights were always dimly lit and never off back when they used oil lamps. She walked across and peered through the woven grass partition and saw that he had already eaten and swallowed one side of [the mother's] breast and the bones beneath.

She walked back across and woke her husband. They got ready in the dark and then left trying not to make sudden loud noises. They put a brace on the door to keep it from opening. When they went outside, they summoned the villagers and they got ready in the dark. They call that old village Qageryalqurmiut. They say there was a trail through the trees behind their village that came out into a clearing. When they were ready, they went through there along with all of the other men in the *qasgi*.

They traveled all night, and the sun came up and they continued traveling all day. They finally stopped the next night. They finally went to sleep. As they were building shelters with roofs, one of them said that he left his knife in the *qasgi*. They say knives were rare back then when there were no white people. They were rare.

They had a fast runner among them, and so he paid him to get his knife in the *qasgi*. He told him that he usually kept it on the side wall next to where he slept. When they woke the next morning, they got ready and left.

Their fastest runner went back to get that man's knife. When he got near Qageryalqurmiut, he started hearing a sound that went, "*Qiyaa.*" When he got to the path behind their village, as he went down, he stopped and closely observed the village. As he observed, a naked baby crawled out from one of the houses on the snow. He turned and headed toward the next house. Just as he was about to reach it, he let his voice out and clearly said, "*Aanakallii ner'aqallii* [I have eaten my mother]." Just as he was about to fall in through the skylight, he would leap into the air and cry, "*Qiyaa,*" before falling in headfirst. He observed him as he did this. He would be inside the house for quite some time. He had almost gone through all the houses.

When he did that for the second time and went into the house, [the runner] ran down to the *qasgi*. Before [the baby] came out, he ran in and searched for the knife and took it when he found it and went back out and kept an eye on [the baby] from the porch of the *qasgi*. After the baby went out and flew into the skylight of the next house, he ran up to the path. He ran and fled from there. When he finally came out of the trail behind the village, he saw caribou tracks cutting across the path of the villagers who fled, and the herd was just crossing over the bluffs.

He followed the path [the villagers] had taken, but turned back when he got an idea. He went back and followed the path of the caribou. Before he got too far, he jumped over the snow into the alder trees on the windward side and waited. As he waited, he heard the voice of the baby who was following him. As he quietly watched, he became visible through the trees. As he crawled, he would leap into the air and would slide forward when he landed on the snow. He was naked and wet, and here it was cold outside. He would say, "*Aanakallii ner'aqallii* [I ate my mother]." He followed their tracks.

When he got a little farther following [the villagers'] tracks, he turned around and came toward him, flying up and sliding on the surface of the snow when he landed. He passed by him, following the caribou tracks. He disappeared over the hill, and after a while, he heard the rumbling sound of the caribou. He then returned and resumed the original path of his people. He reached the people from his village just as night fell while they were building shelters. It took him one day to retrieve the knife. [The baby] didn't come and haunt them all night.

Those people who fled did not return home but traveled up toward the Yukon River.

They say some became residents of Masserculleq [Marshall], but those who stayed at Mastuliaq returned to Akiachak. That is what he said after telling that story. Some became residents of Masserculleq in the Yukon River area, but the ones who lived in Mastuliaq returned to Akiachak.

When those people first arrived, they lived on the banks of the Yukon River in Mastuliaq, but when the original residents of Mastuliaq didn't want them around any longer they moved farther down. They lived there for some time.

When the residents of that other village didn't want them around any longer, and didn't want to feed them, they didn't want to help them any longer. Some of them returned home [to Akiachak] from there, but the majority went down the Yukon River looking for a place to live, a village of their own. They would stop traveling at night and build shelters.

After traveling for some time, they came upon a river that was in the trees. They went down the river, and their leader led them, probably an elder. They stopped when it became dark. After a number of days, they came to a clearing. When they came out, they looked around and saw the ocean down there, the Bering Sea; apparently it was an ocean. They went down that river because their leader led them, following that river.

Not long before nightfall, they came upon open water on the ice, an unfrozen section on the river. Small fish would jump out from down there. Their leader told them to stop there even though it was still early. When they stopped, they built a snow shelter, and one of them possessed a small net, one that could catch small fish. He set his net in that hole in the ice. They went to bed at night. When they woke up the next day, that person checked his small net. It had caught a lot of fish. They cooked his catch before they went on their way.

While they were eating, their elder said that the location was a prospective village site, that he desired it and wanted to stop there. The trees were not far behind them. They complied with him because he was their leader, and they went there to get logs to build houses. After they gathered a large amount, he told them to build a *qasgi*. They chiseled the permafrost and cleared it of snow. They built a *qasgi* because there were many of them, and they worked together for two days building a large *qasgi* and finished it on the third.

After taking a fire bath, when it started to get hot, they finally let their women in with all of their belongings; and that man finally advised them to work on building one house and to fill it with residents when it was complete. They also went to gather logs, and they added them to the ones they had left over and built houses, and eventually they all had places to stay. Their *qasgi* was in the center and their houses around it.

They say they ate from that open hole in the ice for a long time, always eating fresh food, and they probably ate some frozen fish also. That hole in the ice did not freeze all winter long. They would also travel and catch caribou from there as well as other big game. They also learned about the ocean when they started to travel down and reach the ocean that their river flowed into.

When winter ended and spring came, some people started to go down and try to hunt because they had never hunted down on the ocean before, and some of them began to catch sea mammals. They added the sea mammals they caught to their other food. Then people from other villages arrived when summer came, and they built their own kayaks after having those people teach them. And because salmon were abundant in that river, they fished all summer. They caught a lot of fish. Eventually, there were many kayaks built in that village, and each man had his own. And they also made canoes like they originally used and knew how to build. They became a village.

The next year they camped at the mouth of their river during the spring. That place became their spring camping site and they hunted sea mammals down there. They would move back to their village after harvesting fish. That became their custom.

One day, a couple's son's wife became ill, and they had a newborn child. She died not long after she became ill. Her body was the first to be buried. Her remains were placed behind their village. She died in the fall at freeze-up.

Back then, a couple from the Yukon River would come and cut fish with them. They would return home during the fall in a boat. That became their custom. That person died just as they returned home.

When night came, her child could not stop crying even though his father carried him. He would finally quiet down. After a number of days passed, he began to cry at night, and that man got up, and his parents lived in the same house. He took him and stood with him down on the floor. While he was trying to quiet the baby, mist started to come out from under their door and dispersed onto their floor, and he moved back, and when it stopped, his dead wife appeared. When she appeared she said, "I came to get the child because I am feeling sorry for it." Her husband said to her, "I am not giving him to you even though you have come to get him. Go and get *kenitat* [salmon backbones] instead." When he told her this, she began to disappear. They went to bed when the baby got quiet, and when her husband woke early in the morning, he looked inside the entrance hole of the house when he was about to leave and saw that it was filled with *kenitat*. You know what *kenitat* are? They are salmon backbones, the ones that they hang to dry. On the coast, they take the ones that are too dry and soak them in water and eat them. The entryway was filled with fish prepared in that way. He gathered them and went out to the porch, and he saw that it was also filled with [*kenitat*]. When he went outside, those soaked salmon backbones were lined up perfectly all the way to her grave.

He took a small sled and gathered them before people began to move around the village, and he brought them over to her burial site. Then after that, their baby continued to cry nonstop and would finally quiet down at night.

Once while doing that during the night, when he was carrying him and trying to get him to stop [crying], mist started flowing in from the entryway like before, dispersed, and just as it moved back, his wife appeared. Appearing more upset than before, she told him to give her the child, not to hold him back because he was getting too pitiful. Her husband said he would not give the child to her, and he told her instead to get some *akutaq* [a mixture of seal oil or caribou fat, berries, boned fish, and other ingredients] . She disappeared when he told her that. He went to sleep when it was time to lie down.

Since he was an early riser, when he woke up in the morning, their house smelled of nagoonberries. They are the kind of berries they add to *akutaq*. As he stood up and went toward the exit and dropped down into the entrance hole, it was filled with *akutaq* mixed with nagoonberries. He picked up the grass where the *akutaq* was sitting, went to the porch and saw *akutaq* lined up in the porch out the door. He saw that the *akutaq* mixed with nagoonberries continued all the way to her burial site.

He took a shovel and put a covering over the sled, and he picked up and placed all of the *akutaq* near her grave before people woke. She didn't reappear after that. After that incident, their elder who was the leader of the village came into their house during the day and said to him, "Something bad is going to happen to you on account of that child." That man knew what was going on. "If you refuse to let him go the next time, I don't know what will happen to you. You adults are more important and are needed more than that child. You will die if you don't give her that child next time." He told him that he came to tell him that. Then he left.

After a number of days passed, that child continued to cry at night. One evening, mist began to flow in from their doorway. It dispersed onto the floor and moved back, and right when it disappeared, that same woman appeared. She said, even more upset, to give her the child now because he had become pitiful. When he turned toward her, he instantly threw that child and she quickly held out her arms, and when the baby landed here, it gave out one last cry and died instantly. Then she disappeared.

He never saw her again. After that, people started seeing her ghost outside carrying that small child on her back. She would sit naked and breast-feed him, and here it was cold and windy outside.[7]

When they became terrified, the villagers began to confer with one another because she began to walk around before nighttime carrying her baby on her back. And they moved to their spring camp, abandoning their village. They had food storage places for their food that were above ground and had ladders on them. And that married couple who usually moved from another village to cut fish there had one of those. No one lived there any longer, they all left and moved to their spring camp. After the village was abandoned, that couple from the Yukon River area went there to get their food supply, one pushing their sled because they had no dogs, the other pulling with a tow rope.

They arrived at that village, but there was no one there. They say those above-ground storage places, those caches, did not have regular doors, but they had doors on their roofs that opened. They both climbed up there, and the husband put their sled on top as well. Because they were haunted by that woman, they put their sled up on top of the cache. They also took off the ladder because they thought she would climb up. She walked around carrying a small baby on her back. He took a piece of food and dropped it between the cracks of the floor, a small piece of food. It made a large thump down there when it hit the ground. That person down there became excited, "*Aling* [Goodness], thank you for giving us this large amount of food." They looked down and saw that it was a large amount of food, a whole grass basket full of food, but they had actually thrown down [a small piece]. She rolled the basket full of food behind them. While she was rolling it, her husband began to load their sled quickly even though it was sitting on top of the cache.

When they were done [loading], he had his wife stand behind the sled, holding onto the back handlebar, and he tied her onto the sled, fearing that she might fall. After closing the cache, he put on his snowshoes when he was on the roof. He told his wife to pretend to keep walking when they took off into midair, even though her feet were not touching the ground. Because her husband was an *angalkuq* [shaman], after harnessing himself on the tow rope, he took his staff and began pulling as his wife pushed the sled. When he got to the edge of the cache, he did not fall when he got to midair, and her husband walked on air only using snowshoes, pulling the sled, and even though the sled passed over the edge, it did not fall. However, his wife suddenly stumbled, but she was tied to the sled and didn't fall, and she held onto the sled and continued taking steps in the air with her legs as he had instructed her.

After a while, the soles of her feet hit something that felt like ground. It felt different but good. They started going higher. As they got a little higher, that woman carrying her child on her back began following beneath them. They continued to climb and went into the clouds and appeared on top of the clouds. They began traveling on top of the clouds because her husband was apparently a shaman. In time, they started descending. They came out of the clouds and their village appeared up ahead, their winter home on the Yukon River.

Qanitat is what they call the refuse pile where they dump charcoal from the fire pit in the area in front of the *qasgi*. They landed on top of the refuse pile.[8] This was at nighttime. When they landed, he told his wife that they would not sleep at home but in the *qasgi*. After they secured the contents of their sled to keep them from the dogs, they went inside the *qasgi*. When they went in, they got their bedding ready on the floor planks and everyone went to bed. Nothing strange happened the next day, and they went home. That is where this incident ended.

When one of the people who moved to their spring camp returned to their village to get food, he kept on eye out for her, but he did not see her. That was the end of her hauntings. When she stopped appearing, they moved back to their village.

IT IS SAID there was a couple who could not have children, and her husband was becoming older but not elderly yet. They only had a dog that was always tied under their cache. They never had any children, but they were fond of children and would feed them. That was how they were.

Awhile after they moved back to their village, winter came. The hole in the river below their village never froze. Summer would come before it froze. One evening during the winter after a fire bath, while the men were sitting, mist began to flow in through the entryway of the *qasgi*. The mist dispersed on the floor and disappeared after pulsating. It is said that the *qasgi* had a sleeping platform above the entryway. They called it a *quliruaq*, and that was where people slept. The lower-level sleeping platforms were close to the floor, but there was enough space underneath. It is said that their *qasgi* was laid out like that.

Just then, a man appeared at the entryway wearing a bentwood hunting hat, a seal-gut rain garment, fishskin mittens, and waterproof skin boots. He was not quite an elder. After he came up through the entrance hole, another person entered behind him. Five men appeared from below, all wearing the same garments, but here the weather was extremely cold outside. Water dripped down from the bottom of their garments, and it wasn't frozen at all.

Before sitting on the upper platform, they removed their garments along with their bentwood hats. They were normal people and there seemed to be nothing strange about them. And they were wearing hunting clothes that normal people wear. They sat down alongside each other above the door on the sleeping platform. Then someone said to get them food.[9]

One of the young men jumped up and ran out. They had never seen [the five men] before, and this was their first encounter. After being gone a while, he came in holding a very large bowl filled with food. The other dish held *akutaq*. They set them in front of them. The eldest of the five looked at the food, inspecting the two bowls. After looking them over he said, "We're hungry, but we can't eat [the contents of these two bowls]." They told the married couple who prepared the food that they couldn't eat the bowl's contents because they were coated with the saliva and the urine of a child. After saying that, [the eldest stranger] pinched the center of the *akutaq* and pulled up the contents until the bowl was empty. When he let go and it hit the bowl, it quivered like Jell-O.

He said they could not eat that food because of what it contained. After that, he told her, "If you are going to cook from now on, always wash your hands first before you touch the food. We cannot eat this food even though we are hungry because it is mixed with your child's saliva that you handled."

They took the bowls and left. Not long after, he came in with frozen blackfish. He came in with one of those large urine buckets that elderly men used that look like bowls. It was one of the elderly men's urine buckets filled with blackfish. They set them in front along with some seal oil. After that same person observed it, he finally smiled and said that the food was clean and they began to eat.

When it was time to eat, they would serve them food like that, using their urine buckets for bowls. [Their guests] did not mind. But when the men were going to take fire baths, they would go outside and play loudly with the kids.

That went on for quite a while. One day, when they woke in the morning, their eldest man said, "We're craving fresh food. Let's go out and try to get some fresh food." They finally put on the garments they removed when they first came, and they even put on their seal-gut garments. When they went outside, because it was wintertime and [the villagers] were curious about what they were going to do, they went outside with them. When they went outside, they went toward that hole in the ice that does not freeze.

When they got to it, [those five men] lifted their arms and jumped into the hole. They all dove into the water. Not long after, they appeared holding fish, and they ate them raw and dove in again when they finished eating. When they had enough to eat, they went back up to the *qasgi* and boasted cheerfully about having eaten their usual meal.

They went back to the *qasgi* and stayed, but they never took fire baths. After some time, they asked what they were. The eldest among them told them that they were about to reach the end of their cycle. They said they came from the outer world. They said they were actually human like us, but they tried to change form because it allowed them to live longer. They said they were *qununit* [seals that turn into human beings]. The people of the village finally understood what they were; they were actually humans who were trying to change into *qununit* and become sea mammals. When they were about to leave on their journey to transform, they were instructed as follows, "*Kitaki-at ayemqaqsaunaci kangiqutat-llu kangirquaqluki egilreskici* [Now, as you travel, don't take a shortcut, and when you come to bays and coves, make sure you travel all the way around them and don't cut across]." It is said that they swim around the waters of our world for many years. Those who follow their instructions can come out of the water and reach home. However, those who do not live by their instructions die on their journey, or hunters catch and kill them. We humans have holes on our shoulder blades. And I used to see a man named Tanqiulria whose sons are alive today and live in my village. They said their father Tanqiulria caught a bearded seal with holes in its shoulder blades. They say that bearded seal was once a *qununiq*. Those men were apparently [*qununit*].

One day, while they were sitting, their eldest leader jumped up from where he was lying and said, "Oh no, we're going to lose our way home. Our way home is about to be obstructed." They got ready quickly, and their youngest one would whimper out of desperation. They said they were about to lose their way. The men in the *qasgi* had no idea what they meant. When they went outside, they ran down to that open hole in the water and jumped in, and they never surfaced. After a while, word got around that one of the women in the village had a miscarriage. They realized that they actually meant that she was the one who would cause them to lose their path. Nothing like that ever happened again, and those men never returned.

After a number of years, as the men sat in the *qasgi*, one of the young men entered and said that there was a dark figure coming from the direction of the ocean. They were curious and went outside and saw something coming from the direction of the ocean not very far away. When it got close, they saw that there were two people with an Eskimo-style boat with a sled underneath. They got close, and they saw it was two tiny people, one a man and the other a woman, yet they were dragging that boat filled with their belongings.

They went straight to the home of the couple who could not have children but who only had a dog. They stopped outside their home. Their boat was huge, filled with their belongings. And here was a tiny couple with their child wearing a long-tailed duck parka that was not cut open but with sleeves. And that child would probably be about [twelve inches] tall if he had a parka made of a long-tailed duck. And here he was running around, and he was extremely agile and active for his size.

That tiny man greeted the couple and told them that they had come to live with them to share spouses because they felt sorry for them for not being able to have children. [The couple] welcomed them and were grateful. Their child was very cute, and he was lively and active. They told them to arrange their sleeping area across from them, and I don't know how large their house was. (They call the length of the side of the wall of a house *nakiqatak*). They cleared the whole other side wall and laid their bedding down and placed a log down that they would use as a pillow.[10] They did not fill that space with their belongings. I don't know how big their house was, but houses weren't large long ago.

They happily welcomed them. And their dog never bothered their child even though he played around him. He had a harness made out of walrus skin and was tied to the cache. After unloading his boat, when it was empty, that little man put it up on top of the cache, that tiny person.

When it was time to go to bed, they went to sleep and put out the lamp, but it had started to get bright in the room because the moon, the earth's light, was getting full. When [the husband] woke from his sleep, they seemed to hear rustling noises from the other side of the house, from the area nearest to the entranceway close to the wall. The tiny people had laid down at the very top of the bed because they were small, and there was a lot of space left in the center of the room, and the rest of the bed was empty.

While they were sleeping a noise would come from across there, from the area below their bedding that covered the whole side wall. He woke and sat up and because light was shining in through the window, he saw two huge people across there covering the whole side of the house. He realized that the noise came from the movement of their feet. That is apparently how they were; they grew at night and shrank when the sun came up.

When men decided to become spouse-exchange partners, the two couples must be in total agreement, and their wives must also agree to the arrangement. They developed that relationship. One day, the wife of the man who couldn't conceive, the one who could not get pregnant unexpectedly became pregnant. As soon as she became pregnant, that little man [who impregnated her] took off a piece of the skin of a young bearded seal that is usually made into boot soles from the area where the peg holes were placed to dry the skin, and he chewed on it. After chewing it, he sucked out all the saliva and hung it up and didn't say anything.[11]

Before the baby was born, one day he went out to go feed his dog. He went out and saw their small child playing around the dog. He gave the food to that dog. Just as the dog was about to finish his food, when that small child ran in front of him, the dog suddenly bit him. The dog instantly killed and ate him. And here the dog had never bothered the child in the past. When his little father realized what happened, he attacked the dog; and when he grabbed it by the neck and yanked the leash made of tough walrus skin, it snapped instantly. He whacked that dog onto that post on the cache and cut it in half. He quickly climbed up on top of the cache and took his bow that was inside the boat, a huge bow, and here he was small, and he drew the arrow immediately without any effort. He said to the man who became his spouse exchange partner, "If you want to seek revenge for the death of your dog then seek revenge for it." That man said he wasn't thinking of seeking revenge over the dog, but that he was only going to feel guilty over the death of their child for a long time. "Don't worry because we do not grieve over the loss of our dogs." But he said that he was only going to feel guilty over the child who was killed by the dog for a long time. [The child's father] relaxed and came down [from the cache]. They buried their small child.

Her unborn child grew inside. One night, that little man said, "If I am not here while she is having contractions, let me know right away." The little wife summoned her husband while he was in the *qasgi*. That little man went in and delivered the baby. Before he delivered the baby at that time, he took that piece of skin from boot sole hide that he had previously chewed and hung, and he stuck it in his mouth and chewed it, making it moist.

When [the baby] was born, after cutting his umbilical cord, he immediately took the piece of skin he was chewing out of his mouth and put it in the baby's mouth. He then gave that child to them. He said to them that the baby would have the name Anglinarli. He told his parents to store that skin that he was chewing in a safe place, and to give it to [the child] when he asked for it one day. They stored it in a safe place. The little person then said that [Anglinarli] was their child and that he was that couple's child as well. If nothing happened to him while he was growing, they should not look for him if he was gone one day. He told him that [Anglinarli] was their son and the other couple's son as well. He told them not to look for him if he was gone one day, even if he left at night. They said they were going to return home the next day.

Because [the new father] was a good hunter, a *nukalpiaq* [good provider], he filled the boat of his spouse-exchange partner with goods and clothing before they left. When they left, they went toward the ocean and disappeared. That [little man] also told the couple to always warn the boy when he grew older never to harm his peers and not to fight back if they picked on him.[12]

[Their son] was like that when he grew, and he never fought back when they picked on him. And he wasn't very tall because he was conceived by a small person, but he was strong. And he would carry things that were hard for adults, but here he was young. And during the summer, he would carry whole driftwood logs back home and he would take them back to his village before he stopped to rest, even though those huge logs were thick.

They say a young male peer who was bigger would pick on him, but he would not fight back. One day while they were playing outside, that boy who continually picked on him beat him up for no reason. After whimpering, he said, "Why is this one here always picking on me?" That boy was actually bigger than him, but [Anglinarli] took him by the legs and threw him against something and his head fell and rolled away. His neck was severed. Anglinarli killed him.

His parents admonished him never to do that again. The villagers could not do anything to that couple because they respected his father. [Anglinarli] killed the person who picked on him.

Some days, he would be gone for a long time and they did not know where he went. While his mother was working in the early evening, he would come in slowly from outside, hot and covered with sweat. When he did that for the first time, she asked him where he had been, and he said he had been visiting his parents. They never looked for him even though he was gone, and he knew where his parents were, wherever they were. He grew and Anglinarli was his name.

AFTER SOME TIME PASSED, one day a boat from outside their region came their way with two people rowing together and a person sitting in the middle of the boat. Apparently, [the middle person] was their son. Their son who was strong and mighty and should have been taking care of his parents was letting his parents row the boat. They docked, and they saw that the great *nukalpiaq* seated in the center of the boat was actually their son. They brought him into the *qasgi* and had him sit in the back area, and his parents went into the *qasgi* as well. They learned that his parents had brought him to all the villages in the area outside their region, and his parents would bring him to other places when he defeated his challengers.

His father said that he was taking his son throughout the whole region, looking for worthy opponents. No one had defeated him yet. He said that someone from that village who thought he could beat him should challenge his son. Those people did not reply and sat still. After a while, one of them said that they didn't know of a worthy opponent in that village, that he did not know of anyone with the same strength and stamina.

The strong man's father responded, "I thought I heard that you had a strong person in your village from the Kuskokwim River area." After pausing for a while, the grandfather of Anglinarli said that he could not think of anyone in that village with the same strength and stamina, but he said that he could have Anglinarli try to challenge him.

Just when his grandfather said that, that small Anglinarli flew from behind near the lamp post and landed in the center of the floor planks. They took off their clothing. That great *nukalpiaq* whose parents were bringing him to places always defeated his opponents because he was huge. When he came face-to-face with that great *nukalpiaq*, Anglinarli tried to put his arms around his waist, but his arms could not go all the way around his waist and his hands were some distance apart because he wasn't very big. Anglinarli held his arms around him.

Those who ask for a challenge are supposed to hold their ground and try to have their opponent take them down. That is what the great *nukalpiaq* was doing. They were slowly going around in a circle on the floor. Anglinarli had his arms around him like that, but not all the way around.

Then suddenly Anglinarli said, "*Arenqiapaa* [Oh my goodness], wait, wait a second." Anglinarli ran out. His mother or father had never showed him that piece of chewed skin. His little father had only told them to give it to him when he asked for it someday.

His mother was working inside their house when she heard heavy footsteps outside. Anglinarli appeared at the door, asking for his chewed skin. When she remembered where it was, his mother gave it to him immediately because it was just in her bag, and he put it in his mouth and ran out.

He ran in and took [his opponent] by the waist again, continually chewing. He moved him around in a circle, and his arms moved closer together. His hands moved closer together, creating a dent in his [opponent's] skin, and the *nukalpiaq* was having difficulty breathing. When the tips of his hands joined after a while, his arms eventually went all the way around his waist. As soon as his hands joined, they heard a snapping and cracking noise and realized that the sound came from the breaking ribs of that huge person whom he was holding, and the arms of that little person dug into his skin.

Blood started to flow out of his nose. When that happened, his grandfather told Anglinarli, "Okay stop, that's enough!" Then he finally let go of him.

When [Anglinarli] let go, the strong man's father said, "*Avaqutaa* [my son], did he not give you a chance to fight back?" His *avaqutaq* answered him, "Do you want the fight to keep going until I die?" He stopped breathing after saying that.

His parents put him in their boat and left.

This is the end of the story of that one who ate his mother. It is the end. I've told the story like I heard it. It has ended.

Introduction
The Five Sisters

Told by Lena Atkiq Ilutsik

Transcribed and translated by Virginia Ilutsik Andrew

Among the Yup'ik Eskimos oral stories were a very powerful way of instilling life's values into the growing child. This was done primarily at bedtime during the winter months when darkness and the cold of the night came early each day. Many of these oral stories were entertaining but also had very strong messages of how children should behave and treat other children or themselves. The stories were not analyzed as we would find in the modern Western school setting, where one would be drilled on what they remembered or what "bad" or "inappropriate" behavior was depicted in the story. The stories were told and retold without analysis.

The late Lena Ilutsik, who was born October 10, 1919, in Togiak, Alaska, recalls being told stories during the dark, cold winter months as they lay in bed. Her grandfather, who raised her, was the storyteller as, following European contact, the Yup'ik people were in transition and male relatives no longer lived in a separate dwelling. The 1918 influenza epidemic had taken her parents when she was a young child, and her grandfather took her in to live with them. She remembers moving around a great deal, following the different seasonal animals that were caught for livelihood. Her summers were spent at fish camps in Ekuk and Clark's Point. The rest of the seasons were spent off the Snake Lake River, primarily in the now deserted village of Tegin'gaq.

As a young girl I used to listen to my mother, the late Lena Ilutsik, tell my younger sister, Virginia Ilutsik Andrew, oral stories in the Yup'ik language. This was often done at night when everyone was in bed. I would hear my younger sister Virginia beg my mother to tell her a story. Her favorite story was what we have respectfully titled "The Five Sisters."

It is also very interesting to hear this story again as an adult after having not heard it since childhood and to compare what you thought you heard with how the oral story was actually told. (One has to remember that with Western influences many parents literally gave their children to the Western educational system and no longer told the oral stories that had been passed down to them). Within my memory and imagination I had included and remembered incidents in the story that were born of my imagination. For example, in reading and listening to the story my late mother shared, it did not have the "shaman" that I thought was a very magical part of the story. Nor did the sisters only call out the colors, rather they already knew the names of the berries that are depicted in the story. I do remember that my mother would also add tasks or jobs that were currently relevant to our present existence such as washing dishes, etc. She described the tasks or chores, but in the story she shared for another audience, she left those minute details out.

The story my mother shared with my sister had a very powerful effect on how I viewed certain things during my adolescent years. For example, the major theme of the story is that you do not spend time admiring yourself and always attempting to look pleasing to yourself and others. It is more important to think about other people and how one can make a better life or contribution to others and the people of the future generation. I remember as a young teenager when your total life revolves around yourself, reminding myself not to think only of myself and being afraid to linger too long in front of a mirror, fearing that I would turn into something bad. Later becoming an adult and having a daughter of my own brought back memories of this story, and I shared it with her using my memory. Later I will share what my late mother actually told without my imagination taking control.

This story was recorded, transcribed, and translated by my younger sister, the late Virginia Ilutsik Andrew of Aleknagik. We wanted to obtain the actual story that we could use in the classroom with other children. So my sister recorded this story in the privacy of her home with my mother in the fall of 1996. At that time my mother was seventy-seven years of age. When I shared this story with other Yup'ik teachers within the Bristol Bay communities I found that not many of those educators or their parents had heard it. They said that it must be a family story that was passed down within a certain family. In my research I found another version of the story, also titled "The Five Sisters," in the book *Medicine Men of Hooper Bay* written by Charles E. Gillham in 1955. In this version the "clean" sister turns out to be the prettiest berry of them all.

—Esther Arnaq Ilutsik

The Five Sisters

Told by Lena Atkiq Ilutsik of Aleknagik

A **LONG, LONG TIME AGO, THERE LIVED FIVE SISTERS.** These sisters were all very hard workers. The sisters helped their mother clean the house, gather greens, pack water, start the fire, gather wood, split fish, and pluck birds.

All the sisters were very mindful of their mother and worked really hard, except one. She did mind her mother, but was very slow with her tasks. She was too busy looking at and admiring her reflection.

Her favorite task was to pack water from the lake. Once she got down to the lake she would look at her reflection. And she would run her hands through her hair and braid it, pinch her cheeks with her fingers so they would be rosy, and bite her lips to darken them.

Many times an older sister would have to run down to get her as they would be waiting for water for cooking and washing.

One day when all the chores were finished, the sisters were outside playing. They were sliding down the grassy slopes and having a great time, except the one sister who was content to look at her reflection. She was nearby playing or rather admiring herself in a little clear puddle, when all of a sudden they all heard a noise.

It sounded like a swish of a bird's wing flapping together, but much louder. They were all startled and stopped and looked.

They all looked up the hill and there stood this old man with flowing white hair and a pleasant smile. The old man had such a gentle voice that they were no longer frightened. He told them that he had come to grant them one wish. He warned them that this wish would last forever and ever, so that they needed to think very carefully of what they wished for.

He told them that their wishes would be granted only if they followed these instructions. They had to climb to the top of the hill and shut their eyes, jump up and down three times singing their wish, and then slide down the hill.

The first sister ran up to the top of the hill and with her eyes shut, she jumped up and down and sang this song, "Oh, I wish to be something that will help my people forever and ever; something that people will remember me with fond memories. And my favorite color is red-orange."

With that she slid down the hill. To the amazement of the other sisters, who were also at the top of the hill, she turned into a field of big, red-orange, juicy salmonberries (known as cloudberries).

The second sister repeated the same actions, but added that her favorite color was blue. And she turned into a field of big, juicy blueberries.

And so the other sisters proceeded to take their turns with the same actions, with one becoming a field of blackberries and the other becoming a field of cranberries.

Then it was the last sister's turn, but of course, she was still admiring her reflection in the clear water puddle. She was combing her hair with her fingers, pinching her cheeks and biting her lips, and telling herself how beautiful she was. All of a sudden she realized it was her turn. It had become so quiet. She looked down the hill and saw all these beautiful fields of berries and proceeded with the instructions given.

She shut her eyes, jumping up and down three times, and sang this wish, "Oh, I wish to be the most beautiful thing in the world, as beautiful as a raspberry."

And she slid down the hill. And instead of sliding smoothly she went bump, bump, and BUMP!

As she still had her consciousness, she looked up the hill and she saw bits of brown pieces scattered all down the hill, and it had a very unpleasant odor.

She looked at herself and saw that she was also part of this brown stuff and with disgust she put herself back together and climbed back up the hill.

Again, she repeated her actions singing, "Oh, I wish, I wish to be the most beautiful thing in the world, as beautiful as a raspberry."

And again, she slid down the hill. And this time she didn't go bumpity-bump. Instead she went so fast that it sounded like someone spilling out water-swish.

When she reached the bottom of the hill she saw that instead of a trail of bits of brown pieces, this time it was mushy bits of brown and the stench was horrible. Try as she might she could not put herself back together. In a rage she began to cry and shouted, "Let it be as it may. May the people remember me forever and ever by expelling me from their bodies, when they become sick with a stomach-ache. And they will have to do the awful chore of disposing of me everyday with honey buckets."

Introduction
Atkuut Tengaururturalriit / A Flying Parka

Told by Paul John

Transcribed and translated by Marie Meade

As with the earlier tale, "One Who Didn't Think Much of a Man's Stomach," Paul John's intended audience for this story was young people. He told the story on a June evening in 2000 at Umkumiut spring camp, three miles to the west of Toksook Bay on Nelson Island. There he and his wife were staying in a small, one-room cabin, serving as resident elders for Calista Elders Council's first culture camp. Two dozen students, aged ten through fourteen, were attending the camp and were active each day catching and cutting fish, gathering eggs and plants, learning to process and sew seal gut, as well as numerous other subsistence occupations.

The students were also learning how to learn, from a Yup'ik point of view. Not only were they asked to observe and practice new skills, they were taught to listen and remember what they heard. For an hour each evening, all gathered in a circle on the floor of the small A-frame Catholic church located at one end of camp. The five elders in residence—Paul and Martina John, Simeon and Anna Agnus, and Theresa Moses—took turns speaking to them about the old days. They began by telling them ghost stories, as well as narratives about the families who stayed together at Umkumiut when they were young. As the days passed, they spoke at length about good listening—instructing the children to sit without moving, never taking their eyes off the speaker's mouth lest what was said "come out their other ear." Their goal should be to "put what they heard in their pockets so that they could take it out in the future" when need arose. They were admonished that even if they forgot what they heard, someday as they were living their lives it would appear to them and guide their actions.

Each elder spoke in turn, and the evening sessions often stretched for over an hour. As their time together drew to an end, Paul would invariably conclude with a story. "A Flying Parka" was one. Usually his stories were not

Paul John speaking to young people at the Calista Elders Council's Third Annual Elders and Youth Convention in St. Marys, 1999. *Photo by James H. Barker.*

long, and they were often funny. Their function was both to educate and to entertain. Learning was serious business at Umkumiut but also enjoyable.

When Paul told the story of the flying parka, he had no trouble keeping everyone's attention. Children rarely hear these stories today. Moreover, Paul is a consummate storyteller. The theme of the apparently destitute orphan who, through hard work and cunning, succeeds where others fail, is well-known in Yupik and Iñupiaq oral tradition. Also well known is the *nukalpiaq* (great hunter and provider), as well as the proud and inaccessible *uilingia-taq* (unmarried woman). Paul's story is a classic example of a moral tale, resonating with Western as well as Yup'ik oral tradition. Clearly rendered in English by expert translator Marie Meade, it simultaneously entertains and instructs.

—AFR

Words of the Real People

Paul John, with Wassilie Berlin and Marie Meade, examines objects at the Ethnologisches Museum, Berlin, 1997. *Photo by Ann Fienup-Riordan.*

Atkuut Tengaurturalriit

Told by Paul John of Toksook Bay

TUA-I-LLI-WA-GGUQ UKUT NUNAT UITAURARQELRIIT KUIGEM CENIINI.
Ilangqerrluteng -gguq ellira'araurlurmek pitukiitnek. Tua-i ilaunani, taugaam
tua-i nunanun taukunun ilausngaluni.

Cali-gguq taukut nunat nukalpiartarluteng apeqmeggnek. Nukalpiartaq-llu
tauna paningqelliniluni wagg'ur-uumek uilingiatamek. Uilingiatamek piaqluku.
Tua-i tauna uilingiataq cucuyaaqelaraat makut aipangnarilriit angutet.

Taugaam cali taukut nunat atkugnek tengaurturalriartangqelliniluteng
arnartarnek, tua-i assirluteng. Taukut-am tua-i atkuut tengaurturalriit teg-
ustiitnek taugaam uingevkararkauluku tauna nukalpiartankuk panigtek
pilalliniluku.

Tua-i nulirturnarilriit tamakut, atkuut taukut, cucuyaaqluku tauna uilingiataq nulirqeqernaluku, qavairateksaaqelallinikiit, tua-i tegungnatugluki.
Unugmi taugaam paivngaringelalliniameng taukut atkuut, erenrani waten
tanqigcetaqan tua-i pissiyaagpek'nateng. Tua-i tamakut nulirtukunalriit
tegungnatugyaaqngaceteng qimagnaurtut imkut atkuut. Tua-i teguvkaqsau-
nateng tegungnaqestemeggnun tamakunun. Tua-i caperrsagulluki allamek
tua-i nulirturaqluteng arnamek, tauna imna uiliataq tua-i pinricenarluku.
Piyugyaaqengermegteggu-wa, taukut taugaam atkuut tegusciigacuamegteki
tua-i apaqsagucuunaku.

Tauna-wa-gguq tua-i elliraarmek pitukiit tua-i qessailnguq angun, elliraar
tauna ikayuakengyunqeggluni qasgimiunek, kevgarturluki. Tua-i qanellrat
tamalkuan, ciullegtengqessuunani elliraar tauna kevgiulliniaqekai qasgimiut.
Waten pikunaaqata, tua-i-ll' egmian nang'errluni ikayualuki. Taumek-gguq

A Flying Parka

ONCE THERE WAS A VILLAGE LOCATED ALONGSIDE A RIVER. Among the residents of that village lived a lowly orphan lad, referred to as a *elliraaraurluq* in Yup'ik. He was alone and didn't have any siblings, but he was part of that community.

And also in that village lived an illustrious man and an outstanding hunter identified by everyone as a *nukalpiartaq*. That man had an older, unmarried daughter. And the village called her a *uilingiataq*. Over time, as the young men in that village reached marriageable age, they tried to pick Uilingiataq as their wife, but she rejected them all.

And also in that village, there was a fancy woman's fur parka that constantly flew around right over the village. The *nukalpiartaq* and his wife told their daughter that they would only allow her to marry the young man who caught the parka that continued to fly around over the village.

It was only at night that the parka was most active; during the day it became less visible. So all the eligible bachelors, wishing to marry that *uilingiataq*, stayed up late into the night and tried to snatch the flying parka. When a young man decided that he was ready to take a wife and went out to capture the parka, it would fly away from him. The flying parka kept escaping from those who were trying to snatch it. While a young man might wish to marry the *uilingiataq*, being unable to catch the flying parka, he would give up and decide to marry another girl. Uilingiataq remained single, since the young men weren't able to take the flying parka.

Now, that person whom they called Elliraaraurluq was always helping and doing chores for the men who lived in the *qasgi*. He was not lazy. When a member in the *qasgi* announced that he needed something, the orphan would immediately respond and run to get whatever was requested before the other young men stood up. And whenever the community was planning

tua-i tamakut pikalget, neqkalget mencuitelaqaiit camek nernariluku piaqameng kainiqevkar yuunaku.

Pengumek-gguq yaaqlingqertut taukut nunat. Tua-i-gguq tauna elliraaraurluq angutet makut pitatni pissuqunga'artaqata pengum taum kangranun agluni, mayurluni, aqumluni ernerpak tua-i tuani pengumi uitalliniaqelria, tangvallratni taukut nunat. Tua-i-llu-gguq imkut kegga-i pissullret qamigaqullret-llu tekirqekata, nutaan tua-i nangerrluni tailuni nunanun tuani uitaluni. Piciryaraq-llu-gguq tua-i tangvallratni taukut ilami. Tua-i tamakut nukalpiat ilagarluki tuaten piurluni.

Atam-am tua-i cat iliitni qavallinilria. Qavallerminek tupakalliniuq cakneqlli-gguq pik'umi qasgim egalrakun unugcuutmi itqertellrani tuai tanqigcepaa, nunaniqvaa. Aren, inangqayaaqelriim imkut atkuut nuliangnaluteng tegussaaqlaq'ngait nukalpiat umyuaqeqaamiki makluni anlliniluni.

Aren tua-i yuqerrluni piinanrani piqerluteng-am imkut taukut atkuut ak'a agayanga'artelliniat tauna tua-i elliraaraurluq. Agayanga'arcatni murilkenrilnguarluni unaggun kuigem ceniikun uatmurtelliniuq. Tarenrait-gguq maa-i alaitaqluteng taukut atkuut. Tua-i uatmun ayagluni, nunat-llu iquklicamiki pellugturaqerluki, nutaan unugcuun una tua-i cuqluku tarenriakata tunumini tua-i nallunaitarkauvkarluki, analriacetun tua-i uyungelliniuq, kanavaguarluni apqiitnek, anaruarluni. Taukunek taugaam tua-i atkugnek tegutengnaqnaluni tua-i umyuangqerrluni ananricaaqengermi analriacetun taugaam uyungqaluni. Tua-i piqerluni-am atkuut taukut tarenrait waniwa ivgalliniut. Ivgangraata tua-i cumikenrilnguarluni uitluni, cumikluni taugaam tarenrait pama-i tunumini uitiita.

Tua-i canimellingluteng pama-I tarenrameggni. Tua-i canimellingengata alegyagucamiki alqunaq tua-i qetqallalliniluni tungiitunun taukut atkuut, yaq'errluni tuaten. Yaq'ertellria unatai neruvelkitliniut. Aren tua-i taukut atkuut teguliniluki. Maaten piuq aren tua-i atkukegtaraat assilriit.

certain activities or events, he would be the first one who came forward to help out. And for that reason, those who were able always shared their food with him when it was time to eat and never let him go hungry.

Just beyond the village there was a prominent hill. Whenever his peers left to go hunting on the land, Elliraaraurluq would walk over to the hill, climb up and sit on top all day long. Then when the hunters began arriving home, he would finally stand up, climb down and return to the village, where he resumed his residence in that community. That was what he always did when his peers went out to hunt. When the men went hunting, he also left the village.

One night while Elliraaraurluq was sleeping in the *qasgi*, he woke up and, looking up through the skylight, noticed the moon shining very brightly. The light coming in through the skylight was radiant and breathtaking. As he tried to go back to sleep he started thinking about the flying parka and all the men who had tried to catch it and failed. Then he got up and went out.

As soon as he was outside he urinated. While peeing he immediately sensed the presence of the flying parka behind him. When he was finished, he went down to the river and started walking casually along the bank, pretending not to notice the flying parka floating behind him. As he continued on nonchalantly he could see the shadow of the parka appearing and disappearing on the ground nearby. He kept going and soon reached the edge of the village. On the outskirts, after noting the position of the moon and calculating where the shadow might appear again, he squatted down pretending to defecate. He wasn't actually defecating, but merely crouched down to try to catch the parka. While he was in that position, soon the shadow of the hovering parka appeared again on the surface of the ground nearby. He waited, acting as though he did not notice anything, but he was fully aware that the parka was floating right behind him.

By paying close attention to the movement of the shadow, he could see that the parka was getting closer and closer. Then when he thought it was close enough to reach, he suddenly sprang backwards with outstretched arms toward the flying parka. He immediately felt his hands grasp something that felt soft and pliant. He held on tight and realized that he had taken the flying parka. It was a beautiful parka.

Tauna tua-i elliraar imggaarluki atkuut taukut unermigluki qasgimun agnginanermini aren umyuangssanguq, "Aling imalluqaa ukut atkuut qasgim elaturraanun elliluki errnerciqumki, imalluqaa kia teguliki." Cali-ll' qasgimun malikluki iteryung'ermi tangerrnayukluki qamkunun qasgimiunun cali tua-i piluni. Tua-i nanelvigkaunaki.

Tua-i umyugaa tua-i takaryugyaaquq taukunun uilingiatankunun agglerka-minek unugmi atkuut taukut tegumiaqluki. Tua-i taugken tamarinayukluki cali piluni.

Ayumian tua-i takaryung'ermi elaturraatnun ag'uq taukut uilingiatan-kut. Elaturraatnun itrami apqiitnek tua-i pivallagaluni tup'allagaluni qamkut tupagtengnaqluki. Tua-i pirraarluni elaturraatni, iterluni amiatgun. Iterluni igvallinia tauna imna atii uilingiatam, ak'a-ll' tua-i uyaquni makluki takuyarluni amik tangerrluku itellra tua-i nalluvkenaku.

Tua-i nangerrluni taum tua-i uilingiatam atiin pillinia, "Waqaa elliraara-urluuq, caluten tua-i iteryaravakarcit unugmi?"

Tua-i-ll' taum elliraam pillinia, "Ukut-wa atkuut nanelvigkaipakaata, qasgim-llu elaturraanun uitavkaryungramki tangertaitnun tegunayukluki. Cali- tua-i malikluki qasgimun iteryungerma tangerrnayukluki yugnun piama, tua-i waniwa unuungraan takaryungerma taiskenka."

Aren taum tua-i nukalpiartam pillinia, "Arenqiapaa-lli! Arenqiapaa! Panimegnuk tua-i piyuumiq'ngai tegusciulliniut! Kitak tua-i ika-I nuliqsa-gutan panigpuk ikna."

Nuliani pillinia, "Usuuq makluten panigpuk tupagesgu, atkuni kankut ciuniurniarai."

Tua-i aanii makcami tupaggluku piani atkukegtaaraat imkut tua-i ciuniur-luki nuliqsaguartellinia taum elliraaraurluum. Tua-i uitaluni.

Atam tua-i qasginaluni waniwa up'ngarteqanrakun taum nukalpiam pillinia, "Kitaki, nek'elalqa qasgim iluani nallunritan, kia-ll' aqumvikeksaitaa cataileng-

After admiring the beautiful parka, he folded it carefully and neatly. He placed the folded parka under his armpit and embraced it tightly as he headed toward the *qasgi*. While he was walking back he considered where to keep the parka until daylight. He thought of placing it in the porch of the *qasgi*, but decided that someone might discover it and claim it. He thought of bringing it with him into the *qasgi*, but he was worried that people in there might see it. He didn't know where to keep it.

Fearful about losing the parka, he thought of taking it to the house where Uilingiataq resided, but felt shy about going there at night with the parka.

After pondering the dilemma, and although he felt anxious and bashful, he turned and headed toward her house. As he entered the porch he deliberately stomped his feet loudly trying to wake up those who were sleeping inside. Shortly after that he entered through the inner doorway. When he entered, the father of Uilingiataq raised his head up and turned to see who was coming in. He was already awake and immediately recognized Elliraaraurluq at the doorway.

Then the father stood up at once and said, "*Waqaa*, Elliraaraurluq, what brought you here during the night?"

Elliraaraurluq answered him saying, "This parka here, after pondering over whether to leave it in the porch of the *qasgi* or to bring it in with me, I decided to bring it over here even though I felt shy about bringing it in the middle of the night."

With a sudden change of attitude and with a hint of uneasiness Nukalpiartaq said, "Oh my goodness! My goodness! Someone has finally caught the parka our daughter had been desiring for a long time."

Nukalpiartaq immediately called his wife to wake her and said, "Get up right away and wake up our daughter so she could receive the parka she had always wanted."

As soon as Uilingiataq woke up she quickly took the parka, and from that moment she officially became the spouse of Elliraarauluq, who remained in the house with them.

The following day when Elliraaraurluq was getting ready to go to the *qasgi*, Nukalpiartaq said, "Now, you know my place in the *qasgi* where I always sit. A place no one else is allowed to sit. When you go in, take that seat right away.

erma. Itquvet tuavet tua-i aqumekina. Tua-i neksagutan. Wiinga picirraatun nani piciatun aqumelangerma cangaituq. Tua-i tauna neksagutan."

Tauna-gguq elliraaraurluq amiigem quliini tua-i uitauratuuq, nancuunani-llu amiigem taugaam uani kalvagyaram quliini.

Tua-i itrami, qasgiami tuaken uilingiatankunek, itrami tua-i tuavet nukal-piam nek'elallranun yuilan tua-i qavarngailengermi makniaraata inartelliniuq. Inangqaqainanrani unuakuarmi tamaa-i angulluat iliit makluni, qurrutni cayu-kanirluku qurqatarluni waniwa pilriim tangerqallinia. Tangrramiu pilliniuq, "Aling elliraaraurlullermi-lli ik'umi tunriipaa! Nukalpiarput-ll'-am enaillini-luku. Wangkuta-wa takaqelaqvut cakneq, cataitaqan-llu aqumqerciiganata uitalalriakut." Tua-i takailkelluku.

Elllin tua-i taum elliraaraurluum niicugningermiu niitenrilngurtun qavarualliniuq.

Tua-i makqaq'ngarcata makut makluni tauna elliraar, elliraaraurluq. Tua-i-ll' tua-i payugteqatanga'arteqertelluki uilingiataq ugna puggliniuq imkunek atkugnek ellami tengaurturatulinek aturluni.

Aren tua-i itran tangerqaamegteggu umyuarteqliniut angullugaat, "Naliatnun-kiq nukalpiat tuneniartau qantaq?" Tangvakiitni itraami tua-i tuaken amigmek imna tauna elliraar tua-i ciuneqluku itralliniuq. Tekicamiu-ll' tua-i tauna qantaq tunluku.

Aren tua-i qanevyulkitangartelliniut-am angullugaat, "Aling, elliraarall'ermi-ll' nulirqegciqatarpaa! Angutem pissutulim nulirkaariinek nulirqegciqatanga'arpaa!"

Tua-i niitenrilnguarluki nerurallralliniuq tauna elliraar. Taqngan tua-i qantaa teguluku tayima anluni.

Tua-i tamaani uitauq tauna elliraar nuliangarrluni. Atam tua-i piinanermini pillinia tauna nuliani angayuqaagminun nunayutqeryugyaaqluku tauna nuliani. Tua-i angayuqaagni apcakek piyukna pisqelluku, maligquraasqelluku.

From now on, that is where you will always sit. I myself, when I'm there I will sit anywhere there is space. The place where I used to sit, it is your place from now on."

Previously, Elliraaraurluq was only allowed to sit in the space above the entryway. That was the place where he always stayed.

When he got to the *qasgi* it was still early morning and the men were still sleeping. As instructed, he went straight to the place where Nukalpiartaq always stayed and lay down, though he wasn't intending to sleep. Shortly after Elliraaraurluq lay down, one of the elder men got up, and as he pulled his urine bucket toward him he noticed Elliraaraurluq lying there. As soon as he saw him the old man became agitated and embarrassed and said, "My goodness! Elliraaraurluq, where is your respect and dignity! How shameful it is to see you lying there in that place of our Nukalpiartaq. We've always shown the utmost respect to him and avoid sitting there even while he is gone." He was criticizing Elliraaraurluq for his disrespectful behavior.

Elliraaraurluq, though he heard the man talking, pretended not to notice and kept lying there as if sleeping.

Then when the rest of the men began getting up Elliraarauluq also got up. Soon, when the usual time came for women to start bringing food to their men, Uilingiataq appeared at the entryway wearing the beautiful flying parka.

When she entered the elder men in the *qasgi* started to speculate about whom she would give the dish she was bringing. As they warily and attentively watched, holding their breath, she walked toward Elliraaraurluq. She came to Elliraaraurluq and handed him the dish.

Then everyone in the *qasgi* relaxed and began talking to each other. Someone remarked, "My goodness! How fortunate it is for Elliraaraurluq. He is now the husband to a woman of high class and only accessible to a great hunter, a man of the same superior rank."

Elliraaraurluq began to eat the food in the bowl, ignoring the comments made by others there. When he was finished eating, Uilingiataq took the bowl and left.

So, Elliraaraurluq remained in the community with his new wife. One day he politely told his in-laws that he would like to take his wife to visit his own parents. They gave her permission to go with him.

Ayakataagnek cakian piyaaqellinia ikamragni aturyukakek atuusqellukek. Uksuullinian tamaani. Kiullinia ikamrangqerrniluni aturngaitnilukek. Nauwa ikamrak? Ikamragkenek-llu ciungani tangyuunateng.

Ayiimek tua-i tauna imna aqumgayarani ciuneqluku ayangartuq. Ayangarcagnek ciuneqluku tua-i tauna aqumgayaraa tangvallratni, tekicameg-negu tauna imna pillinia taum, una patuullinilria pengum qainga, patungqell-inilria ikircarauluni.

Ikirtaa maaten qemaggvik kan'a, can'get-wa kankut. Taukut imkut can'get ancamiki pillinia, "Waniwa tang ukut, aqumgauryukaqavcia waten pissurnam nalliini, wani aqumgauryukaqavcia ernerpak, uumum waniwa atkullraaramnun imiulluki aqumganguartura'arqelrianga, pissulriit malig-taquaqamki. Tangllerpeceni ernerpak wani aqumgangaqurlua, amta-llu wii yuilqurcaaqlua."

Qemaggviim taum imai antai aturaqegtaaraat. All'uki pillia, "Waten waniwa aturlua ukunek pissulalrianga aqumgauryukaqavcia tangllerpeceni." Aren tua-i taukut atkuni all'uki ayagtuk.

Tua-i nutaan tuavet taukut quyurrluteng uitaluteng. Maaten tua-i tauna elliraaraurlurmek pitukiit nutaan tangvagtelluni ilani pissullgucirluki piss-urtuq, aling picularyaaqellinilria tua-i. Aren tua-i ayagneqluku tauna piss-ungengami pissunguq angayuqatek taukut quyungqalriit kaigcecugnaunaki. Nukalpiameggnek-gguq kiituan piyaurtaat taukut nunat. Tua-i nualpiaru-yaaqengermi-am tauna elliraunguarturalliniaqluni taukuni nunani. Atkuni-llu tauna cimiyuilnguarlalliniluki waten nukalpiarulliningermi.

Tua-i-am taukut atkuut kia tegungailaki tayima elliin teguyugngacini nall-unrilamiu tauna nulirkani nayurturallrullikii atkuut taukut tegunatkaminun. Man'a maa-I qanemciq tuaten pitauq. Tua-i.

When they got ready to go, his father-in-law offered Elliraaraurluq his sled to use. It was in the winter. He told his father-in-law that he had his own sled. Since no one had ever seen him using a sled before, they wondered where his sled might be.

When they left the village, they headed right toward the hill where he always sat. When they got to the top of the hill, she noticed a cover there on the ground. It was a flap that you could open and close.

When he pulled the flap, there was a hole below it with a pile of loose grass at the bottom. He took some grass out and said, "See this grass, I use it to stuff my old parka with. I set it on top of this hill here when I go out and hunt like the rest of the hunters in the village. The stuffed figure that sits on the hill all day long is seen by everyone in the village, while I am actually out hunting."

He also pulled out brand-new garments from the hole. He put the clothes on and said, "These are the garments I use when I go out hunting." After he put on the outfit, they left.

Then the parents of Elliraaraurluq moved to that village, and they began living as a family from then on. Elliraaraurluq started going out hunting with the other men. The other hunters then realized and observed that actually he had always been a skilled and experienced hunter. Eventually, people in that village no longer viewed him as a poor orphan lad and started calling him a *nukalpiaq*. He had lived in that village wearing old garments and everyone thought he didn't have a family and was an orphan.

Since he knew other young men couldn't capture the parka, perhaps he had continued to stay in that village where his future wife resided waiting for the right time to take the parka. This is the end of the story.

Introduction
Uraqural²rig / Sibling Brothers

Told by Nuratar Andrew Noatak

Transcribed and translated by Nakaar Howard Amos

At the time this story was recorded in 1986, Nuratar (Andrew Noatak) was the oldest resident of Nunivak Island. The story was tape-recorded among a series of interviews conducted by Ken Pratt of the Bureau of Indian Affairs' Alaska Native Claims Settlement Act (BIA ANCSA) office to gather information related to historical place and cemetery site investigations on Nunivak Island. "Interview" is not quite the right term, as this particular recording purely captures Andrew doing what he loved to do—storytelling.

Pratt and Howard Amos held Nuratar in the highest regard with an appreciation of his depth of knowledge and his skills as a raconteur. Prior to his death in 1990 at about the age of one hundred—his exact age was unknown and recorded birthdates range from 1889 to 1900—roughly thirty hours of recordings over twenty-one sessions with Andrew resulted from the BIA site investigations. Today many of these tapes have not been fully or carefully translated. One reason is that Andrew's speech remains partly enigmatic for Yup'ik language scholars. Few individuals (Amos is one) possess the ability to translate Nuratar's Cup'ig.

The evolving work on the translation of this story provides a good example of the difficulties involved. Our dear friend Irene Reed, along with Sophie Shield, first began translating Andrew's material in the late 1980s. Challenged by the differences of the Nunivak dialect from the more familiar General Central Yup'ik, Irene admitted to sometimes being completely befuddled by some of Andrew's speech, and she first postulated that he was speaking a subdialect of Cup'ig that had previously gone unrecognized. In 1994 she wrote, "His speech has some phonological idiosyncrasies that may reflect a subdialect which he alone maintained. In his recordings we find some unique lexicon. He also exhibits certain stylistic devices…which appear to be used especially in the presence of individuals with whom he had kinship ties" (Drozda 1997).

Reed enlisted the help of Cup'ig speaker Margie David of Anchorage and Mekoryuk, who then redubbed this particular tape while interspersing it with English translation and editorial comment. Still, the resulting translation lacked complete accuracy before Howard began to work with it. He commented, "Here is what I worked on. Retranslating what [they] translated. It appears to be better, because I understood Andrew more than the ladies."

Howard's comment is in no way a slight to those women; in fact, he and his wife, Muriel, as well as a number of other Nuniwarmiut (particularly Dorothy Kiokun and Prudy Olrun), worked closely with Irene in the modification of the standard Central Alaskan Yup'ik orthography to better reflect the unique Nunivak dialect. Steven Jacobson of the Alaska Native Language Center (ANLC) continued that work, and recently the ANLC published the *Cup'ig Eskimo Dictionary* (Amos and Amos 2003). Those familiar with Central Yup'ik orthography will immediately see the difference in the presentation of the Cup'ig text.

Amos may be the one person best suited to translate Andrew's recordings since he was not only present during most of the sessions, but also because most often Andrew spoke directly to Howard, as in the tale recounted here. The kinship tie alluded to by Reed is present between Amos and Nuratar, and we were informed by Andrew that his paternal great-grandfather's sister had a child named Nakaar whose name was given to Howard. He was not simply repeating the stories that he knew, he was instructing Howard and passing on his knowledge to him.

Andrew was born at Narulkirnarmiut, in the Tacirrlag area of south Nunivak where much of this tale takes place. He and his family, however, resided at Tacirrarmiut, a remote settlement nestled among the high, rugged cliffs of western Nunivak. There he learned fully the skills of cliff hanging for bird netting and egg gathering from his uncles and relatives. There, too, he learned the traditional stories, history, and geography of his people told in an older form or now extinct (sub)dialect of Cup'ig.

There is much that remains to be understood about Cup'ig, particularly its relation to other Bering Sea Eskimo languages. One point that may require immediate clarification is the relationship between Nunivak Cup'ig and Chevak Cup'ik. It is true that while Cup'ig shares some lexical and phonological features with Cup'ik (as well as other Yupik languages), they are quite different dialects. The Cup'ik spoken in Chevak is closer to other Central Yup'ik dialects than is the Nunivak Cup'ig (Jacobson 2003), and despite the similarity of their names, they should not be confused.

Nonspeakers such as me or strangers to Nunivak may miss obvious and subtle cultural understandings that are not or cannot be accurately translated into English. Although I have not made a thorough study of the Nuniwarmiut *qulirat* (legends) and *qanengssit* or *univkangssit* (stories), it strikes me that

Nuratar (Andrew Noatak) with a mask he made in the Nunivak Island style. The central carving represents an *ircig*, a half-human, half-animal spirit. *Photo by Robert Drozda, Mekoryuk, 1987.*

Words of the Real People

the majority I have heard or read in translation are not only enriched by knowledge of Nunivak geography but have an actual physical component in the landscape.

There are many examples of this narrative/landscape bond within the corpus of Nuniwarmiut traditional stories. For instance, in the tale recounted below Andrew offers a number of place names that provide a geographic context to the story. This is not unusual in Yupik narratives, but in this Nunivak Island story we also have physical objects, both man-made and natural landforms, that have their locations as well as their origins explained to us. The final resting places of the story characters have been firmly and physically identified. Andrew also makes this point that they were seen and known; the brothers, their sister, and her dog are there on the land, or were there before succumbing to weathering, gravity, erosion, and/or theft by outsiders.

Now that the physical remains have disappeared we are fortunate to have the story to recall the tradition. We are reminded that the physical world and humanity are transitory, impermanent, and intricately bound in ways that may seem paradoxical. The storyteller also reminds us of those who have passed on by providing his references at the very beginning of the tale and by respectfully naming those who told the story to him.

Likewise Andrew is no longer with us. When he spoke his words in front of the tape recorder he was keenly aware that his knowledge of the traditional stories, histories, genealogies, natural history, lifeways, and geography of his earlier years and those of his ancestors were being eroded by the Western world. He was continuing a tradition in a nontraditional setting and lamenting as well as savoring the past. Although this and other traditional stories are now written we would do well to remember them and encourage their repetition as intended within the context of oral tradition, as they may provide a welcome antidote to the insidiously pervasive American pop culture.

—Robert Drozda

Uraqural²rig

Told by Nuratar Andrew Noatak of Mekoryuk

NUT'AN TAKEL²RIAMEG.

Nut'an-am cali uumeg univkangssit'artur angulluarag taukug An'uliksenam atra, Qiawig'ar, univkangssit'artur tauna-llu imna-llu Lurtussiikar-llu, ak'allakacagarmeg.

Qiini-ggur tauna nukalpiat ill'it, cun'era'ar, Askinat negratni etliniur, nunangqelliniur. Piyal²rim kuten cun'eraraulini nulirturyuumallermini, picuqapiarauluni. Picuqapiarauluni piyal²rim pinaringani nulliangllliniur. Kuten angayuqertuumal²riameg, aanatuumal²riameg atatuumaluni-ll'u. Tauna-llu cakia cali piculiulun'i. Picuqapiarauluni, nukalpiaqluku nun'at. Taugg'am kuni etellra taum nalluaqa, Tacim awatiini qiini pingatur.

Nut'an-am kuten tegucini up'nerkaryartullrani uksuaryal²ria, cakian qayillinia qassiami miklermeg. Mikellrungran. Kuc'urkek'ngengremiu anuraqluni tawa-i cakimi pilingani piuralliniur.

Tawa-llu pinaringan up'nerkarngan qayarturluni piyal²rim, pinrit'ur! Kuksukapiartur imna qass'a. Pingran cavkenaku, tawa aturluku piliqluni-am up'nerkarpag.

Kiagluni, kiagluni, tawamta-llu-am uksurluni piyal²ria nut'an-am cakian qayillinia imum qassan mikpall'anran'eg. Tawa-i mikelkengremiu anuraqluni qaneqsaunani ayagai makut nanicukcuareneg, iqkicukcuarem'eg.

Tawa-llu nut'an nulliani anuraqsaqvimineg pillinia caluni allragnirpag qayitaallermineg mikcukcuaren'eg, maktayugnaatur-kur kwa mermun ek'uniu.

Sibling Brothers

A LONG ONE THIS TIME.

Then again, the two elderly men used to tell this ancient story. Kay Hendrickson's[13] namesake, Qiawig'ar, and the other person, Lurtussiikar.[14]

There was a young man, a very good hunter, who lived up north. He had a settlement somewhere north of Askin'at.[15] As a hunter he excelled. He was at the age for getting married, so he acquired a wife. His wife had parents; a mother and a father. His father-in-law was also a good hunter. He was an experienced hunter indeed. I don't know the exact location. It may have been in the Tacir [Norton Sound] area.

Then after acquiring his wife, early spring turned into spring season. His father-in-law made a kayak, one that is smaller than a normal size. Although it was smaller than usual, and very unstable, showing respect for his father-in-law's work he persisted and followed along.

So the time came in the spring, when he was seal hunting, he made a sharp remark, "This doesn't cut it!" His kayak was terribly unstable. Even though he had this problem, he continued using it and caught much game throughout the spring.

Summer passed and winter came again. This time, his father-in-law made him another kayak even smaller than the one he had previously made. Even though it was too small for him, he didn't say anything out of respect for his father-in-law. The kayak ribs were short and very narrow.

After patiently showing respect for his father-in-law, he finally made a comment to his wife, "Why has my father-in-law made me very small kayaks in the past two years? I will not be able to keep my balance if I launched into the water!"

Pillinia nulirran, "Tawa-tar naklekluten pikiiten, anuqenguskaten tenget'nayuklut'en."

Nut'an-am tawaten pingran amirluku cavkenaku. Ancat-ggu tawa-i, anca-miu tupekluku piurallinia, qayar tamana, kinracirturallinia.

Taum-ggur cakian una nengauni inglukevlerqurara, nengaukmiluku-llu ciullegyaqiini tawani.

Nut'an-am pulenglluku qamigalliniur pinaringani ekenrarerlun'i. Piyal^{z}rim ayemnera'armun kanaryal^{z}rim legcigpani teguluku, (ektut tamaani eksutek'ngamegteki legcigpit) pegcarpiarumaaquniu-ggur-am unawet-llu-ggur palluarcarpiarnaurtur ayemnera'aremun. Pulenglluni-ggur ellirrarluku anguarutni teguyaaqekuniu paluciarpiaqernaurtur. Piyugnaalami legcigpani tegungamiu utermun yuulliniur. Yuungami qayani qamu'urtellinia ikam'errsuucirnaamitun-llu ikarallitmineg pingami legcig-pamineg-llu, imarniterluni-llu, napautalliniur. (Napautatullrut maklagtel^{z}rit anguyararaqameng.)

Aqvaqurluni tagyal^{z}ria ciunra quyaluni, pinaciarwanritur-am nengaugar. Ayagluni, ayagluni, nunat kua tekiciqiaqerluki en'yeng yaa-i tumkerrarluku, yatruarrluku ayakalliniur nunam tungiinun pawawet.

Nulirran-ggur awawiarluku maliumangnaqerluku piyugnaalamiu cangu-luni, qunukeqerpakarluk'u.

Nut'an-am nuna ayemqerluku ayalliniur pingkut, Askinat, amkut kel-luatgun egil^{z}ralliniur. Egil^{z}rayal^{z}rim tawamta-llu-am qanikcaarulluni man'a nanwat cen'it taugg'am ellmaaremeg qanikcararalirluteng, nanwat imangluteng amatiinun kanarpaalegmi.

Nut'an-am pingkut tangerrnarinratgun ingrit caciqminaurtur metrap'ig, imna nanwista qaterpag. Asguuqeryal^{z}ria… imkut nulingqerrsukut metrap'it tunguryagneg. Ketvaqercal^{z}ria imkut tukliniluteng qetuncuarai aqvalirtu-myugtut emrem qaangani, pivv'il^{z}ngut an'era'arat kayangum'eg. Tawa-ggur uyungqerrluni taukut ineqsuarauteklukii atekaanirluku una elqini atuutai kuten taukut: "Ayaa-raa-aa-aa-ayaangaaraa, aangi-rrii, angii-ii, augii, augii."

His wife replied, "It is because he loves you, and doesn't want you to drift away when winds start to blow."

The skin hull covered the frame with ease. It was then taken outside and cared for as it dried.

His father-in-law had ill feelings toward his son-in-law because he had beaten him with a first catch.

So the time came again when he hauled his kayak over the ice and initially launched it into the water. When he arrived to the newly opened water lead, he grabbed his large gaff and boarded. (When embarking, a large gaff was used to steady the kayak.) At the moment of releasing his gaff he nearly capsized into newly opened water. Again placing his gaff down, he grabbed his oar but nearly capsized once more; he repeatedly attempted this maneuver. Since he was unable to achieve it, he set his large gaff and disembarked. He pulled his kayak up onto the ice pan. Using a typical method, he loaded the kayak onto a flat sled. He then took his grass-mat seating, tied it to a gaff, donned his waterproof sealgut raingear and erected a makeshift flag. (When a bearded seal was caught early in the day, makeshift flags were displayed to show pride.)

As he ran up, his welcoming party was happy. "It sure didn't take long for my son-in-law!" He heard, but continued to run on and on. Entering the village, he ran directly to his house then intentionally averted and fled inland.

His wife ran after him for a while, but couldn't catch up to him, so she turned back. Her sudden emotions were to be with him.

Using shortcut routes, he traveled inland of Askinat mountains. He traveled on and soon the snow melted. Some snow remained around lakes. The lakes melted before he reached south of Askinat mountains.

When Nelson Island became visible, of all things, a common eider duck appeared; a white colored one, one that resides in ponds. The eider ducks have mates that are blackish. When he resumed walking facing the wind, he veered toward the pond. The eider ducklings had already hatched and skipped along on the surface of the water; tiny creatures just hatched from an egg. He squatted down and cooed to them. He wore his wooden hat. As he cooed, he tightened down his visor and sang this song to them: "Ayaa-raa-aa-aa-ayaangaaraa, aangi-rrii, angii-ii, augii, augii."

Tengmiat aagiiratuyukut yaaniqlit imkut, qal⁷riuruciat uputarluki tawaten pilliniur.

Nekevngami nut'an ayalliniur. Taukut imkut metrayagat aanita kusgullrani nanwarra'armi tawaten atuuqarluk'i.

Ayagluni ingrit pingkut kelluatgun uyangtur Taciullinil⁷ria, pingna pia-i kangirrluar'er. Maaten uyangta enluqvag'ar, kan'a qikertami pussiartur, kenirlun'i.

Nut'an qawaggun kiatiikun at'erluni, cikungqerrngan tayima pikutagtur. At'erluni tekitag arnagneg nevviarcararagneg cungqelliniyal⁷ria tawa, imkuneg uquneg ciwanriluteg pillinil⁷rig, uquutekiullinil⁷rig. Tekicaqiiteg tawa cunriqutekqerluku tupkeqapiarluku neqliuyarluk'u. Qayangqelliniluteg-llu. Nutaraneg pitaqnera'arneg imkuneg taqukaneg ciwatuggluteg maklit uquitneg. Tawa pussuag tangllinia tawani tamakullragni. Pilliniag, tamatu-meg ciwatugtameg meciicaqiini ciwacugnilarqeng'an, caluku makut pillritneg. Qassautungata-ggur, nalqigtelliniag. Qassautungata-ggur tawa egaluki pituit.

Tawamta-llu pivkenani, tawa narurtevkenakeg. Alerquaguryaqkiiteg ekluki pisqellukeg caqutmun maligartenrit'ag.

All'erngami-llu tawamta-llu waawet kangirrluarkun imkugni piani qik-ertaugagni pilliniur, pingkug nunaulteg tawa-i nunacillengqerrsugnal⁷ngug, imkug pingkug qikertaugag kangirrluaram qukaani, siimag. Aaluugigneg taugg'am cungqertur. (Cungqet'ug takumegni.)

Nastur piaken, Englul⁷rarmiut ik'ut tangllini-i atakuarem'i. Kenirturyal⁷riameng-ggur kuaten pussuit napaurtut. Nunat kana-i tangerr-rluki ingrit ciuqerratneg piyaqiiteng.

Nut'an-am umyugarmini alegyukauterpakarluki ek'ernaluni. Atraqertelliniur, at'erngami-llu tawa-i atakumi ketvartualliniur tayima akulurriurluni puqlaner tuwinrakun nut'an all'arluteng tawa-i pia-i. Qawallinilut'eng.

Tekicarturrai Englul⁷rarmiut ika-i ik'ut nunauluteng etliniyal⁷rit kiani kiatitni enluqvagar atauciar yaqsig'arluki taukut etlinil⁷ria. Taukunun ciunirpek'nani, tauna atauciar ena tumekluku, tekicarturluni aciakun yuulliniur.

He was imitating the sound of the ducklings, and echoing back to them.

He stood up then and resumed his journey, after singing to the common eider ducklings being protected by their mother.

As he continued his journey using the inland areas of Nelson Island, a bay came into his view. The one back there, a small bay. Down below was a house on an isle, its fireplace billowing smoke, cooking.

He then walked down through the inland side of the bay; perhaps the bay still carried ice. When he arrived he met two young women who were apparently the residents. The two were in the process of cooking seal blubber to render as seal oil. Dropping their chore, they proceeded to care for and feed their guest. They also possessed a kayak. The ladies were processing freshly caught bearded seal. He saw from above the billowing smoke as they worked in that process. He said to them, because he was served that particular seal oil and it tasted of cooked blubber, "Why is it prepared like this?" They replied, "Because it is raw it is cooked."

Nevertheless, he did not stand in their way. He gave them instructions to fill a seal poke with blubber, but they did not immediately respond.

He then walked out to the estuary. Apparently he was at the two islands back there by Nelson Island; two strips of land that look like nothing will be there. On two small isles in the middle of a bay were rocks. The only creatures that occupy them are seagulls. (I witnessed what resides there.)

From a high elevation, he surveyed the area from Nelson Island in the early evening. Across Etolin Strait he saw Englul'rarmiut [Cape Manning]. While they cooked, their smoke billowed straight up. The settlement was seen down there from Cape Vancouver at Nelson Island.[16]

In his mind, his adrenaline was at its peak to go across. He sped down below from his lookout. It was in the evening when he crossed Akulurer [Etolin Strait]. The sun was setting when his destination appeared in the horizon. The residents of that settlement were asleep.

He reached Englul'rarmiut, the place across there, a settlement, where farther inland stood a lone house separated from the main village. Instead of stopping at the main settlement, he went directly toward the lone house and disembarked.

Yuungami mayurturalliniur. Cugmeg-llu tangerpek'nani tayima. Mayurluni mayurluni amiluqvatagagnun itrum'artur kumauralliniluni qamna enem illua.

Pinginanermini qamani arnalquaraungalˀngur qanlliniur, "Tututgirrlug, tarum ityuilkiikug, itraakug, curraumaarru."

Tawaten pim'arnginanrani nevviarcara'ar una anqerrluni tangerqallinia tawawet. Tangemciksagterluku itliniur.

Iterngami qamani niicugniqeryaqiini pilliniur, ukuni-ggur nunami tan-grrumayuilˀngur ugna tekitelliniur tallurnarqerwalˀria cun'era'ar.

Pillinia, "Amci nanikualˀriarulliur itresqiu. Nanikaulˀriarukuni-ggur iterciq'ur."

Imutun anngami tangerpek'naku pillinia tungiinun kingyaumarlun'i, "Nanikualˀriarukuwet-ggur iterciqquten."

Tawa iterciqngan maliggluku en'itnun iterlun'i. Imna itertur maaten mar-rlugarmi akiani wiitalliniluni. Marrlugan nut'an waatiinun aqumum'arlun'i. Piyalˀria ellmikun qanerturaqaqerluni pillinia, "kangiiyugngami arnalquaram taum nanikaulˀriaruluku piyukluk'u?"

Pillinia kua-i nunami yaqsigwangran kua tukuiturluni piniluni tauna-am nut'an tutgarra amatngurtengremi kua tukuqnaluku pillinia. Piyaqi, marrlu-gan pillinia tauna ang'un: "Amatngurnarqenrituten tawai ell'i kiimi ikai ikna amatngurnarqur."

Imkut awani ciuliaqat'ut nevviarcararat cumanarriaqameng tarperra'artut tawigtaneg taperrnan'eg. Tamakuciullinilun'i. Kangmikun taugg'am pussiare-luni. Cumanamineg kugg'un. Nut'an ayagniqataarluni pingami.

Nut'an qanlliniur tawa taggrarluni tekitenqigciqniluni nut'an erenrem qukaani, ˀakeqlukeg tawai. Anngami nut'an pivvalˀgatni tangerpalˀgatni uter-mun tagluni taukugnun nulliagminun tekitelliniur. Erenrem nut'an qukaani ertevkartelluku.

Pilliniag nut'an kanawet ketvarciqiarniluni nunanun kelluagnun camani-llu tukurkangellrunilun'i.

Imna qunukengragni tawai, tawa-ggur meciicaqiini taum nerqeryalˀrim neqniqitelˀria uqumeg meciameg. Qiini pillernaamitun ayuqelˀriameg.

After landing, he slowly went up. Not a single person was seen. He went up and up. Approaching the door, he entered and noticed that a light was lit inside.

At that moment a person who sounded like an old lady spoke from within, "Grandchild, a being never comes in on us before, someone is here, go out to meet him!"

At that moment a young woman suddenly came out and met him face-to-face. Attempting to recognize him, she reentered.

When she entered, he heard her saying to her grandmother, "Someone who has never been seen in this village is at the door, a young man who looks very respectable."

Her grandmother said to her, "Hurry up! He may be a person in need of help, ask him to come in. Kindly ask him to enter if he needs help."

When she re-exited she didn't look at him face-to-face as before. Without facing him, she said, "If you are in need of help you may enter."

He knew that she would go back in, so he followed behind her. Inside, he discovered that she was situated across from her grandmother. He sat down beside her grandmother near the door. After talking about unimportant matters, she curiously asked, "Are you in need of help?"

He told her, "I am from a faraway place and seeking a host." Her grandchild, although feeling unworthy, was prepared to be the host. Her grandmother said to the man, "You are not unworthy, the one across there; she should be the one who is considered unworthy."

In the days of our ancestors, when young women menstruated, they wore braided grass for menstrual pads. She was one of those, and was emitting smoke from the top of her head. She was a source of smoke emanations. Her unwanted event arrived, because she was just beginning her menses.

He then said, "I will go back to Nelson Island and return again, this time in the middle of day." He made that promise to them. When he exited, prior to others seeing him, he went back to Nelson Island and reunited with his two wives, at the middle of the day in broad daylight.

He then said to them that he was going to a village down below and has found a host for himself there.

They did not want him to leave; when he was served seal oil, he liked the taste. It was similar to what he had up north.

Nut'an-am ayalliniur tawai tamta-llu, akulurriurluni nut'an erenrem qukaani. Ayagluni ayagluni all'arngamiki nut'an ket'aryarturluki maaggun ketekcuaratgun itrallrani, imkut-ggur ciinag ciunerkan pitakarrai ketvarngameng maawet cenamun kuten qanenglliniut, "Nalimtenun-kir kua ciuniurciq'a." Ellait tawa-i ciuneqertassiarlut'eng.

Kiturturyaqiiteng kiawet, imna kiugna enluqvagam tungiinun, kuten-ggur-ciinag piquyalˀriameng, "Uuyuyurram kangra wa-aa." Tawa cumacirrauteklukU. Pulenglluku piaqluku, "Uuyuyurram kangra wa-aa." Una kangra pussiaralˀria aglenrarraungan cumacirrauteklukU.

Pingratni tawa-i ciuniullinia. Ciuniurluku, tawa-i imkut ciknaluteng kaliwartengremeng callunritliniat taugg'am tawai.

Imkut kinguliag ciknaqerpakarluteg qunukeqerparkarluki-llu imkut makut paciteklukI tawa-i unicateg ciwanrat egqaqlertulliniakeg ciwaliteg, uquuciateg, egaluki imkut pillret. Ciwanrat egqaqlertulliniyaqiiteng nunam qaanganun tutmartuallinliut tawaten. Maa-i nunam qaanga tamalkurmi ciwanraneg tamakuneg maawet-llu nunamun tutmarluteng mat'umun nunamten'un. Qakmai egqaqelkegneka ayuqnguarait ciwanrat maani nunami wiitaut, ciwanrat, tamai-ggur. Piani elˀngug taumeg wiimegneg Ayugta'arimeg ciknaqerpakarluteg egqaqelqak'eg.

Nut'an-am nulirqelluku piyaqniu kiagunginanrani imkut pitakarragnekeg qanrutliniat-am tawa, camna kua-ggur Cingigglagmi camani nukalpianeg pitangqelˀria cuirlineg, cuirliqapiareneg, uyuraqelˀrianeg talliman'eg. Arnamegkur kuten tallimangqertut, tawai—imkuneg akguawar quliraqallmegneg.

Tawai kangiiyugturallinia nateqvaqapiar etellran'eg. Cingigglim-ggur ciuqakacaggaani tayima wiitaut. Ullagtemeggneg-llu-ggur tawai ciullegtengqessuitut. Kiiran Cingigglim cam'um cukluk'i. Paqumiyukalliniur tawai nut'an.

Tawamta-llu-am nulliani unilluku tawa ayalliniur. Tung'arluki taukut, tangerrsarturluki, kiagmi. Ayagluni ayagluni piyalˀrim tawamta-llu-am, Cing'ig kanai kan'a, qipcamiu maaten piur ingri akemna mermi uyangqalliniyalˀria. Uyangqalliniyalˀria qikertaullininluni akmai kellua emruluni. Taaguraqerluni kellua nunatangurallinliur tawai. Nunam mat'um cali iqukngani ilakliniluk'u.

So, he again departed, crossing Akulurer this time during the middle of the day. He traveled for some time and finally reached his destination. As he paddled close to shore, young women in the same age group as his host-to-be were blurting, "Which one of us will he go to?" Each of them hoping to be the chosen one.

When he passed them going toward the little house, they exclaimed, "Uyuyurrar's top, bad, bad, bad." That was their expression for her repulsiveness. Again they'd said, "Uyuyurrar's top, bad, bad, bad." The top of her head was emanating smoke, indicating her initial menses and was used as a means for warding off strangers.

Although she was verbally attacked by others, still she hosted him. Others were very jealous of the young woman but did not act violently against her.

The two wives [at Nelson Island] he left behind were very jealous because they didn't want him to go. The two blamed his departure on the cooked seal oil blubber. They angrily threw the containers used for cooking blubber and the seal oil they had rendered. As the cooked seal oil blubber was thrown, it splattered all over the tundra. For that reason, the tundra has what appear to be vegetative patterns all over, including Nunivak Island. Up to this date, the evidence of this enragement is seen on the tundra. The wives at Nelson Island became so jealous of their husband, Ayuguta'ar, they trashed their personal belongings.

He wedded her [his host] as his wife during summer. His peers told him that there were skillful siblings, *nukalpiat* [great hunters] down at Cingigglag [Cape Mendenhall]. The four sibling brothers were very skillful people. They had a fifth female sibling—the tale I related yesterday.

Because of his curiosity, he sought information for their exact location. They are located at the very tip of Cingigglag. It was said that their visitors have never beaten them in anything. They were the only inhabitants of Cingigglag. His curiosity became more intense.

And once again, it was during summer he departed, he left his [third] wife behind [at Englullrarmiut]. He went down to go see them. He traveled on and on. After reaching Cing'ig [Cape Corwin], he went around the cape to see a distant island. A mountain was visible above the water. Its form revealed it to be an island; water enclosed its inland shore. When he had traveled for some time, its inland shore became visible and appeared to be part of mainland

Nut'an tawa niitellrungamiu, naken-kir tayima ketvarta, Kuigaarmeg pici-qur. All'erluni tawa pillerkirluku, tawamta-llu all'erluni Igwaryarameg iiraarai kanaken nunasqa'arat mayurrwigtalirluteng etlinil'rit. Mayurrwiggneg kiir-ran pitalirluteng, imkuneg equgneg tawai entalirluteng-llu. Kangiraarkun kanaggun cin'garyaaqumallrani at'erterutelliniut cun'eraaral'gutai cetaman arnar-kua una tallimit. Qimugkararangqelliniluni, qimukcuaremeg tawai angenril'nguarem'eg.

Tawa-llu tagulluku allanilluku. Allanilluku piyaqitni taumeg-am nut'an arnameg nevviarca'armeg cali, arnaunratneg, nulliangllliniur.

Piyal'rim imkut cakirani tangerrsaqiiteng erenret ayagturatulliniluteng. Ayaggarluteng tekitnaurtut nulqarluteng tamalkurmeng pitliniluteng tawai. Tawai tangellrat caperrnarqepigallininluni.

Kiagungran kan'a Tacirrlag taqukangqetungan, issuriyagarneg amirkar-tetungata-llu. Cali tuntuneg makuneg ayaggarluteng tekiskuneng tuntutlini-luteng tawten amllertatkural'rianeg. Tawai ill'it-llu pitevkenani tekicuunan'i. Ayuqluteng tawaten piuratulut'eng.

Nut'an-am umyuggiulliniur ell'i up'nerkarmi taugg'am tawai pissullerkani una enqakluku, taum nalliini pissu'urkaulun'i. Qayiluni-llu tawai piyal'rim, qay-angqellinil'ria tarr'i tayima nutarameg taugg'am tayima qayiluni pikutagtur.

Up'nerkaryarturluni piyal'ria … imna nut'an up'nerkarpal'gan nulirra qum-ingellrungami tawai qetungrangllliniur up'nerkallrani, arnaunrat taukut.

Taukut-llu tupkeqatarluku cakirain piluteng quyakqatarluku arnaunerteng wiingellran'eg.

Up'nerkarluni piyal'ria, picit ill'itni tawai ertur utumaluni, quuniqatarluni. Piyal'ria, upqaqlertuucal'riameng, ayuqluteng ukut malikluteng piyal'riameng ell'i malliinani tawai. Taukut taugg'am cakirai malikluteng tayima ayaglut'eng. Pingrata kiimartuarang'ermi ketvarluni pitarkameg tangerrngami pitliniur.

Piq'arluni tawa tagtungata anguyararaqameng, tagluni maaten piur imkut cakirai tekiteksaatelliniluteng tawai tawawet. Tawai ell'i kiimi picestenguluni, maklagcestenguluni.

Piyal'ria-ggur tawai nut'an kinguakun tekitut tawai tekiqurapaculliniut tawai. Tawai pitenritlingermeng castun piqerluteng tawai ciknaqalliniut

Nunivak. It is also the end of this land; therefore it is attached to the main island of Nunivak.[17]

He previously heard about it; therefore, he made his plans to go down to the cape probably from Kuiga'ar.[18] He further went down to Igwaryar'er,[19] to see a tiny village. The community was situated with a way to ascend from below. There were only elevated and gabled wooden storage sheds visible. When his kayak touched shore, inside the cove, his peers rushed down to meet him. There were four men with a woman as their fifth sibling. She owned a puppy, a small puppy.

They brought him up and welcomed him as a stranger. When they welcomed him he took their sister as his wife.

He found out that his brothers-in-law departed every day. After their long day's trip they returned home each having caught something. He observed, and thought of them as meticulous individuals.

In summer Tacirrlag[20] usually has seals, spotted and baby bearded seals. Still, after going on short trips, the brother returned home having caught the same number of caribou. None of them returned empty-handed. Their methods were all similar.

He thought to himself, in the spring when the time comes he will hunt. Therefore he constructed a kayak. He fortunately had a new kayak, apparently he had made one.

Early spring emerged on them. His wife was already pregnant, and therefore bore a child in the spring, the female sibling of the four.

The brothers-in-law took care of him well; they were pleased that their sister had acquired a husband.

One day, spring arrived and an acceptable calm morning dawned on them. The siblings immediately prepared to hunt and were to travel together. He did not pair with any of them. His brothers-in-law departed as a group. Although alone, he paddled out to the sea and pursued and secured game.

After securing his catch, he returned home, because those who caught a seal early in the day usually returned soon thereafter. He returned home to find out that his brothers-in-law had not returned. He was the only one who caught a bearded seal.

They finally returned home after he did, miserably they came home. All returned empty-handed. Somehow they became jealous of their brother-in-

ciullelinruluteng taumeg nengaumeggneg. Ciumeggni pitellra tagellra pitekluku nut'an ilutekqalliniut. Atam tawai tekicestemeng-llu ciullessuilateng all'am. Ciullelinruluteng, ciumeg pical'ria tauna pitekluk'u.

Nut'an-am tawa qaallikutkarrarluteng ayumian peksarquutelliniut. Peksagquucal'riameng anngarpa'arat pikawet Qemirrlagmun mayulliniur. Mayuryal'riameng siimaurtelliniur tawai. Atra kwai una Taamituryag, Tauna anngarpa'arat.

Aterngameng tawamta-llu malikluteng tawa pirr'arluteng pilliniut. Kanawet nanwarrlim kucuanun kuigan paangan, kuiluraram ceniinun ekurpaurtelliniur tawai Kanangar'er. Kanagarer-kur tawai tungeqlia anngarpa'arat'a.

Tawamta-llu ayagyal'riameg taukut uyuqlig, uyurpaaraata, anngaata-llu tawamta-llu tung'ig tawa. Tungkutacirmeng piuralliniut. Yaawet Ingigutet kelluatnun tawamta-llu-am siimaurtelliniur. (Siimaurcal'ria taugg'am ataucimeg nenermeg kwi tangeqsaatua, qalliryugtaneg taugg'am siimaneng tangertartua. Tawa tauna nallunalkutaqluki piyukluki taugg'am umyuggarteqtartua. Siimaurtengran caneg castun qallilirluku pikutaggat terlagmi el'an.) Tawaggur Cung'ar.

Tamta-llu uyu'urpaarat ek'ralliniur. Ketvarngami unaggun pengut ket'itnunggur ek'rerngami ikawet qikerta'armun (kellua qaugyaugur taugg'am), ketvarngami kanawet keteqva'arnun qikertam ket'in tungiinun, aqumlliniur. Amyag, Amyag kua atra cal'i. Siimaurcimaalliniur. Nut'an tauna caumall'irluni et'ur. Qanengqertur-llu, tangertaaraqa tawani.

Cuum atra Amyag. Taum qikertam ateqsagulluku tauna.

(Piyal'rim akguawar uyurama tangenrit'a. Piirutliniur-kur tangertallrungamiu. Taukug imna-llu Mell'arpin yugguaran ill'it pikani etqam waatiini ecal'ria, kua tangenrit'ag taukug-kur piirutliniug tayima. Tauna angtuarussaaqur teguluku pikutaggat tangertain. Caumallirluni kuten ayuqur, ayuqsaaqur.)

Nut'an piyal'ria tawaten arnaunrat imna tauna peksagcal'rit naklegyukarparkarluni taukuneg angutngunmineg ciullegciuryal'riameng peksagtel'rianeg, itralliniur nut'an kiawet. It'erngami Nunaumirutet ek'ut qauqeratnun. Atengqertut taukut Nunaumirutet. Tawa-ggur tarr'i, nekumaryal'rim siimaurtellinil'ria amayagani kenucessra'artelluku, nepiyengqerturluni tawa piur cal'i. Siimar cukayunaar angenrit'ur.

law because he outhunted them. It was because he caught a game animal and returned home before they did, they were heartbroken. Even visitors have never outhunted them before.

After deliberating they scattered in all directions. When they scattered, their eldest sibling climbed up to Qemirrlag.[21] After climbing the hill he turned into a stone. The name of the eldest sibling is Taamituryag.

They went down together. Down to Nanwarrlim's river mouth,[22] Kanagar'er turned into a tussock there. Kanagar'er is next to the eldest sibling.

And so the younger siblings and his older brother walked. These occurrences were according to age sequence. There inside of Ingigut'et,[23] one of them also turned into stone. (Although they turned into stones, I have not seen any bones, though I have seen rocks that were piled up. I believe that this was used as a landmark. He may have turned into stone; a pile was probably built to cover it, as it was probably situated in a low-lying place.) His name is Cung'ar.

Then the youngest sibling went across. When he went down, and walked on the beach below the sand dunes to an isle (the landward side of the isle is sand), walking down he sat down at the seaward side of the isle. Amyag is his name, who then turned into stone. This one has a face and a mouth, and I have seen it there before.

Amyag is a person's name. It is now the name of the isle.[24]

(Yesterday, my younger sibling did not see it. She said it vanished, because she has seen it before. Those monuments including one of Mell'arpag's[25] stone balls, the location is up there and inside a natural pit. She did not see them; what used to be there vanished. That particular one Amyag is large; it was probably taken by someone who saw it. It has facial features on it.[26])

The female sibling showed emotional pity for her male siblings who scattered, because they were outhunted by someone. She walked inland to the top of a tussock; the name of it is Nunaumirutet. When she stood up she turned into stone carrying her baby as it protruded on her back. It has features like that. The characteristic of the stone is not big.

Tawamta-llu-am imna qimukcuara alliayukarpakarluni kiimi elli'ircal'rim ciugcimarluni mauryal²rim, ciugarraartacirmi tawaten siimaurtelliniur. Nepiyengqerturluni cali quletmun cugg'eg ayuqur. Cali-llu taum qimukcuaram tumai qawani Nunaumirutet kuteng kiatitni siimani caligerni tamakunun taum murrualqellini-i, murruallri-ggur tawai. Murruallerneg tamakuneg atengqertut cal'i.

Tawaten ayuqur. Tawawet niitetaaraqa enekniluku. Cali-llu qasgillra tawa tauna kiani Kangirarram egkuani laanellerpag angtuar Ayuguta'arin tawa qasgianeg apertutuat, tawa tauna. Tawa tar aminkuggumarngami qasgingqellinil²ria taumeg angtuarwarmeg.

Nut'an-am cali piyal²ria castun tawa tawawet uunguciitaqa. Nulliani aqvaaqa tawa, kiimartuaranritlil²ria.

Tawewet tawai picarnalquranun arularucima'arpug.

Then her puppy was so saddened because it was now alone. When it raised its snout to howl, it also turned into stone. The characteristic of that rock is formed with a snoutlike feature raised upward. Also, the tracks from the puppy at Nunaumirutet can be seen on huge flat rocks. Its tracks are embedded on that rock surface. The name of this particular place is called Murruallret.

That's the way it is. I have heard that he possessed a house. Also, his community house, *qasgir*, up there at Kangirarram's edge, is a large pit. Ayuguta'arin's community house is mentioned and located there. Because he was the only inhabitant remaining, he owned a huge men's community house.

It is here I am not certain what happened next. It may have been that he went to get his wife; he probably was not alone then.

I am stopping here where it is solidly remembered.

Notes

1   *Ingulaq* was a harvest festival celebrated in many coastal and Kuskokwim villages, often in the fall following the berry harvest. Families worked together to refurbish the *qasgi* after returning to their winter home. Following these preparations, people gathered for a celebration and feast. Women danced to *ingulautet*—slow, old-style songs—and presented the men with bowls of *akutaq*.

2   When a man died, his sled or kayak was often placed over his body and his tools hung or nailed onto a post to mark the grave. Here the woman marked her son's grave with the tools he would have used had he lived to be a hunter.

3   Frances refers to the admonishment never to eat large amounts of food following a period of starvation.

4   Nakaciuryaraq (the Bladder Festival, literally, "way of doing something with bladders") marked the opening of the winter ceremonial season. At the time of the winter solstice the bladders of seals and other animals killed that year were inflated and brought into the *qasgi*. These bladders, believed to contain the animals' souls were treated as honored guests. Finally, at the close of the festival, men deflated the bladders and returned them through a hole in the ice to their underwater home, where the seals' spirits would boast of their good treatment and subsequently allow themselves to be taken by hunters the following season.

5   Tununak is seven miles from Toksook Bay, over a low mountain on the north side of Nelson Island.

6   Frances is referring to the contrast between the woman's long, hard journey away from home and her short return trip.

7   Women were admonished in the past never to lie down and nurse their children in bed but to sit up and remove their parkas, thereby giving strength to their sons later in life. People did not view this as immodesty, as it was a way to help one's child.

8   Many stories describe people rolling in refuse and human waste to make themselves visible to their fellow humans and to counter the effects of haunting. Passing gas or farting (the reverse of the social act of eating) was also believed to neutralize the power of either a shaman or a ghost. In everyday life, aged urine was a cleansing agent used to remove grease and dirt from both a person's body and clothing.

9   Offering one's guests food was an essential gesture of hospitality.

10 A log typically marked the outer boundary of the sleeping area in a sod house and was used as a head rest. Grass mats covered with skins and clothing made the area a soft and comfortable place to lie.

11 Here the man is providing his son with an *iinruq* (amulet) that will protect and empower him later in life. Today the word *iinruq* is normally translated "medicine."

12 Parents routinely advised children who were being picked on not to retaliate to avoid injuring the minds of their contemporaries. The warning is especially important in this case because of the strength that the child inherited from his tiny father.

13 Kay Hendrickson (1909–2001).

14 Possibly Abraham Luktusegok (Lurtussiikar), born ca. 1869.

15 An area encompassing the ancestral village of Hooper Bay and the Askinuk Mountains.

16 The old village site of Englul'rarmiut on Nunivak Island, a distance of about eighteen miles from Cape Vancouver on Nelson Island, would be easily visible on calm, clear days.

17 Cingigglag is connected to mainland Nunivak by a narrow, low-lying isthmus.

18 Kuiga'ar, a small site or stream between Cing'ig and Cingigglag.

19 Igwaryar'er, an old settlement on the easternmost point of Cingigglag.

20 Tacirrlag (Duchikthluk Bay), the large bay and estuary of southern Nunivak.

21 Qemirrlag, a large hill, the highest elevation on Cingigglag.

22 Nanwarrlim Kuiga, a small stream with an outlet on the east coast of Cingigglag.

23 Ingigut'et, a sandy beach with large, wave-sculpted volcanic boulders or rock formations on the southeast coast of Cingigglag.

24 The southernmost point of land on Nunivak Island is indeed named Amyag. At lower tides the isle is connected to the main island by a low-lying strip of sand and gravel.

25 Mellarpag, the legendary giant juggler of Nunivak lore (Noatak 2004).

26 The stone figure Amyag was well remembered by Nunivak elders, who believed it was taken from the island around 1945 (US BIA 1995:217). Kalirmiu (Peter Smith, 1912–1995) made a drawing of Amyag from memory in 1986 (Drozda 2002).

Works Cited and Suggested Reading

Ager, Lynn Price. 1971. *The Eskimo Storyknife Complex of Southwestern Alaska.* Master's thesis, University of Alaska Fairbanks.

Amos, Muriel M. and Howard T. Amos. 2003. *Cup'ig Eskimo Dictionary.* Fairbanks: Alaska Native Language Center, University of Alaska.

Bethel Regional High School Students. 1975–76. *Kalikaq Yugnek / Book for the People.* Bethel, AK: Lower Kuskokwim School District.

Curtis, Edward S. 1930. *The North American Indian, Being a Series of Volumes Picturing and Describing the Indians of the United States, the Dominion of Canada, and Alaska*, Vol. 20 (reprinted 1970).

Drozda, Robert M. (compiler). 1997. *Qikertamteni Nunat Atrit Nuniwarmiuni: The Names of Places on Our Island Nunivak.* Manuscript. Native Village of Mekoryuk, Alaska IRA Council.
  2002. *Nunivak Cultural Map.* Illustrated by Hultman I. Kiokun. Mekoryuk, AK: Nuniwarmiut Piciryarraata Tamaryalkut'i (NPT) (Nunivak Cultural Programs), Inc.

Fienup-Riordan, Ann. 1983. *The Nelson Island Eskimo.* Anchorage: Alaska Pacific University Press.
  1988. *The Yup'ik Eskimos as Described in the Travel Journals and Ethnographic Accounts of John and Edith Kilbuck, 1885–1900.* Kingston, ON: Limestone Press.
  2000a. *Hunting Tradition in a Changing World: Yup'ik Lives in Alaska Today.* New Brunswick, NJ: Rutgers University Press.
  (ed.) 2000b. *Where the Echo Began and Other Oral Traditions from Southwestern Alaska Recorded by Hans Himmelheber.* Fairbanks: University of Alaska Press.
  2005a. *Wise Words of the Yup'ik People: We Talk to You Because We Love You.* Lincoln: University of Nebraska Press.
  2005b. *Yup'ik Elders at the Ethnologisches Museum Berlin: Fieldwork Turned on Its Head.* Seattle: University of Washington Press.

Gillham, Charles E. 1955. *Medicine Men of Hooper Bay, or, The Eskimo's Arabian Nights.* London: Batchworth Press.

Griffin, Dennis G. 2004. *Ellikarrmiut: Changing Lifeways in an Alaskan Community.* Anchorage: Alaska Anthropological Association.

Hoffman, Brian. 1990. "Bird Netting, Cliff-Hanging, and Egg Gathering: Traditional Procurement Strategies on Nunivak Island," *Arctic Anthropology* 27(1):66–74.

Jacobson, Steven. 2003. "Introduction to Cup'ig Eskimo Dictionary," in *Cup'ig Eskimo Dictionary.* Muriel Amos and Howard Amos. Fairbanks: Alaska Native Language Center, University of Alaska.

Lantis, Margaret. 1946. "The Social Culture of the Nunivak Eskimo," *Transactions of the American Philosophical Society* (Philadelphia) 35:153–323.

   1990. "The Selection of Symbolic Meaning," in *Hunting, Sexes and Symbolism*, Ann Fienup-Riordan, ed., supplementary issue of *Etudes/Inuit/Studies* 14(1–2):169–189.

Mather, Elsie P. 1985. *Cauyarnariuq / A Time for Drumming*. Alaska Historical Commission Studies in History No. 184. Bethel, Alaska: Lower Kuskokwim School District Bilingual/Bicultural Department.

McGill, Lillian Michael. n.d. *Akaguagaankaaq*. Told by Olinka Michael, illustrated by Teri Sloat. Bethel, AK: Bilingual Education Center, Bureau of Indian Affairs.

Meade, Marie and Ann Fienup-Riordan. 1996. *Agayuliyararput, Kegginaqut, Kangiit-llu / Our Way of Making Prayer: Yup'ik Masks and the Stories They Tell*. Seattle: University of Washington Press.

   2005. *Ciuliamta Akluit / Things of Our Ancestors: Yup'ik Elders Explore the Jacobsen Collection at the Ethnologisches Museum Berlin*. Seattle, WA: University of Washington Press.

Nelson, Edward William. 1899. *The Eskimo about Bering Strait*. Bureau of American Ethnology Annual Report for 1896–1897, Vol. 18, Pt. I. Washington, D.C.: Smithsonian Institution Press (reprinted 1983).

Noatak, Andrew (Nuratar). 1986. Taped interview and transcription. Interview by Ken Pratt and Bill Sheppard; translation and transcription by Howard T. Amos, Margie David, Irene Reed, and Sophie Shield. June 25, Mekoryuk, Alaska. Tape and file 86NUN003 BIA ANCSA Office, Anchorage and Nuniwarmiut Piciryarraata Tamaryalkut'i, Mekoryuk.

   2004. *Mell'arpim Yuggualra*. Retrieved December 4, 2006, from Nuniwarmiut Piciryarraata Tamaryalkut'i web site: http://www.nunivak.org/narrative/Mellarpag.html.

Orr, Eliza Cingarkaq and Ben Orr. 1995. *Qanemcikarluni Tekitnarqelartuq / One Must Arrive with a Story to Tell: Traditional Narratives by the Elders of Tununak, Alaska*. Fairbanks: Alaska Native Language Center, University of Alaska.

Orr, Eliza Cingarkaq, Ben Orr, Victor Kanrilak, Jr., and Andy Charlie, Jr. 1997. *Ellangellemni / When I Became Aware....* Fairbanks: Alaska Native Language Center, University of Alaska Fairbanks.

Oswalt, Wendell. 1964. "Traditional Storyknife Tales of Yuk Girls," *Proceedings of the American Philosophical Society* 108(4):310–336.

Pratt, Kenneth L. 1990. "Economic and Social Aspects of Nunivak Eskimo 'Cliff-Hanging,'" *Arctic Anthropology* 27(1):75–86.

   2001. "The Ethnohistory of Caribou Hunting and Interior Land Use on Nunivak Island," *Alaska Journal of Anthropology* 1(1):28–55.

Rearden, Alice, Marie Meade, and Ann Fienup-Riordan. 2005. *Yupiit Qanruyutait / Yup'ik Words of Wisdom*. Lincoln: University of Nebraska Press.

Shield, Sophie and Ann Fienup-Riordan. 2003. *Qulirat Qanemcit-llu Kinguvarcimalriit / Stories for Future Generations: The Oratory of Yup'ik Eskimo Elder Paul John*. Seattle: University of Washington Press.

Sonne, Birgitte. 1990. "The Acculturative Role of Sea Woman," *Meddelelser om Grønland, Man and Society* 13:3–34.

Tennant, Edward A. and Joseph N. Bitar, eds. 1981. *Yupik Lore: Oral Traditions of an Eskimo People*. Bethel, AK: Lower Kuskokwim School District Bilingual/ Bicultural Department.

United States Bureau of Indian Affairs, ANCSA Office. 1995. *Nunivak Overview: Report of Investigation for BLM AA-9238*, Calista Corporation, Vol. 2, Site Abstracts AA-9238–AA-9289. Kenneth L. Pratt, compiler, editor, and principal author. Copies on file at BIA ANCSA Office, Anchorage and Archives, Alaska and Polar Regions Department, University of Alaska Fairbanks.

United States Bureau of Indian Affairs, ANCSA Office. 1986–1991. Nunivak Island Oral History Tapes. Recorded in support of ANCSA Section 14(h)(1) Historical Places and Cemetery Sites for Calista Corporation Application, Nunivak Island. Copies on file at BIA ANCSA Office, Anchorage and Archives, Alaska and Polar Regions Department, University of Alaska Fairbanks.

Vick, Ann, ed. 1983. *The Cama-i Book*. Garden City, NY: Anchor Press.

Woodbury, Anthony C. 1984. *Cev'armiut Qanemciit Qulirait-llu / Eskimo Narratives and Tales from Chevak, Alaska*. Fairbanks: Alaska Native Language Center, University of Alaska Fairbanks.

Worm, Mary. 1986. "The Crow and the Mink," transcribed and translated by Elsie P. Mather and Phyllis Morrow, in *Alaska Native Writers, Storytellers, and Orators*, special issue of *Alaska Quarterly Review* 4(3–4):46–58.

PART II

Iñupiaq Narratives

THE IÑUPIAT COMPRISE hunting and gathering societies whose members speak different dialects of the same language and live in Northwest Alaska, along the Arctic coast, and eastward into northwestern Canada. Iñupiaq is taken from the root word *iñuk* ("person") and the suffix *–piaq* ("real"). Iñupiat (plural) means "real people."

Within this region were once found 150 or so settlements. Settlements ranged in size from fifty people to about a thousand, and several settlements might be allied into "nations." Each nation controlled its territories and was identified by the territory name and the suffix *-miut*, which means "people of." Thus, the King Islanders are Ugiuvaŋmiut from the name of the island, Ugiuvak, and *–miut*. Other examples include Kiŋikmiut (Wales people),

Qikiqtaġruŋmiut (Kotzebue people), Tikiġaġmiut (Point Hope people), and Utqiaġviŋmiut (Barrow people). Today, the Iñupiat have settled into approximately 35 villages (see http://www.kstrom.net/isk/maps/ak/alaska.html). Before contact with Europeans, there was an estimated population of 8,500 Iñupiat. Today, an exact number is difficult to ascertain, but census experts give estimates of about 13,500 Iñupiat (see http://sled.alaska.edu/akfaq/aknatpop. html or http://www.uaf.edu/anlc/stats.html).

The people of Iñupiat island and coastal villages hunt large sea mammals, such as bowhead whales and walrus, from large skin-covered *umiat*. Bowheads are still hunted today, in spring and fall, primarily at Point Hope, Wainwright, and Barrow. Walrus are hunted in spring, when the Arctic ice pack breaks up. Groups around the Kotzebue Sound also hunt beluga whales. In winter, several varieties of seal as well as polar bear are also killed. In addition, Seward Peninsula Iñupiat eat king crab, and all consume various species of birds and fish. Greens, roots, and berries round out their diet.

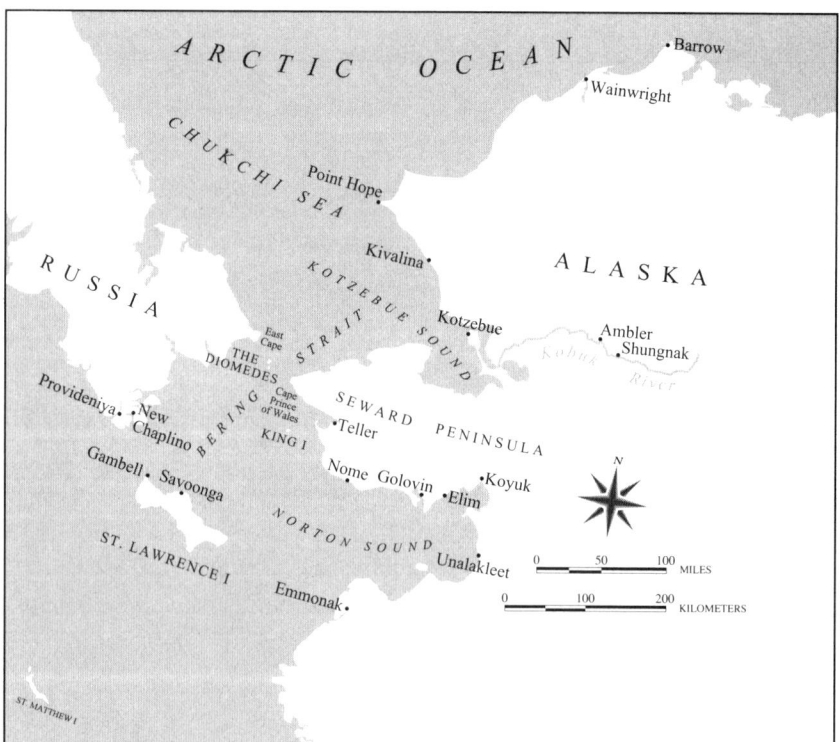

Northwest Alaska with major Iñupiaq towns and villages indicated.

Words of the Real People

Inland Iñupiat subsist primarily on caribou and fish, although grizzly and black bears, as well as moose, are also eaten. Ground squirrel, hare, wolf, wolverine, fox, lynx, land otter, mink, muskrat, and weasel are hunted and trapped for their fur. Ducks and geese provide meat and eggs. Greens, roots, and berries are gathered in summer.

THE IÑUPIAQ LANGUAGE is a member of the Eskimo–Aleut language family, which comprises six languages, four of which are found in Alaska. Iñupiaq/Inuit is spoken across the North American Arctic, from Alaska east across northern Canada, all the way to Greenland, and goes by different names depending on dialect. While Iñupiaq is the Alaskan name of the language, it is called Inuvialuktun in western Canada, Inuktitut in much of eastern Canada, and Kalaallisut in Greenland, to give just a few of the local designations. Iñupiaq extends as far west and south as the Bering Strait area of Alaska, and the border with Yupik is found in the region of Norton Sound. It is believed that Iñupiat moved into the Norton Sound borderland beginning some two centuries ago, first from the southern Kotzebue Sound area and later from the western and interior Seward Peninsula. The result is that Yupik and Iñupiaq people lived in close proximity to each other and often learned each other's languages. Iñupiaq words are found in Norton Sound Yupik, and Yupik words and sound patterns have penetrated the Iñupiaq dialects of this area.

Alaskan Iñupiaq comprises two major dialect groups: North Alaskan and Seward Peninsula. North Alaskan Iñupiaq is made up of the North Slope dialect, spoken all along the Arctic coast north and east from Kivalina, and the Malimiut dialect spoken around Kotzebue Sound, along the Kobuk River, and with a southern extension in the Norton Sound villages of Koyuk and Unalakleet. Seward Peninsula Inupiaq includes the Qawiaraq dialect, originally in the interior of the peninsula but now also in the coastal Norton Sound villages, and Bering Strait Inupiaq, spoken in the villages on the Alaskan shore of Bering Strait and on Little Diomede and King islands. The *ñ* is not used in the Seward Peninsula dialect, where "Inupiaq" is used. In all there are about 2,500 speakers of Iñupiaq in Alaska.

The spiritual world of the Iñupiat was animistic in nature, and they believed that the forces of nature were spirits, who were both good and evil. Generally, the spirits worked for good until humans angered them with neglect and/or disobedience. There were many different kinds of spirits, including the "Great Being" or "Spirit of the Universe," *siḷam iñua*, who would reward or punish as needed.

Like their Yup'ik neighbors to the south, the Iñupiat have a well-established tradition of storytelling. Since communication in this society is primarily oral, stories have great importance and serve as a tool of education to pass on history, culture, and other information necessary to live life as an Iñupiaq. Young people listen to stories and learn from them, finding out how their ancestors lived in earlier times, before modern machines and systems changed their world. An important theme is survival and how hunters conquered the challenges of Arctic weather and ice and snow conditions. Some stories are about sea ice hunters who found themselves drifting over the ocean on an ice floe and how they managed to reach land and return home. Other stories discussed how food was gathered, prepared, and stored, often as a backdrop for other events such as supernatural occurrences. The land of stories was often inhabited by strange creatures, including a dragonlike reptile and a ferocious wild baby. Phantoms and dwarves might appear at any time, and stories told people how to deal with them. Shamans were prominent in stories, which told particularly of their powers and practices, their performances, and their role in the community, as well as of competition between shamans. In addition to purely magical beings and shamans there were powerful individuals who might be orphans, grandmothers, or unmarried women. Although they lived like ordinary people, their powers were greater than those of others. There were long stories and short ones, humorous and serious. For example, the Iñupiaq epic *Qayaqtuaġiṇñaqtuaq*—often called *Qayaq* for short—is said to have been told every evening for a month, consisting of multiple episodes. It is the story of a heroic and powerful man who travels across country, overcoming obstacles such as fantastic creatures and dangerous landforms.

A story like *Qayaq* is called *unipkaaq* (*unipchaaq* in the Kobuk dialect) meaning "legend" or a story that tells about a time far removed from the present, of people and beings not directly remembered by anyone alive today or their parents or grandparents. Another type of story tells of historical events, experiences of the storyteller or his/her family and has another name, for example, *quliaqtuaq* or *uqaluktuaq* on the North Slope or *quliapyuk* on King Island.

Traditional storytellers are extremely concerned with the accuracy of the stories they tell in the sense that stories must be told the way the storyteller heard them. Although stories in English typically rely on a written version as the "official" version, oral cultures rely on the integrity of storytellers who learn stories accurately and completely and often will not tell a particular story if they doubt their own knowledge of it. Highly regarded storytellers do not tell stories that they have learned incompletely.

Iñupiat people may criticize inaccurate tellings of stories. Storytellers often credit their source: "I learned this story from my uncle." What is known as copyright in literacy-based cultures is also respected in Eskimo culture, through acknowledgment of sources.

There are different versions of stories, and these may be transmitted within families or villages. Storytellers are not free to embellish or make up parts of stories, although some do tell different versions of a story.

In my own work with Iñupiaq speakers I have been repeatedly impressed by the power of the human memory as illustrated through storytelling. Relying heavily on reading and writing, highly literate societies seem to deemphasize memorization skills. Listening to my preliterate children memorize and recite books they had heard read to them a few times pointed out to me that I am no longer capable of the same feat, although I probably was at their age. In traditionally oral cultures without books and newspapers, note pads and filing cabinets, a well-developed memory is a valuable asset and the only way of preserving information and oral tradition.

THE FIVE IÑUPIAQ CONTRIBUTIONS that follow this introduction exemplify different types of Iñupiaq stories and narratives. Minnie Gray's text "My Name is Aliitchak" is oral history, another genre favored by Iñupiaq storytellers. She tells the history of Ambler village where she lives and where her family was among the earliest residents. "The Story of the King Island Wolf Dance" combines oral history with insight into the spirit world, explaining how the Wolf Dance was borrowed from the mainland Kawerak people, the relationship between the two groups, and how animals are involved in the life of both communities. Jimmie Killigivuk's "A Long Unipkaaq" exemplifies the legendary story that recounts events from a time not remembered by anyone living. Modern values and technology are absent from this old Iñupiaq world, in which supernatural events occur in a land where giants live in *iglus* and animals can take human form. Frank Ellanna's three short stories illustrate a diversity of styles, with family history in "My Great-Grandmother, the Shaman" and a beast fable in "The Oldsquaw and Her Ducklings." A fluent Iñupiaq speaker, Herbert Anungazuk from Wales on the eastern shore of Bering Strait writes about traditional culture and worldview, emphasizing the role of hunters and the importance of hunting traditions to the Iñupiat, helping define their relationship to the land and the animals, as well as the spiritual universe and the ancient past. These five pieces serve as an example of the diversity and creativity found within Iñupiaq oral tradition. Although they are changed by being translated into English and put into written form, the contributors have done their best to render as much of the flavor of the original as possible, resulting in texts many of which have a decidedly oral feel.

—LDK with Deanna Paniataaq Kingston

Introduction
Uvaŋa Atiġa Aliitchak / My Name Is Aliitchak

Told by Minnie Gray

Translated and edited by Tadataka Nagai and Lawrence D. Kaplan

This story is part of a narrative by Minnie Aliitchak Gray of Ambler, Alaska, originally told in Iñupiaq to Tadataka Nagai in July 2001 in Ambler. The storytelling was filmed by Takashi Sakurai and transcribed and translated by Nagai with Gray's assistance. The original Iñupiaq version is about an hour long.

Minnie Gray is one of the best-known and most highly respected Iñupiaq elders in Northwest Alaska. She taught Iñupiaq language and culture for many years in the Ambler School and coauthored books on topics ranging from folk remedies (Gray et al. 1976) to handicraft (Gray et al. 1981; Pulu et al. 1981) and traditional beliefs (Gray 1981). Her contribution also covers dictionary making; she helped linguist Wilfried Zibell compile a dictionary of Iñupiaq (Webster and Zibell 1970) between 1964 and 1967 and later became a compiler of the *Kobuk Iñupiaq Junior Dictionary* (Sun 1979). Gray is also a well-known storyteller and has authored works on Iñupiaq folklore (Gray 1978a, 1978b). This gift she inherited from her father, Robert Nasruk Cleveland, who used to tell stories to his children in the evening. She transcribed and published his stories from tape recordings (Cleveland 1980). Now retired from teaching, she is as active as ever in passing on her cultural knowledge to younger generations, teaching the subsistence lifestyle at Iḷisaġvik Camp, and holding sewing classes at home.

In this five-part text, Minnie Gray tells her life history. Part One is the history of Ambler as Minnie heard it from her father and outlines her life in the village. Part Two tells of her life up until her school days. In Part Three she reminisces about her childhood and adolescence, from her school days until her marriage. In Part Four she recounts her life from her marriage to becoming a bilingual teacher. Part Five is devoted to her days as a teacher and her retirement.

—Tadataka Nagai and LDK

Uvaŋa Atiġa Aliitchak

Told by Minnie Gray of Ambler

Ivisaappaat Aliitchaum Uqaaqtaŋi

Uvva Ivisaappaanik uqaaqtullaŋniaqtuŋa tusraaŋurakkapkun. Taataga uvva uqaġaqtuq. Taimangguuq *1898*-mi naluaġmiut aggiqpauraqmata. Tarani iñuuniaqtut naluaġmiut. Uvva tamauŋaqpatigun qauġri'apta taapkua Kilvaġiatkut tarani iñuuniaġniqsut. Taimma taatna taruŋali nunannaŋniqsuk Kilvaġiatkuk ukuak qitunġaqtuummaġmik. Taatna tarani iñuguqtutli qitunġaŋik. Tara Ivisaappaaġmiuŋuniqsuat taapkua Kilvaġiatkut. Tasramma tatqamakŋa Nuurviuramiñ iḷaraġaqhutiŋ. Taatna qaluŋniaġvigikhuni naaggaqaa aŋuniaġvigikhuni tuttunik naaqaa makuniŋa pisruktuanik piñiaġvigikhuni. Taatna nayuġaqniġaat.

Ukiumi auraġmi tara taapkua Kilvaġiatkut tara tarani ittaqniqsuat. Taatna taimma taipchua iqatikaaŋich piiġaluaqtut. Tarani taatna iñuuniaqtut taimma pitḷaiġataḷiġmiknunaglaa. Uvva *1943*-mi taimma tarakŋa iġñiŋaknik iḷaqatniktuŋa. Taruŋa tara iñuuniaqapta tarani auraġmunaglaa taatna iñuuniaqtugut. Qanuqtai uvva *three years* taapkunani taatna iñuuniuraallaktuŋa iliŋitñi. Uvva aasrii qamuŋa nuutlunuk qitunġauraqaqhunuk paniuraqaqtuguk. Uvva aasrii paniuranikmiuguglu taavruma unitchaaŋa.

Tara Ivisaappaat una iñuuniaġvigikhuni inniqsuaq. Tara *1958*-mi uvuŋa nuuttut qamakŋa Nuurviuramiñ taapkua tallimat malġuŋnik qitunġaġiich. Taruŋa nunaksraqhutiŋ nunnipḷutiŋ taruŋa inillaktut. Tara una nunaaqqiuraġuqtuq *1958*-miñaglaan. Uvvali aasriiñ uvaguk iḷaqatnitqikama taruŋali uqaqtautyaqtuguk *1963*-mi. Tara uvuŋŋitñamali taruŋa taatnatunaglaan iñuuniaqtuŋa. Taimma tuvaaqatma unitchaluaġaaŋa *pastor*-ŋuŋŋamnuk. Aglaan *three years pastor*-ŋuuraallaktuŋa tarani. Aasriiñ aglagviŋmun savviqḷuŋa tasramma *1973*-mi. Aasriiñ aglagviŋmun savviqḷuŋa tasramma *1973*-mi. Ivisaappaaġmiut tara ukua taatna Ivisaappaaġmiut tara ukua taatna aullaġniisaqqaaġataqamiŋ aglagviitchaluaqtut, aŋaayyuviitchaluaqtutaglaa. Taatna aullaġniirut.

My Name Is Aliitchak

Part One   Ivisaappaat / The Village of Ambler

I'm going to tell about Ambler, according to what I have heard, as my father used to tell about it. In 1898, white people came and then they lived there in Ambler. And later, when we were old enough to remember, Kilvaġiaq's [Happy Jack's] family lived there too. Kilvaġiaq and his wife chose land with their children, and their children grew up there. Kilvaġiaq's family were Ambler people. People from Shungnak came to join them there also. It is a good place for fishing and hunting caribou and a good place for hunting bears. They remained there.

In winter and summer, the Kilvaġiaq family always stayed in Ambler. The people who used to stay with them died. Even then, Kilvaġiaq's family stayed there until they got old and couldn't do much. In 1943 I married their son, Ugiaġnaq [Teddy Jack]. We lived there even in summer. I stayed with them about three years. And we moved upriver when we had a little baby girl. After we had our baby girl, my husband died and left me.

Ambler was a good place to live. In 1958, people moved here from Shungnak, the seven families. They marked off the land into lots and started living there. Ambler became a village in 1958. As for us, when I got married again, we moved here to be pastors in 1963. From that time on, I have lived here. My second husband died while we were pastors. I worked as a pastor for three years, and after that I started working for the school in 1973. The Ambler people had no school when they first started living here, and they had no church. That's how they started out.

Ukiaġmi sikumataaqtuġnaqmiuq. Tuttuliqman tuttunniaġnaqmiuq. Suli upinġaksrami tamarra itchuġvik tamaani inniqsuq. Iñuuniaġvigikhuni. Taatna nuurvigigaat.

Taimma taimakŋaniñaglaa nakiñaglaatai iñuich iñuuniaġviginikkaŋat taatna. Uvva qauġri'apta taapkua Kilvaġiatkut tarani iñuuniaġniqsuat. Uvuŋatunaglaa taatna iñuuniaġvik nakuuruq. Qaluŋniaġvigikmiuq. Aŋuniaġvigikmiuq. Taatna iñuuniaġvigiuraġniaġikput uvva taimma tuvaaqatipta unitchaluaġaatigut. Aglaan taatna iñuuniaqtugut.

In fall they fish under the ice. When caribou come, they hunt for caribou. In spring there's a place for hunters to watch for game. It's a good place to live. That's why they moved here.

Since long ago people have lived here. Since we were old enough to remember, the Jack [Kilvaġiaq] family lived here. And right up until today, living here has been good. It's a good place for fishing and a good place for hunting. We stay on here, even though our husbands have left us. That's the way we live.

Part Two   Uvaŋa atiġa Aliitchak / My Name is Aliitchak

My name is Aliitchak, and I was born upriver in Kobuk. Kobuk was the first village in this area. I was born there in 1924. In the year I was born, people moved down to Shungnak and moved the school there also. We were raised there in Shungnak. The Iñupiaq name of Shungnak is Nuurviuraq. When we reached school age, we started school there. They moved the school from Kobuk, because it always used to flood in Kobuk, and so they moved to Shungnak. When I reached school age and first went to school, in January, 1931, our school burned down, just when I started school. When it burned down, we cried for our school. It burned quickly because it was so old. After that we went to school at our church in Shungnak. The church was a log building, all made of wood.

So we started school at our church and went to school for a whole year. We had writing tablets. When the school burned down, people managed to get out the tablets and books, and so we had books, tablets, and pencils. That's how we were able to continue with school, and we went to school all year. We used to go to school from October to April, because it was the BIA. We went to school at the Bureau of Indian Affairs school, but I didn't finish the seventh grade. Maybe I finished the sixth grade, though. That's why I can't speak English very well.

We used to live at Black River [Imaġluktuq], and we were raised there. There at Black River we had a summer camp where we used to spend the summers, and after freeze-up we had a winter cabin on an old channel. We spent winters over there, and we really loved our winter cabin. We sure liked our place, Black River, and our winter cabin. We used to set snares for ptarmigans and rabbits, and we were always happy. There were no caribou, but we needed to eat game meat and so we snared for rabbits and ptarmigans.

In summer we lived by seining and fishing with nets. We lived through the summer, using dogs to pull the boat along the riverbank, and that's how we went upriver. We used oars and paddles when we went downriver. That's how we lived. When we traveled upriver, we hitched dogs to the boat. How many were there, I wonder? Three or four dogs must have been tied to the boat. That's how we went upriver with a boat, because we didn't have a motor. Pushing off with our arms, rowing, and pulling the boat with dogs and ropes is how we went upriver. In winter, we drove our dog team and went to get wood. That's the way we lived.

When it was muskrat hunting season, we went to spring camp, after school ended in spring. Then we would start hunting muskrats. Since it was the only way to get money, we hunted muskrats. We sold their pelts to the store.

In winter we set traps for foxes, weasels, and minks, so that we could sell them, because we had no other way to get money. There was no work, no jobs. That's how we grew up. I think that's all.

Part Three   Aglaguiqama / When I Quit School

When I quit school, I was seventeen years old. I had brothers and sisters, and there were thirteen of us, including five girls. There were eight boys and five girls. That's how many of us there were. When we were growing up, the oldest brothers and sisters died. And my older sister Paaniikaaluk [Clara Lee] grew up with other people, since she was adopted. I was the oldest one when we were growing up, and I grew up with the boys. The youngest one of all was a girl. I learned how to cook, because my mother showed me how. When she was pregnant and couldn't do things, she showed me and I started cooking. She explained about cooking, and I started cooking according to what she told me.

Making mukluks is another thing she showed me how to do. I learned how to make mukluks from my mother. When I sewed, I used to rip out the seam if I made a mistake. When my mother wanted me to rip it out, I did as she said. As for parka making, I first made a parka out of rabbit belly fur. Getting enough rabbits together and tanning their skins, I made a parka out of rabbit bellies, stitching cloth over them. I wore that parka for a long time. Rabbit skins are very good for parkas.

I always used to like to go to spring camp. When we went out to camp in spring, I learned to shoot muskrats. When we started hunting for muskrats, we would go to lakes and stay there all night. Each time we got muskrats, we brought them home. We slept during the day, and the next night we went hunting again for muskrats. I liked to fish too. I liked seining for fish, since seining is fun. And I liked to play, too. When we spent a year in the village, we would play football together, and we sure liked it. Playing baseball was fun for us too. In summer, handball was our favorite game. Those of my age group were my favorite playmates, including two girlfriends of mine. When we traveled, by dogsled and by boat, we were happy to move out to camp. It was fun for me to travel by boat and dog team in winter. I didn't travel much to Ambler here, when I was young, but one time I drove a dog team and came to Ambler. When my uncle Inuqtuaq [Johnny Cleveland] wanted me to go get fish, I followed him with dogs and went to Happy Jack's family. Kilvaġiaq's family had an extended two-room house, and they were fun to be with. They are all gone now, but I often remember them.

I still remember corralling reindeer. In Shungnak, right before the Fourth of July, reindeer herders always corralled reindeer with us, and took the reindeer there. When they brought them, we always had a good time corralling them. We children got wedged in among old people, middle-aged men and women, and we held hands and pushed reindeer into the corral. That's what I always remember, the fun I had during corralling. Because we ate reindeer, reindeer herders killed fat reindeer and fed us. When they were done with the reindeer, on the Fourth of July, we gathered at the village, where all the people were, and they played handball, ran races, and had boat races, and we always had fun. People our age or older people, or even very old people, when they started playing handball, they would stay up all night.

In winter, we played at Christmas. When we got together and we reached the people from our winter cabin for Christmas, we had fun. We would stay up all night playing football and hide-and-seek. That's how we used to play. Those were our games when we were young.

I learned to sew from my mother. I sure loved to sew, and I have always sewn. Even now, I still love to sew, and I love making baskets. I learned how at school from our teacher Iyaġaaluk, and even today, I love to make baskets and still do make them.

Corralling, Christmas, and the Fourth of July, I used to play on all these days, and I have loved them all my life. Still now, I love to play handball. But I'm getting weak, so it's getting kind of hard for me. That's it. I have talked for quite a while.

Part Four   Iḷaqatniktuŋa / I Got Married

I'm going to tell how I have lived. When I was twenty years old, I got married to Ugiaġnaq [Teddy Jack]. When spring came, they came to get me from our winter cabin. In those days people used to arrange for their children to get married, choosing spouses for them. In that way, when I was twenty years old, Kilvaġiaq came up from here in Ambler to our winter cabin. That winter cabin of ours was called Aanaruaġiik [which means "grandmother and grand-child"]. In spring, in the month of April, Kilvaġiaq came. He didn't even come into the house. He came to ask my father about me. I didn't know what was going on. I didn't understand. They talked to each other, and, without ever coming into the house, he went away. My father came in and told us about it. Kilvaġiaq had come to ask for his son to marry me. My father had said yes to him. I was not happy about this, because I didn't know anything about it. That's how I started my life.

In spring, when the snow started melting, they came to get me. Then I moved to Ambler though it was lonely. That's how they lived. I tried to live with them. I didn't know much, but I could sew and cook. We started living in Ambler in summer and winter. I started living with them, and I learned how to live from them, how they lived here in Ambler, how to fish or pick berries, some of which I already knew. I started living the way they lived.

Sometimes, I couldn't eat what they ate, but I learned. I tried to live like them and not do anything wrong. We lived here and it was quiet. We had one daughter in May, 1947. We stayed together for only four years, because when our daughter was four months old, my husband Ugiaġnaq died. He was sick the whole winter. While I was pregnant, he got sick, and in September, in the fall of 1947, he died. I was a widow then. I was twenty-three years old when I lost my husband. Our two teachers helped me. Mr. and Mrs. Warbelow, Marvin and Willi Lou, were our teachers at that time. When my husband was sick, the two of them helped me, giving him food and giving me sewing to do. I made mukluks and other things, and that's how we lived. When he became unable to work, he was working as a janitor at school. He got sick and quit working. When we moved to summer camp—we spent the summer two bends upriver from Shungnak—he got sick again and didn't last long. He died with bad lungs from tuberculosis. In those days there were no doctors to help us. There was no way to help if a person got that sickness. Teachers, the Warbelows, helped me out, as I was trying to raise my daughter. Those teachers were responsible for starting a store and a post office, telling people that the village should have these things. The people agreed with them and held meetings. That's how the Warbelows got us a Native store and post office and had them set up in the village. They sure helped us.

My daughter was getting bigger. I started trying to get my brother Aŋarraaq [Levi Cleveland] to go to school. I wanted him to go to school. Mother and Father always spent the winter at their cabin and didn't stay long in the village. I started sending my brother to school. I made money by sewing and so we had food. Those teachers helped me. And a CAA aviation weather site was put at Kuutchiaq [between Kobuk and Shungnak]. It was for weather reporting. Those two teachers helped me when I started living alone. At that time we had no phone or TV, but we had radio. We always listened to radios, since we had them. That's how we lived. When my brother became old enough to go to high school, he went to high school at White Mountain. But the army drafted him soon after, before he finished high school. He didn't finish high school at that time. When he quit the army, he started working on his GED and finished high school, and then he joined the National Guard. I don't know how many years he was in the National Guard. He was in the army for four years, and when he finished those four years, he joined the National Guard.

After five or six years, I got married again. I got married to Qatlu [Arthur Gray], and he started helping me make a living. I helped him by sewing. He started working in other places like Dillingham and Bornite. After that, we started working at the Native store, and we worked there for some years, I don't know how many. Elsie and Hugh Thomas were our pastors at that time. They told us we should go to Bible School. In the first year after they told us that, we didn't go. The next winter, when they came back and told us to go again, we started going. We went to Bible School in Noorvik for three years. After those three years, they sent us to Selawik to be pastors in the fall of 1960. In the spring of 1963, we moved back home to Shungnak. Qatlu didn't feel very well. We didn't even go to Kotzebue for a conference, since he really didn't feel good. So they wrote us a letter from the Kotzebue conference telling us to be pastors in Ambler. We said yes to them, and we became pastors there in Ambler. While we were pastors, in 1967 he got sick and went to see a doctor. He went to the hospital, and they sent him straight to Anchorage. There they performed an operation on him and removed one of his kidneys. They must have told him that he had just one year to live. He lived for only one year, and in October, 1968, he went back to the hospital in Anchorage and died there. I kept on working as a pastor till 1971, and in 1972 they asked me to be an Iñupiaq teacher. When they asked me that, I said yes. I worked as an Iñupiaq teacher till 1994. That's the story of my life.

Part Five   Qanuq Iñuuniaŋŋamnik Ivisaappaani / My Life in Ambler

I'm going to tell about how I have lived here in Ambler.

When I started working at school, one of the school board members came to ask me if I wanted to be an Iñupiaq teacher. I answered him that I didn't know how to speak English very well. They told me that I wouldn't be speaking English but that I would speak Iñupiaq and teach children. They wanted people to teach Iñupiaq, and they had meetings about it. When they decided, they came to ask me, and I said yes. That was in 1972.

After that, when spring came, in April, they sent Tilak [Truman Cleveland, Sr.], Tatqaviña [Katherine Cleveland] and me for training. We went by airplane. I used to go to Kotzebue, but I had never flown to other cities. We flew by jet to Anchorage. I was scared to fly by jet for the first time, and I had never ridden in a car. That was when I started riding in cars. I was scared that we might crash into something. I even moved around when I got into the car for the first time. They put us in a hotel, and then we started our meeting. Having come to a big city for the first time, I was worried, since I had never lived in a place like that before. From eleven villages, three, two, or one from each village were brought to this meeting. They sent them from a number of villages. We gave the names of things in Iñupiaq. We got together from different places and stayed there for one week. When the summer of 1973 came, they sent us to Nome. They brought us together in Nome from the villages, and we learned how to write Iñupiaq words. We stayed there for the month of July, and the next fall, in August, we started teaching. We started teaching Iñupiaq, and though it was not easy, we started. We worked the whole winter, and in late spring, they asked us to go to Nome again in July. I missed mentioning something else: in July, after our classes, they sent us to Barrow. When they sent me there, I stopped in Fairbanks on the way. They brought me to a young Iñupiaq woman that I knew. I stayed with her, and she took me over to some other Iñupiaq people she knew. 'Let's go visit people over there,' she said, since there were some Iñupiat that she knew. We visited them and stayed there for a while, and then she left to go home. I didn't know what to do in a city. When I went out of the house where I was staying when we went out for a visit, I didn't check the house number. I went to visit just as if I had been at home, in the village. After she left me, I visited for a while longer and then tried to go back, only I didn't know how to get back to where I was staying. I got lost. Luckily, those people I was visiting took me in a car to find the other woman's house, but it was in vain. I stayed overnight there with the people I visited. A person I knew had taken me to the place where I was to stay when I arrived in Fairbanks. I called her up, since I was going to fly to Barrow in the morning, and she took me to the place where I was to leave from. That woman called the person I was supposed to stay with.

I went to Barrow and stayed for one month, till the end of August. And that's how we studied Iñupiaq writing. There were not many of us, just Aaluk [Amelia Gray] and I. They sent Aaluk and me up there to study. The next summer, after we had taught the whole year, in 1974, they sent us to Nome again. We stayed there for a month. We began traveling a lot. When we were teachers, we went to Anchorage for meetings in February, and we always stayed for one week or three or four days, at meetings. Afterward, we started teaching what we had learned. Every year, we went for meetings, and we always traveled by airplane.

One time in summer, Tupou Pulu, our education teacher, the Tongan woman who we gave the Iñupiaq name of Qipuk, started telling me to transcribe my father's stories that were at the University of Alaska Fairbanks archives. In summer I went there to work on the stories that my father had told. They made my father's stories into a book. When we became teachers, we taught from 1973 till 1994, and were always traveling and studying. We kept on studying and teaching.

When I quit working and retired, they took us to Oklahoma. I went a very long way by car. These Baptists took us over there for a trip, me and my older sister Paaniikaaluk [Clara Lee]. We stayed there for one week, and then we came back, traveling for one week. We got tired from traveling for so very long.

When I worked in Anchorage, Kitik [Bertha Sheldon] and I first went to Hawaii, in 1988 I think. We stayed there for one week and then came back. Hawaii was hot and had lots of bugs too. And my daughter, my youngest daughter Qałhaqpak's [Helen Roberts'] husband was a soldier there. I went there twice. Since her husband lived there, my daughter lived there in Hawaii for seven years, and she has two children.

I have been traveling for a long time. Right up to today, I still go to meetings. I have gone to meetings for the Alaska Rural Systemic Initiative, I don't know for how many years. Maybe for three or four years, every year, when it's time to have meetings, I go to meetings. We have meetings twice a year. How to handle children is one thing I go to meetings about.

And then I went over to Vancouver Island, Canada, when Barbara MacManus took me there, after I'd quit working. She has a house on her land, on one of the islands, Cortes Island. She once took me over there, and we stayed at her house for one week. People there were very good. Children don't mess up things nor steal. They leave their houses unlocked and leave their things outside. That's how their lifestyle is. They can't kill animals on that island, either. Deer were eating outside the houses. We saw them. When the tide went down, when the tide went down around the islands, we gathered what are called "clams" for food. They were very good when Barbara cooked them and fed us. We used to go around the island, around to the other side of the island. The next year, she took Paaniikaaluk [Clara Lee], Saiḷaq [Sarah Tickett] and me over there again, and we stayed there for one week. It was very good to stay there, since just like up here, it was cool and good. We used to pick up seashells. The shells there were very good. That's how I have lived. That's how people have helped me and taken me on trips.

We started gathering birchbark, going to Fairbanks for birchbark. When we got permission, when the foresters gave us permission from the Bureau of Land Management, we started going to get birchbark. Paaniikaaluk [Clara Lee] and I went first to find the bark. Panitchiaq [Grace Huff] and her husband would help us get birchbark in Fairbanks. After we got some, we mailed what we had, and from then on we kept gathering birchbark, every summer, going to Fairbanks. Later, Saiḷaq [Sarah Tickett] started going with us.

I have four children, three girls. The oldest child is my own daughter from my first husband. The other three are adopted, and the one boy is the youngest. I have eleven grandchildren from them. One grandchild died, Tiriq's [George Gray's] oldest daughter. And I have sixteen great-grandchildren. I have lived for seventy-six years, and that's how my life has been. That's all.

Introduction
A Long Unipkaaq

Told by Jimmie Killigivuk

Transcribed and translated by

Carol Tukummiq Omnik and Tom Lowenstein

This story from Tikiġaq (Point Hope, Alaska) was told in March 1976 by Jimmie Asatchaq Killigivuk (1891–1980) and translated from Iñupiaq by Carol Tukummiq Omnik and myself. The cassette recording is held by the Alaska Native Language Center, Alaska State Library, the Omnik family and myself. *Unipkaaq* means "old story, myth, legend." The story, so far as I know, did not have a title, and we referred to it as the "long *unipkaaq*."

At the time of the recording, Asatchaq was the Point Hope elder most deeply engaged in traditional lore. The majority of Asatchaq's knowledge was inherited from his maternal uncle Samaruna and from Niġuvana, his mother (born ca. 1875). He learned the present story, the longest that he recorded, from Samaruna.

In addition to his reputation as storyteller among Iñupiaq people, Asatchaq also became known to twentieth-century students of Iñupiaq culture. In 1940, with his mother Niġuvana, he contributed to Froelich Rainey's account of traditional Tikiġaq, *The Whale Hunters of Tigara* (1947). Asatchaq was also principal Point Hope informant to Don C. Foote's geographical studies in 1960–1961. But long before this, Asatchaq had also worked with Diamond Jenness on Iñupiaq folklore when employed as a hunter and guide to Stefansson's Canadian Arctic expedition in 1913. Auditing some of these sessions aboard the ill-fated *Karluk* was the Scottish meteorologist William Laird McKinlay. Following the wreck of the *Karluk*, McKinlay kept with him some rolls of film and a diary. When I met him in Glasgow in 1978, Mr. McKinlay produced a photograph of the twenty-two-year-old Asatchaq with his Point Hope friend Pauyuuraq on board the *Karluk*, and also a (so far unpublished) transcript of a passage from the present story in Jenness's translation. References to Asatchaq may be found in *Arctic Odyssey* (Jenness 1991).

When Asatchaq recorded the present story we were in the fourth month of our work in Tikiġaq, and after a clear February, March brought blizzards. At the height of the stormy weather, Asatchaq's fifteen-year-old granddaughter, Nancy Timothy, went missing on the sea ice. On the evening after Nancy's disappearance, Asatchaq launched into a recitation that would fill three hour-long sessions. I felt, perhaps wrongly, that this story of ordeals and transformation, often on sea ice, provided a context—formal, spiritualized and remote—from which we could contemplate Nancy's passing. I dedicate this translation to the memory of Nancy, to her family and to the storyteller. Asatchaq's circumstances at the time were also difficult. He had recently returned to the village where he lived alone in an isolated cabin. Sometimes cold and hungry, but studiously preparing for our evening sessions, the storyteller spent each day reconstructing a narrative he had not told for many years. The telling, like all his recitations, was a model of concentration and unhesitating narrative memory.

THE SUPERNATURALISM OF THE STORY is in keeping with many ancient Iñupiaq narratives (*unipkaaq*). But as in many myths and legends, details of recognizable life also abound. People wear parkas, live in *iglus* and sometimes even belong to communities. Animals, likewise, make species-recognizable appearances.

The story is, nonetheless, almost wholly non-naturalistic: The narrative takes place in a presocialized and protoshamanistic dreamtime when, for example, men marry animals, *iglus* have moving "mechanical" parts and humanized animal families socialize in submarine *iglus*. The lives of "real people" (Iñupiat) are conducted within a fantastic light: giants carry whales on their backs, sexual intercourse leads to death, boys have copper genitals and women toothed vaginas, skins on the drying rack come to life and fight.

The story's supernaturalism is suggested in the opening scene as an anonymous hero sets out on his journey from Tikiġaq. This name immediately falls away and appears only once more, as do the names Kobuk, Nuvuk (Point Barrow) and other areas of traditional settlement. None of these places are, however, topographically recognizable and geographic reality becomes, on the whole, subordinated to the evocation of nonspecific and imaginative narrative space. While a Tikiġaq audience will once or twice recognize places such as the Cape Thompson cliffs (Imnat) and Aqalulik River (just north of Tikiġaq), it is the foreground action and briskly changing movement between episodes that engage the attention.

The two heroes who travel this somewhat abstract environment are also without name and identity. What matters at the story's outset is the first hero's rejection of communal life and his solitary quest for experience. The nature of this search is suggested in the statement that in leaving Tikiġaq and walking south, the traveler is "looking for something." This "something" is at first definable only in that it lies beyond the community. But one feature of Tikiġaq lore, found in the parallel Tikiġaq story of Ukuŋniq (Lowenstein 1992:21), does help define the present story's journey. Ukuŋniq also leaves Tikiġaq to wander south "in search of something." In Tikiġaq thought, the south was identified with the female and the generation of life. Animals migrate from the south; the midwinter sun first rises south of the village next to Imnat cliffs. In the present story and in Ukuŋniq's, the south shore leads beyond communal life to personal encounters, in a spiritualized unknown, with the supernatural. As in the present story, Ukuŋniq's first experience is at Imnat. Here the audience learns that Ukuŋniq is an *iḷiappak*, "poor boy," "orphan": invariably, in Iñupiaq stories, a solitary shamanistic candidate, sometimes already an initiated practitioner. While many details differ, the encounter in the present story with giants at Imnat similarly reveals the hero's quasi-shamanistic status. This man, like Ukuŋniq, has neither kin nor community. He journeys south and struggles with a succession of antagonists: giants, monsters, murderous denatured humans. As long as he travels, the encounters proliferate. Returning to Tikiġaq he and his adopted son take off once more and extend their experience, this time to the north.

As regards the story's supernaturalism, the narrative suggests a number of different levels and genres. On one level, we might say that this story is an Iñupiaq version of the hero saga found in many Native American traditions. In these, the protagonist is a warrior figure whose task is to "fix things up" by killing predatory mythic animals or monstrous humans who ravage a primordial just-post-creational landscape. In this respect, the Iñupiaq hero resembles trickster creator figures such as Manibozo and Gloosnap of northeastern woodland societies. The hero as trickster also appears in many Inuit/Iñupiaq myths. Figures such as Aliŋnaq, the Moon Spirit, who controls the game, and the Raven of many creation stories were semidivine humans or human/animal hybrids who accomplished their creative work by deception and often trickery.

The hero of this story is different from these figures in that he and his son are viewed solely as human figures with dreamlike dimensions of power. In the epic of *Qayaqtuaġiŋñaqtuaq* ("he who always travels by kayak"), often shortened to *Qayaq*, from the Seward Peninsula and the subarctic rivers, the protagonist is unambiguously a heroic warrior. In the *Qayaq* story, the world is at a delicate post-creational stage. The dangerous monsters (*iñua*) are represented as part of a landscape that the hero undertakes to pacify and render safe. Tikiġaq's own creation story follows this pattern. In this, the Raven Man, Tuluŋigraq, harpoons a sea beast that transforms to "Tikiġaq *nuna*" (land). The hero's achievement converts supernatural threat to the service of society and thereby consecrates and defines Tikiġaq peninsula.

The present story, like that of Ukuŋniq, differs from these narratives in several ways. First, its heroes do not pursue communally oriented careers. True, they dispatch giants, habitual murderers, giant birds, and the like. But unlike the monsters of *Qayaq* or Tikiġaq's sea beast, the beings in the present story neither threaten society nor pollute the human/animal landscape. Instead, as though in response to the traveler's search for "something," each antagonist or animal companion appears as though in response to his presence. Unlike the infested world of *Qayaq*, the environment here is a neutral space. The volitional nature of each encounter is particularly vivid in the case of the son. While the father simply meets, or is summoned by, antagonists along his journey, the son leaps or dives toward each adventure. "My mind wants me to jump," he cries. And while the supernatural exerts its pull, he himself appears internally compelled.

IN CONCLUSION, BRIEFLY, the two heroes' experience suggests that their ordeals are symbolic of shamanistic experience and in particular, of initiation. While shamans of the historical period usually worked in, and for, the well-being of their society, initiatory experience was often nonsocial. Significantly, however, the word *aŋatkuq* (shaman) is absent from this story, no doubt partly because the presocial dreamtime of a legend like this predates historical village organization with its recognizable institutions. It is shamanistic *experience*—dream, vision, out-of-body states, psychic conflict—rather than shamanism as a socioeconomic phenomenon that suffuses the narrative. Even in the context of the Iñupiaq *unipkaaq* (old story, myth), this one, with its entirely supernatural content, must be very ancient. The story may thus perhaps be read as an archaic representation of the visionary ecstasies, aspirations, and terrors of the shamanistic imagination which underlay the world of shamanism as it was historically practiced. Finally, it is worth noting that many of the events in the story conform quite clearly to shamanistic patterns of initiation that are widely distributed both in the Inuit world and other shamanistic societies: repeated dismemberment by animals or spirits; the gathering of amulets for shamanistic use; human/animal marriages; journeys into animal spirit realms; death by dismemberment or ingestion by animal followed by revival; human transformation into animal form; inner earth and submarine voyages; appearances of spirit helpers or healing children. (For discussion of these archetypes see Eliade 1964: chapter 2.)

A small number of the tropes above occur in other stories told by Asatchaq, but it is also worth noting that investigators at Point Hope have recorded very few parallel instances. Two exceptions stand out, both from Froelich Rainey's field notes of 1939–1940, which are archived at the University of Alaska Fairbanks. In one, a neophyte is initiated by a shaman with a club (Frank's story:79). In a second, two child initiates are consumed by a polar bear (Frank's story:109.). In contrast to the proliferation of dramatic initiatory events in the present story, the paucity of parallel information highlights the unique interest of Asatchaq's narrative, and also perhaps suggests that it may represent an amalgam of tales from native sources beyond Tikiġaq.

—Tom Lowenstein

A Long Unipkaaq

Told by Jimmie Killigivuk of Point Hope

I'M GOING TO TELL A STORY. The story's long, but it will end. A man left Tikiġaq. He walked south by himself. He walked the south shore, looking for something. When he came to the cliffs, he met a giant. The giant lived there; he lived at Imnat. And this giant had a kayak. He had many other things. And he had whales—not butchered; they were cut in half and laid on the beach along the cliffs.

The giant also had an *iglu* [sod house]. He asked the traveler to stay there with him. When the giant went in, he put his arm up. He pulled the traveler through the *katak* [entrance hole]. The man couldn't get through the *katak* himself. When they were inside, the giant said, "I want to play games." The giant didn't offer him food. He challenged him to games. "All right," said the man. So they went outside and started to play. The giant put half a whale on his back, and ran up the cliff face. When he'd done this, the man had to copy him. "Put that whale on your back," the giant said, "and run up the cliff." The man did it; but the game exhausted him.

"Tomorrow," said the giant, "we'll go and hunt whales. We'll see who gets one first." The traveler refused his challenge. He didn't even have a kayak. (I'm sure he would have hunted if he'd had a kayak.) So the giant challenged him to fight. The man was small. Perhaps that's why the giant challenged him. The giant put his arm out to wrestle. They started to fight, but the man could do nothing. But when the giant was going to throw him, the man planted his feet. And when the giant tried to throw him, the giant's arm broke.

The traveler left. He'd seen the whales, and how the giant cooked half a whale at a time. He pushed a piece of wood inside and held the whale above his lamp. That's how he cooked. (Women used to cook this way. They held meat above their lamps. I used to eat it; it tastes very good.) The man went on.

He met another giant. This giant asked, "Did you see my younger brother?" "Yes," said the man, "I met your brother." "What did he say?" "We did nothing. I broke his arm. His arm is broken."

Then the older brother wanted to play. He too had whales that he'd cut in two. They played the same game, and then they wrestled. When they wrestled, the traveler set his feet on the ground and broke the giant's arm. Now he'd broken the arms of both the brothers; but he didn't kill them. (This story is a long one.)

Now when he'd broken the giant's arms, the man went on. He traveled on foot. He reached Qikiqtaġruk. But no one there challenged him. He went on upriver. As he traveled, he met some people, and one of the men was an *iñuqaġnaiḷaq* (a man who is always killing people). This *iñuqaġnaiḷaq* liked playing games with strangers. The *iñuqaġnaiḷaq* owned a whale's skull. There's a hole in a whale's skull; a man's head fits inside it. When the *iñuqaġnaiḷaq* found a player, he forced his head into the skull hole, pulled off the head and left it in the whale's skull. But the man pushed the *iñuqaġnaiḷaq*'s own head in there. He held his legs and jammed his head in. The skull-hole's edges were made into teeth. The *iñuqaġnaiḷaq*'s own game killed him. After he'd killed the *iñuqaġnaiḷaq*, the man asked who else might want to fight him.

The people said, "There's a man upriver: the *iñuqaġnaiḷaq*'s older brother: he's even stronger. He too has something he kills people with." The man left those people to go upriver.

He traveled all day, and in the evening he came to some people. "What have you come for?" asked the people. "I'm looking for a man who kills," he answered. The first evening they did nothing. But next day they said that he'd meet him for a foot race. "The one who loses will offer the next challenge." The men started running. After a time, the *iñuqaġnaiḷaq* stopped.

"We'll run back to the people. The first to get there will be the winner." They started running. At first they ran abreast of each other. But after a while, the Tikiġaq man outran the killer.

He left the *iñuqaġnaiḷaq* behind. He was the winner. He came in first, but the people did nothing. They acted as though nothing had happened. Then the loser told the people to go to the *qalgi* [ceremonial house].

The man who'd lost was the first to enter. He was a member of the *qalgi*. "Since I was the loser, I'll start a new game." The game was at the *katak* (entrance hole). A pair of whale jaws was fitted to the *katak*. The jaws had teeth; they moved in the *katak*. The murderer started the second game. He took a bead and dropped it through the *katak*. Then he jumped through the *katak* and picked the bead up. The jaws in the *katak* opened and shut. When he'd picked up the bead he came back to the *qalgi*. The man did it nimbly. He was good at his game. There was blood on the whale jaws. The traveler saw it. "Now you do what I did. Drop the bead through the *katak*. Go down through the *katak*. Pick up the bead and come back to the *qalgi*." Now it was his turn. He dropped the bead. As the jaws opened the man jumped through them. He picked up the bead and returned to the *qalgi*. He came back safely.

Now the jaws moved faster. The jaws had sharp edges. There was blood on their edges.

Now the jaws were moving faster, the Tikiġaq man thought he wouldn't make it. Then his host dropped the bead, dived after it, and came back safely. The jaws moved faster. Then the man dropped the bead and went down again safely. He picked up the bead. But as he came back the jaws caught his ankles. He feels his feet; they've been cut at the ankles. He feels his feet have been cut at the ankles. When he looks through the *katak*, he sees two hawks' feet on the passage floor. Then the host tried again; he threw the bead. They saw him go down, but when he came up, the jaws caught him by the thighs. Then the Tikiġaq man killed him. The owner's own trap caught him. The Tikiġaq man won. The killer tried to trap him, but he couldn't. The Tikiġaq man asked if there was another killer.

But they answered, "There is no one." He told them he would go upriver. "When I wake in the morning, I will travel upriver." When he woke, he left. He traveled up the Kobuk River.

At first he met no one. But after some time, he saw an *iglu*. When he reached the *iglu*, he found a man and woman living there. The man and woman welcomed him. They didn't look like murderers. They treated him well. They gave him meat. The man stayed a while. But one morning when they woke, the Kobuk man said, "I want to wrestle with you." The Tikiġaq man agreed to wrestle. The man spread tent skins. They were made of caribou.

But before they started, the Tikiġaq man spread a walrus skin on top of the caribou. They started to wrestle. The man watched his challenger. He watched the Kobuk man. He studied his method and let himself be thrown.

And as they fought, he saw the woman circling the skin. She walked counter-sunwise. The Tikiġaq man watched her. As they fought they tore the skin up. Their feet tore the skin up. When the skin was torn, the man let his host throw him.

He wanted to know what his host would do.

And when he was down, the woman attacked him. She grabbed his penis. The woman grabbed his trousers. But while she held his trousers, the Tikiġaq man kicked her backwards. She ripped off his trousers. Her head came off when she fell backward. She ripped off his trousers as he kicked her backwards. Her husband did nothing. The husband was happy. The woman had torn the traveler's balls off. The woman was the *iñuqaġnaiḷaq*. Her husband did nothing.

The Tikiġaq man was sorry for the husband. He knew the woman was an *iñuqaġnaiḷaq*. Then the Kobuk man said, "When we wake in the morning, we won't wrestle with each other. We'll fight with clubs, with branches from trees. Our clubs will grow thicker as we fight." "*Ii*, yes," said the man. He agreed to fight again. In the morning they picked up branches and they started to fight. Both men had sticks.

They fought. But when the man hit his enemy, his club hit nothing. He felt nothing when he hit him. The branch went through his body. But when the Kobuk man hit him, he broke his club. The club broke on his body. When he saw what had happened he ran away. He ran to the river. He jumped in the water and started to rub himself. The Tikiġaq man followed. (That man from Tikiġaq had an amulet of rock.)

The Kobuk man rubbed himself with fish slime. (Live fish are slimy. That's why his enemy felt nothing. It was the fish slime. And it was the rock charm [that] made his club break.) They fought and then stopped. They couldn't hurt each other. But during their fight, the Tikiġaq man was hit on the body. His rib was broken. He told his host he'd go back to Tikiġaq.

He spent the night there, and then started walking. He walked north, toward home. He passed the cliffs where the giants lived. The giants were well; they had plenty of meat there. When he met the older giant, he cut off his little finger and took it with him. When he came to the younger he did the same. He took his little finger. He just took their little fingers. He wanted the joints of their fingers as amulets. "I'll keep those joints as amulets, and give them to my children, even to adopted children."

He reached Tikiġaq. All he brought with him were giants' fingers. Now he was in Tikiġaq, he worked in his *iglu*. He spent his time there making arrows. He came home to his *iglu* and stayed there making arrows in the evening.

Now before, when he was younger, all the women he slept with died when he was with them. The women he slept with never woke in the morning. He would wake up but the women didn't. Now he's making arrows in his *iglu* one day, and he hears a movement in the entrance passage. His parents were dead. And a voice came up from the entrance passage: "Give me back my little dog! Give me back my puppy!" When he heard this, he went to the *katak* and looked down. There was a young polar bear in the passage.

"Get it yourself," he said through the *katak*. He didn't want to give the dog back. Then the bear came in through the *katak* and changed into a woman. She had two long canines. She had two canines showing. (People with those teeth are called *qamaugigraq*. People used to say that I had teeth like that. When I was a child, they told me I had teeth like that. Sukannana used to say that.)

The woman who came in had canines that showed. The man took her. They slept together. She gave birth to a polar bear. The cub was their child. The child was a polar bear. After they'd been married for a while they quarreled. The woman lost no time. She left the *iglu*. She took the child on her back. The man did nothing. (What she did was normal.) The man did nothing. He just slept in the *iglu* by himself.

The next day the man went to find her. He looked in the passage. But there he found nothing. He looked outside, but didn't find her. He went to other people's *iglus* looking for the woman. But he didn't find her. She hadn't gone to anybody's *iglu*. Then he walked back and found her footprints. The tracks went south.

The man followed them. The tracks took him to the sea ice and went south again. He followed for a while. The bear tracks stopped at open water. Now there was only one way ahead. He jumped into the water. He was on the seabed. There were his wife's tracks. He followed them. Now as he traveled, he saw *iglus* in the distance . . . his wife's tracks continued. They stopped at the last *iglu*. The tracks went in. The man followed. He went into the *iglu*.

Inside he found many people. It was his woman's parents' people. Her parents were there. And men were playing with the little polar bear. When he entered they said nothing. And the man said nothing. He saw them playing with their nephew. They were polar bear people. They had bear snouts on their foreheads. Tukummiq asked, "Were they humans?" They were human. They were people; but they wore polar bear snouts. Wolves and wolverine can do this too. These people were passing time at home; they were doing nothing. The man had come to his wife's parents' *iglu*.

Now someone called through the *iglu* skylight. The voice said, "Your *aŋutauqan* [co-husband or lover] has challenged you to diving in the morning." "How could he have an *aŋutauqan* when she didn't have anyone before this?" said her parents. "He never came to see us when she lived here before." They never lived together, but since the *aŋutauqan* challenged the Tikiġaq man, the father called up, "Yes, he'll do it."

When they woke next morning, the father said, "My parka's in the entrance passage. It's a polar bear parka. Take it when you go. Your *aŋutauqan* is a polar bear. He wants a contest with you. Whoever catches a seal in his mouth and first climbs back onto the ice will be the winner."

So the man changed into a polar bear. And they went to the place, and the *aŋutauqan* dived. The man dived after him. He'd turned into a polar bear because he wore the polar bear parka. "He's never beat me at diving," said the father, "but this time I don't know who'll come up first."

Now the man dived. And as he went down, he saw dark shapes in the water. His wife's father had told him, "when you see a black thing, get it in your mouth and come to the surface." Now he saw dark shapes all around him in the water. But he didn't try to get one yet. But when he turned toward the surface, he bit one and held it. And when he climbed back on the ice, he found he'd taken a small *ugruk* [bearded seal].

It wasn't a large *ugruk*. When he came up, he threw the *ugruk* on the sea ice. The polar bears were watching. The woman's brothers said, "The other hasn't come up yet." But soon he too came up with an *ugruk*. But he'd lost his own contest. They went home. The loser said nothing. When they went into the *iglu*, the man told the father what he'd seen in the water. "While I was diving, I saw dark shapes in the water. But I didn't immediately try to catch one. When I started to come up I bit one." The father said, "Ii, yes. You did what I told you."

Now someone called through the skylight again, "Your *aŋutauqan* wants to meet you tomorrow." When they woke in the morning, they went to the sea ice. They faced each other from a distance. The father said, "Now you have to run. As you pass him, tear his skin off." They started and raced like this for a time. He was sure he'd torn the other polar bear. (Polar bears are left-handed. Some animals are like that. Brown bears are left-handed too.) When they ran at each other, the *aŋutauqan* struck him. The man felt the blow, but his skin wasn't opened. And as they competed, the man tried hitting left-handed. But this failed too. But the third time, the man ripped the polar bear's shoulder as they passed each other. He tore his *aŋutauqan*'s parka. The woman's brothers stood around and watched. They said, "Now you ripped that parka you have won the contest. Now your *aŋutauqan* will think up a new challenge."

They went home again. Then someone called in through the skylight, "His *aŋutauqan* has no more challenges."

The Tikiġaq man stayed for some time. He was treated kindly. Then the father said, "You should go back to where you came from." They left the next morning and traveled toward Tikiġaq. So he took the polar bear home with him. When they reached Tikiġaq, he still had the woman. But the woman and child were still polar bears. (I don't know if the child was male or female.)

They stayed for a time, and the man said, "When whaling starts, I'll take my woman with us." And he started to build a skin boat. Spring and he finished the skin boat. Whaling started. He left for the sea ice, and took his woman....

Summer came, and the man and woman traveled north in the skin boat. They traveled by day, and made camp at night. They traveled for some time, the Tikiġaq man and his polar bear woman. They traveled till they reached the point beyond Utqiaġvik. The place was called Nuvuk. It's like our point at Tikiġaq. And the Tikiġaq man stopped at Nuvuk and decided to live there. They built an *iglu*. No one else lived at Nuvuk. So they lived there. There were no other people.

And while they were living there they started to quarrel. Then they started fighting. The woman tore her husband to pieces. She was a polar bear.

Now he realized he was dying, he decided to kill her. As he lay on his back, he put his arms round her neck and snapped the vertebrae. That's how he killed her. He pulled the vertebrae apart. He lay on the floor helpless. He could do nothing. The woman had torn his body to pieces. Then one night as he lay doing nothing, he heard someone in the passage. A small girl entered.

He'd thought he was alone at Nuvuk. The girl said, "My *aana* (grandmother) told me to come. She told me to come and see how you were. You'll die if we leave you. You'll die unless you lie down on the polar bear skin." (He might die anyway—or maybe survive—on the polar bear skin.) "If you want to die, just die there on the skin. If you want to live, then live."

So he lay on the skin, and during the day the girl looked after him. He started to recover. She tended the oil lamps and prepared his meat. At last he recovered, lying on the bearskin. (That's what they did then if a polar bear or brown bear hurt you. You lay on the skin of the animal that wounded you. They said it was its soul that cured you.) And so it happened now. He lay on the skin and started to get better. He recovered and his body healed. He continued resting on the skin.

One evening as he lay there, someone came in. He said, "They told me to fetch you. So I've come." The man answered, "How did you get here?" Then he went out and he followed the visitor. He followed the messenger. They went far. The Tikiġaq man was led to an *iglu*. He saw people there with brown bear snouts on their foreheads. He saw that they were brown bear people. There was an old man among them. The old man said, "It was I who sent for you. I want you as a husband for my daughter. Here is my daughter. Take her if you like her." "It doesn't matter," said the man. But when they showed him the woman he was grateful. He didn't have a woman working with him.

Now that the woman was to marry, she told the men in her *iglu*, "Go and put up tent skins in the *qalgi* [ceremonial house]." And the old man said too, "put tent skins in the *qalgi*." (This must have been the woman's father.) So they hung skins in the middle of the *qalgi*. (In those days, tents were made of caribou skin.) When the tent was up, the woman called to him, "come in. Come inside now." So the man went in; he went into the tent. When he was inside, the man saw sleeping skins. The woman was already lying there. The man lay down with her.

He went to the woman and started to fuck her. But even before he'd entered the woman, she began screaming. And when she screamed, the man heard growling in the *qalgi*. It was the brown bears growling. The growling grew louder. The woman called out, "*Naagga*! No! Don't hurt him! It's just that he's hurting me here!" The woman was lying. But the bears stopped growling. And when the growling stopped, the bears went out perhaps. Before they left the *qalgi*, the man had fucked her. Then they took the skins out. The woman said, "Look, I won't follow you to your place unless I have caribou skins to walk on." "Sure," said the man, "there are plenty of skins at my place on the meat rack."

So skins were laid all the way to his *iglu*, and she walked there on them. But before he left, the man thought of the people he'd had at home, two people who had tended the oil lamps. "I forgot to tell them that I was going. I was wrong not to tell them." But the father said, "We'll take care of the lamps. We'll send someone to take care of them." And the messenger who'd called for him told him that they'd find someone for the oil lamps. They were sent from the brown bear's *iglu*: yes . . . a white fox and a red fox circled the entrance hole, they circled and were gone, the red fox and the white one.

So the man and the brown bear went home on skins. And on the way they met the two foxes. The foxes said their place was lit already. "The lamps are burning. They stayed burning in your absence." They arrived at his *iglu*, the man and the brown bear. When they entered, they went inside and the bear became a woman. And when they got inside, there's a noise from the rack. (There's a drying rack above the oil lamp: wooden.) The man had kept his first wife's skin on the drying rack. And the noise they heard was a polar bear moving. When the brown bear entered, it became a woman. And when the woman came in, the bearskin starts moving. It turned into a living animal. A polar bear rose in front of the oil lamp.

And now the woman turned into a brown bear again. The polar bear was jealous of her husband. The bears stood facing one another. Before they started fighting, the man said, "Don't fight on my account. I can't handle it in here!" So before they'd even started, the bears fell back. Now the brown bear said, "When we wake tomorrow, we'll gather all our people and count them. Then we can judge which family is the greater: the polar bear or the brown bear. Tell your people to come here," said the brown bear. When they woke in the morning, they left the *iglu*. And the brown bears started coming from inland. And from the sea ice, polar bears were coming.

And the polar bears were so many that they stretched to the horizon. But there weren't so many brown bears. So the brown bear woman lost.

And the man saw one polar bear with a black spot on its haunch. And he knew it was his son. It must have been: for once, as he ran round the *iglu*, the cub had scorched his fur on the oil lamp. That's how he got the mark on his haunch.

Now when they had all seen their families and were back in the *iglu*, the brown bear asked the man to bring her caribou meat. Yes, she wanted her husband to fetch it for her. And when she's eaten caribou, she asked for another thing: she wanted to drink water that tasted of copper. The man said, "If it can be reached, I'll get it." And he turned himself into a peregrine falcon. He flew north to the river where this water could be found. He carried a water pot. He carried the pot to fill with water. He took this back to her. (She asked too much of him.) And after he had brought the copper water, they sat alone in the one evening. The man said nothing. He had nothing to say to her. She had asked too much of him. The woman spoke. "Why are you silent?" The man said, "I want to eat meat with blubber on it." The woman just said, "Yes." (She would get what he asked for.) She brought in cooked meat; there was fat on the meat.

It was brown bear meat. She had killed a brown bear. She'd cooked brown bear for her husband. And when he'd eaten, he said, "I want to drink water that tastes of copper." The brown bear woman said, "Yes... I'll try and get it...." And she picked up the water pot. Now she was a woman. And the copper was far off, very far. (I don't know how she got there.) But she found the water for him, and he drank it. After that he asked for nothing, and they lived together. The man kept this wife who came from the brown bear people. They stayed there for a long time. They lived as man and woman. Then one day they quarreled. The brown bear got angry with her husband. He didn't let the brown bear live much longer. He killed as he'd killed his first wife. He was torn up badly by the brown bear. And again the girl appeared. Her grandmother sent her to heal him. She wanted him to lie down on the brown bear skin. But the man refused. He didn't want want to lie down on the bearskin.

Some time later when he was alone one evening, two people came in. They came in and said, "We're here to fetch you. Will you come?" "Yes," said the man, "I'll follow you. Where are you taking me?" "We've come from the whales," replied the two people. "We want you to have a wife who is a whale." So he traveled with them to the whales.

They left his *iglu* and left Nuvuk for the sea ice. They walked till they came to an *iglu* entrance on the sea ice. When they'd found the entrance, they went in. Inside, the man saw whale flukes. Then he remembered: he had left his *iglu* without telling the people who tended the oil lamps. But the people with him said, "We'll send someone to take care of the lamps." And an old man said, "*Ki*! Go! Send someone!" And two black [winter] guillemots flew down from the ceiling and started circling the *katak*. "These are the two who'll tend your oil lamps," they said.

The man left with his wife. They traveled inland. He lived with the whale. But unlike the brown bear, she asked for nothing. (You can see those birds around here in the winter.) When he got home with the whale, she became a woman. But before they reached his *iglu*, they saw the guillemots returning. The *iglu* was lit. The lamps had been burning. It was as though the man had never left it. When they reached the *iglu*, they went to bed. The woman's skin seemed dark to him. (The whale's skin's black, you know.)

They lived together for some time now. But one day the man grew angry in his mind. He thought, "Why do I always take wives from among the animals? If this goes on, I'll never have descendents." Before he'd said a word, the woman understood his thinking.

She said, "We meant you no harm. We just wanted you in our families. Your first wife was a polar bear, and your second was a brown bear. I am a whale. We wished you no harm. We wanted only to befriend you. We shall not kill you." They [two] did nothing. This put an end to their quarrel. But one evening while they sat alone, they weren't of one mind. The woman knew his thoughts before he spoke them. She said, "You're thinking, why must I always have animal wives? Why must my wife always be an animal? But listen. We meant you no harm. We did it for your good. Nor can you harm us." But after she'd spoken, the woman grew angry. She turned into a whale, right there in the *iglu*. Her flukes lashed the walls. The man was in danger. So every time the flukes came near, the man jumped away. The rest of her body was no danger. But because of her flukes, the man had to catch her. So he made up his mind. He grabbed her waist and broke the whale's backbone. That's how he killed her.

And after he had killed the whale, the small girl appeared. She went and told her grandmother. Together they cut the whale up in the *iglu*. There was plenty of meat there.

Then they cleaned the *iglu*, and the old woman told him, "One day soon, you'll get a warning. You'll be warned the bears are coming to get you. Your wives' families are coming, and they'll want to kill you. What will you use against so many?" He knew he had no weapons, so he took the jawbones of his bowhead whale wife and started to carve them. He carved handgrips in each jaw bone. He made clubs from the jaws to beat the bears with. Now he was ready for anything that happened.

One day the old woman sent the girl to warn him. "Tomorrow the polar bears and bowheads will be after you," she said. "How will you defend yourself against so many?" "Tell your *aana* that I've made a weapon. When the polar bears and the brown bears come, I'll kill them with these whale jaws." Later the girl called in through the skylight. She told him she'd seen the animals coming. "Polar bears and brown bears are coming, and bowheads too!" The whales couldn't get to land, but he could see them swimming in the water, backwards and forwards opposite his *iglu*. But the polar bears were coming off the ice toward him. And the brown bears came from inland. The man struck them with his whale jaws. He struck them on their heads. And though they were many, his weapons protected him.

He did nothing to the whales, because he couldn't reach them. Now when his struggle with the animals was over, he decided he'd go back to Tikiġaq. He decided that he'd go next morning. He told the old woman. He'd go in his skin boat: the boat he'd come north in with the polar bear woman. So he took the skin boat and traveled toward Tikiġaq.

When the man reached Tikiġaq, he adopted a boy. He wanted a child; he wanted descendents. He still had no woman. The boy grew up. And one day as he played outside, he killed another boy. Someone went to the father and called through the *iglu* skylight, "Your boy has murdered someone. Not on purpose, but he's murdered someone." The father waited. When the boy came home, his father said, "Never harm the people whom you live among. Don't kill anyone from now on. If you want to kill someone, up there, upriver is a man who broke my ribs once. You can go there and kill him. Come home when you've killed him."

The young man left Tikiġaq on foot as his father had done. But along the way he saw nothing unusual. He came to the river where the man who'd hurt his father lived. He killed the man, and went back to Tikiġaq. When he got home he said to his father, "I killed the man who lived on the river." "If you really killed him, we will shut you in the *iglu* and block the outer entrance and the entrance passage. Then you'll have to escape from the *iglu*." And he told the people to block the whole *iglu* with his son inside.

When the people had blocked the *iglu*, the man called in, "now try to get out!" And the Tikiġaq people stood outside and watched. After a while someone said, "I can see someone coming. There's someone coming up behind the *iglu*!" The son had burrowed through the frozen ground; he came up behind the *iglu*. The father did nothing. His father did nothing. His son had passed the test he'd set him.

Sometime later the boy started thinking of his father's life at Nuvuk: how he'd taken wives from among the animals. The son decided to visit that place and his father's old *iglu*. He couldn't remove this thought from his mind: "I must go and see my father's *iglu*. The place where my father had lived with animals." When he told his father, they started to quarrel. The son killed his father. But before he died, the man said, "When you kill me, cut up my body and throw the bits in the sea." The son did as he was told. After he had killed his father, he built a skin boat—or maybe he used the boat his father traveled in.

That summer he left. He left for Nuvuk where his father had lived, he left while the ice still lay round Tikiġaq. There was ice in front of the boat as he traveled, but somehow the path ahead was always clear.

Now while he was traveling, he saw a polar bear. The bear was his father. It climbed into his skin boat. After it got in, the bear took its hood off. The young man saw it was his father. They traveled together. When they had passed Uivvaq, the young man said, "My mind: it makes me want to jump ashore." His mind kept telling him to jump. His father said nothing. Since his father made no answer, the young man jumped. When he landed he ran inland. He was running along when he saw a great bird. It was flying toward him. The young man turned and ran away. But the bird caught up with him and pushed him forward. The man was killed. But he wasn't dead for long. He got up and ran: he started running toward the sea. The bird pursued him. It pushed the man with his breast and he fell. After he'd been killed a second time, he got up quickly and ran for the skin boat. He hadn't gone far when he saw the polar bear approaching. The bear was his father. A third time the bird pushed him. The young man died and came alive. The polar bear reached him. He saw the bird. He reared up and snapped. He caught the bird's claw.

The bird dragged him along, but it couldn't fly off with him. The bear was being dragged along. The bird started rising. It seemed to be tiring; the son thought of ways that he could kill it. He found a long stick, but he couldn't find a place to strike the bird. So he went to the back to get at the anus. The young man pushed the stick up its anus. That's how he killed it. After he had killed the bird, the father said, "Come, let's take a wing. The shortest part, the forewing." They worked at it and finally broke off the forewing. When they had broken the wing the father said, "Let's try to put the wing in the skin boat. The wing will shelter us when it starts raining." They had a hard time getting the wing in. But when the rain came, the wing was their shelter.

They went a bit further. Then the son said again, "I want to jump onto land again." His father said nothing. Then he said, "If you jump, I may not be much help to you." But the son jumped ashore and started running. In front of him he saw a hill, and a gap along the front of the hill. The gap was wide enough to crawl into. The young man approached. But just as he got there, the hill fell on him and he was trapped. He was trapped by the hill. He knew what had happened. As he lay there, he saw a man approach. He was carrying a long-bladed knife. The man stopped and said, "This fellow must have been here some time in the hill trap."

He felt the body; it was frozen. The flesh didn't move when he pressed it with his finger. Now when the father had adopted him, he'd given him a rock charm; also the two giants' fingers. And now it was the rock charm that saved him. Next, the man with the knife took the body from the hill trap. But when he came out, the dead man was living. And the man laid his knife on the ground beside him. And the young man put it in the other's mind that he should walk away a little and leave his knife. He watched the knife man through his half-shut eyes. The man moved away. When he'd gone far enough, the young man jumped up. He ran for the knife. He killed the man who owned the hill trap.

The man thought, "What shall I do about the hill trap?" Then he saw a path. It led into the mountain. He decided to take it, to find out what there was in there. As he walked he saw a little girl and boy. They came toward him. "Father!" called the children. The man left the path. The children followed. When he'd drawn them a little way off the path, he killed the two children. Then he started to examine them. He looked at their genitals.

The boy's *usuk* [penis] was copper. The girl's *utchuk* [vagina] had teeth inside it. And the boy's copper penis had scratches all over it. This must have happened when they were playing: the brother and sister had fucked each other. When he had seen the children's bodies, the man returned to the path and followed it. He hadn't gone far when he saw an *iglu*. When he saw the *iglu* he approached it. A woman came out. As soon as she saw him she said, "Come in quick! Or we'll be caught by my husband. He'll soon be home!" The man still had the long knife with him. He'd killed the children with it. She went into the *iglu*. The man followed her. When they got inside, the woman said, "Quick, let's go to bed, or we'll be found out." She took out some skins and he watched while she took her clothes off. As the man watched he heard noises coming from her *utchuk*. The noise was the sound of teeth in her *utchuk*. The teeth were grinding. It came from the woman. She had teeth in her *utchuk*. The noise was the teeth as they ground one another. The man got ready to lie down with her. He still had his knife. He kept it by him. Now the young man got on top of the woman.

But instead of putting his *usuk* in her *utchuk*, the man thrust his knife in. The knife was in, and her *utchuk* teeth bit it. The man lost no time in getting away. But as he left the *iglu*, the edge of his parka caught in the passage. The two sides of the passage were moving in and out. He escaped from being squeezed to death. He escaped being crushed and went back to his father.

The two traveled on. They hadn't gone far when the young man said, "I want to jump. I want to jump toward the land." "*Ii*, yes. Go ahead and jump," his father said. "If I can help you, I will help you. If I can't help you, I won't help you." The young man jumped, and again took off running. After he had run some way, the man saw a pond. In the pond there was a walrus. He ran toward the pond. The walrus floated on the water surface. And a girl was sitting on the walrus's head. The girl was beautiful. The man ran toward her, he went for her immediately. But suddenly a polar bear appeared between the land and water. It took the walrus in its mouth, and went down in the water with the walrus. The bear killed the walrus which made that place dangerous. The pond had nothing in it now. Father and son returned to their skin boat.

They traveled along. The water in front of the skin boat stayed clear of ice. And the son said again, "I still want to jump. I want to jump toward the land." His father said, "Yes. If I can help you, I shall help you. If I can't help you, I won't help you."

The young man jumped and started to run. He was young. He liked running. He ran on the tundra. As he was running he came to a mouth. A human mouth stood on the tundra. The mouth was open, and when it inhaled, he had to run faster, he was drawn toward it. And the mouth was also singing. Every time the lips inhaled the man ran faster. When he got to the mouth, he was sucked inside it. But just as he entered, he grabbed hold of the lips. If he hadn't grabbed the lips he would have been swallowed. What was this mouth, now? It was a mosquito, a human mosquito, a singing mosquito. The young man got out; he wasn't trapped this time; he wasn't swallowed. He went back to the skin boat. They continued to travel.

They hadn't gone far, when the young man said, "I want to jump into the water." His father said, "Yes. It's all right to jump." The father said quickly, "I can help you in the water." The son jumped into the water. He got to the sea bed. When he landed, the son found a path.

The path led through the sea. He followed the path. Ahead of him he saw an *iglu*. The young man ran toward it till he reached the entrance. When he reached the entrance he decided to go in. He went into the *iglu*. Outside the *iglu* he had seen nothing, not even a meat rack. When he went into the *iglu* there was an old woman. The old woman said, "*Ii* . . . ye-e-s! Here's some food come my way! Just when I was hungry! Here's some food come my way!" As the young man stood there, a falcon flew past him. The peregrine falcon was his protector. As the man stood and watched, the woman caught the peregrine. He grasped its neck and strangled it. Then she wiped the oil lamp with it. The lamp was sooty. She used its body to wipe the oil lamp. As the peregrine was flying, the young man noticed it had no feet. Once, in the past, when his father met a killer, he'd looked down through some whale jaws in the *katak*, and seen hawk's feet, not his, at the bottom. That's how the falcon had lost its feet. As the man and the woman looked at each other, the polar bear came in. The bear bit the old woman and picked her up. He carried her outside the *iglu*. His son had found a jellyfish *iglu*. The old woman was a jellyfish. This time the young man would have perished, but his father saved him. That was the last time he met anything, inland or on water. They went on in their skin boat going north. And though it was winter, the prow moved freely through the water.

Now they met some people at some breathing holes. When he saw them, the father got out. He swam from hole to hole and came up through each, and killed all the hunters.

He killed many that way. He killed the women too. The people at home in their *iglus* he also killed. He killed the whole village. He left only a couple; he spared one man and woman. They left that place when they'd killed all the people. They traveled on and came to a river mouth. There were people on both banks. They were little people. Now earlier when they'd gone past Uivvaq (Cape Lisburne), they had found a walrus, and taken the ivory. And while they'd traveled, the father carved the ivory. He had made little figures, he'd made images of men from one tusk. These he stood upright on the other walrus tusk. Now when they reached the place where the little people lived, he took out his carvings, his images of people. And in the boat he had his bird's wing. He took the wing and knocked the figures over. And when he did this, the people on the riverbanks fell over. The father watched. Then he took the wing and stood the figures up again. He said, "Stand up!" And when the images stood up, the little people on the bank stood up. Then as they watched them, the little people fled inland.

Neither father nor son knew what kind of people these were. After they had met the little people, they went on. They continued to travel and saw nothing unusual. They were still in their skin boat. They continued north, and the prow was always clear of sea ice. As they traveled they saw a gull on the water. It was a giant seagull, and it picked them up and swallowed them. They were swallowed by a seagull. They continued north inside the seagull. As they went along, they noticed they were sliding down inside the seagull. And when the gull shat, they were free again. Their hair had fallen out because they'd been in the seagull's stomach. Then the weather got rough and they drifted to a little island. There was nothing on the island they could live on. No wood, no animals. They suffered greatly. After some time the father said, "We can't stay here. We'll go back to Tikiġaq. Put your arms round my neck and I'll dive into the water." And his father told him, "When you're out of breath, squeeze my neck." The polar bear dived and the son held his breath. When he couldn't stand it any longer, he squeezed his neck. He was riding on the bear's back. When he needed to breathe, he tightened his grip and they surfaced. Then they dived again and came up near Tikiġaq, at Aqalulik River. There are two small lakes here, a little way inland. It was by one of these lakes that the two of them surfaced. They dived no more. They didn't dive, in case they lost their way. This is where they stayed, and when it was winter they went to Tikiġaq. Now in their absence, the Tikiġaq people had prepared something for them.

They knew they must watch carefully when they got to Tikiġaq. They knew the people would want to kill them. So before they reached home, they got ready for anything that might happen. And the Tikiġaq people made a set of *niulut* (wooden figurines).

They made of a set of *niulut*, in two sets of six. They'd use them next autumn on the young sea ice. The *niulut* would stand in two rows. Someone would be chosen. He'd throw the *niulut* into open water saying, "When someone walks between the two rows, let the *niulut* close in on him!"

So the *niulut* were thrown in the water. Now when winter was approaching and the weather was fair, the son went down to hunt seals on the sea ice. And while he was out there, he saw twelve people. They were standing upright, in two rows of six. The young man thought they were watching for seals. The twelve hunters faced each other. When the man saw them, he walked through their middle. But they were not men. The figures were *niulut*. And the *niulut* fell inwards on him. Now his father had grown old. He could hunt no longer. They killed his son.

Asatchaq concluded, "Old people said when I was younger, 'Be careful of figures standing on the sea ice. For those *niulut* were thrown into the sea at Tikiġaq. The *niulut* are there still. When a man walks through a line of *niulut*, the images collapse on him, and he's buried beneath them.' *Tavra.*" [That's all.]

Introduction
The Story of the King Island Wolf Dance

Told Lucy Tanaqiq Koyuk and Earl Aisana Mayac

Transcribed by Deanna Paniataaq Kingston

In 1982 and again in 1991, the King Island Iñupiaq Eskimo community revived the Wolf Dance. They had not performed the Wolf Dance in its entirety since 1930. I (Kingston) became intrigued with the Wolf Dance (both performance and story) when Marie Aakauraq Saclamana and Auntie Margaret Iiŋaq Penatac told me that the Wolf Dance was dangerous because one of the Wolf Dancers died. I became even more interested when a friend (Karen Brewster) found the version told by my great-grandfather, Aġnazuŋaaq (my mother's mother's father), to Knud Rasmussen in 1924 (Rasmussen 1932:17–33; 1952:255–260). This chapter includes my great-grandfather's story, followed by two versions recorded from Lucy Tanaqiq Koyuk and Earl Aisana Mayac during my dissertation fieldwork in 1997 (Kingston 1999).

Knud Rasmussen's work among the Eskimoan (Inuit) peoples is generally regarded as accurate and reliable, since Rasmussen was part Greenlandic and could speak the Inuit language. Burch claims that Rasmussen's greatest contribution to Alaskan Eskimo ethnography is in folklore (Burch 1988:151). He also believes that we should regard Rasmussen's work as the "most authoritative" (Burch 1988:153) on the subject. I assume, then, because of Rasmussen's fluency in Inuit, that Aġnazuŋaaq told the story in Iñupiaq to Rasmussen. I do not know whether Rasmussen then wrote it down in Iñupiaq, Danish, or English. However, the stories first appeared in a Danish publication in 1929 (Rasmussen 1929) and then in English in 1932 (Rasmussen 1932).

In contrast, both Koyuk and Mayac told me the story in English because I know only a little bit of Iñupiaq. The two storytellers, Koyuk [Quyuk] and Mayac [Maayaq], are bilingual in English and in Iñupiaq. Thus, when they told the story in English to me, they gave their English translations of what they were thinking in Iñupiaq. In addition, both told me the Wolf Dance story while I was sitting in their kitchen after a meal or tea. Both told me the story in response to the questions, "What do you know about the Wolf Dance? Do you know the story?" I assumed they were familiar with the subject because Mayac was a Wolf Dancer in the 1982 performance and the box drummer in 1991 and Koyuk performed as Mayac's partner in the 1982 performance. When answering my questions, both made a point of telling me from whom they heard the story. Koyuk learned it from her aunt (who was my mother's mother) and Mayac learned it from his father. This practice of reporting from whom they heard the story is common to Yup'ik, Iñupiaq and Inuit storytellers and stems from the cultural value they place in not claiming to have more expertise than others. As Mather (1995:17) points out, the stories do not belong to individual people, "It is not their story. It was passed on to them. They claim no authority about what they will tell you."

In addition, I vividly remember that Koyuk incorporated me into her telling, saying, "I was only fourteen years old when your grandma-to-be told me this." My "grandma-to-be" is Koyuk's mother's sister. It's interesting that Koyuk referred to the aunt as my "grandma-to-be". At the point when she first heard the story, I was not even born, so Koyuk projected a future state onto the person who told her the story, her aunt and my future grandmother. I have not seen this before in English translations of the oral literature of the north. However, I suspect that this foreshadowing of future states of people mentioned in the stories is due to the grammatical structure of the language, which has postbases and other endings that make the language very precise and detailed.

As is often the case, particular dances and rituals are linked to certain myths and legends. Interestingly, both Koyuk's and Mayac's tellings are blends of the story itself and how and why the Wolf Dance is performed. Both, for instance, mention that the dance is hard, that it is "not a play thing to do" in between telling elements of the story. They do not separate the story from their own participation in Wolf Dance performances. In other words, performing the Wolf Dance and the story of the Wolf Dance are so intertwined that they cannot be separated from each other. In contrast, Rasmussen includes not only the story as paraphrased here, but also a separate description of a Messenger Feast that Aġnazuŋaaq participated in (Rasmussen 1932:39–55). Based upon my experience with Koyuk and Mayac, I suspect that Aġnazuŋaaq also blended the story with a description of an actual Messenger Feast/Wolf

Dance, although we will never know for certain. Rasmussen's recording of Aġnazuŋaaq's story also does not include an acknowledgment of the person who taught him the story. This again shows that Rasmussen probably edited Aġnazungaaq's account for publication.

A major difference between Koyuk's and Mayac's versions is that Mayac also makes the point of stating that the King Islanders learned the Wolf Dance from the people of Kawerak, which corroborates Oquilluk's [Ukalliq] claim (he was from Kawerak) that it was his people who started the Wolf Dance (cf. Kakaruk and Oquilluk 1964; Oquilluk 1973).

Although Rasmussen represented the story in prose form in both the 1932 and 1952 versions, I chose to paraphrase Aġnazuŋaaq's version of the story below into stanzas and breaks. I did not make the stanzas and breaks arbitrarily; rather, in reading the story to myself, I made a line break wherever I paused and I created a new stanza after a longer pause or with a break in topic. For Koyuk and Mayac's story, I try to represent the shorter (line break) and longer (new stanza) pauses that they gave when telling the story to me in 1997. I also try to give a few other performance cues, such as when Mayac twirled his finger around in circles, in order to give readers a taste of the telling of the story. Finally, I created parenthetical statements for some phrases in which the tellers gave additional information not directly related to the story. Phrases contained in brackets are information I added for clarification.

In closing, I want to thank the following people who made this article possible: first, the storytellers, Lucy Tanaqiq Koyuk and Earl Aisana Mayac, who shared this story with me. Not only did they tell me the story, but they also shared food with me, which was greatly appreciated at the time. I also thank the King Island Native Community and the King Island Native Corporation, organizations that gave permission for me to pursue the Wolf Dance research and who helped me financially while I was in Nome. There are also many others in the community too numerous to name that helped me: I want you to know that I thank you as well. Finally, I thank the National Park Service for supporting this Wolf Dance research. As the King Islanders say, *Iliġanamik*!

—Deanna Paniataaq Kingston

The Story of the King Island Wolf Dance

Told by Lucy Tanaqiq Koyuk of Nome and Earl Aisana Mayac of Nome

Aġnazungaaq's version, 1924, paraphrased

A hunter from Kawerak was out hunting, when an enormous eagle started
circling over him.

He killed the giant eagle with three arrows.

He dried the skin skillfully and it became his amulet.

He put offerings of meat into its claws.

He became an even better hunter.

Some time later, when he was out hunting,

he met two strange men who had fox noses on their hoods.

The two fox-men told him they were going to take him to a strange land.

So, they made him close his eyes and they went swiftly through the air.

When they landed,

they walked further inland

until the hunter could hear a loud knocking sound.

The fox-men said the sound was the heartbeat of the mother of the eagle
that he killed.

When he arrived, he was feasted outside the house.

Then, when he went into the house of the eagle mother.

The eagle mother thanked him for taking care of her son.

The eagle mother told him that he must hold a great feast and dance for her
son's skin, including messengers and exchanging wishes.

Since he didn't know how to do this, the eagle mother taught him how to sing
and dance and how to feast.

The hunter promised to hold such a feast when he got home.

He was given two caribou heart-sacks as a parting gift.

One was filled with the corners of caribou ears;

one was filled with the corners of wolverine and wolf ears.
The eagle mother told him not to lay the heart-sacks on the ground.

The fox-men took him back near his home.
He was tired and when he came to a river,
he stopped to rest.
A steep slope in front of him was full of small round holes.
A large flock of swallows flew up and down the river.
Suddenly, they went into the holes!!
A moment later, the heads of wolves peered out.
He watched this vision with wonder.

Then, he started to leave, but he discovered that he dropped his gifts on the
    ground in his amazement.
Because of this, the heart-sacks had become so heavy that he could not lift
    them.
They were full of meat and the skins of caribou, wolves, and wolverines.
He would have to leave them where they were and go home,
where he would ask young men of the village to get them.

After that, he went back to his village.
He started to make preparations for a feast and he and three other men sent
    out messengers.
To imitate the eagle mother's heart, he made a four-sided wooden box drum.
He also decided to represent the swallows and the wolves that he saw on his
    way home,
so he built a bluff of planks and bored holes into them.

The swallows were represented by ornamenting the dancers with feathers.
During the dancing, the dancers will slip into the holes and come out as
    wolves.
He finished the preparations and went out hunting.
He shot an arrow at a caribou but his arrow flew high.
When he went to look for the animal, he discovered that he had shot his own
    sacred messenger.
He became sad and confused.
He did not want anyone to find out what had happened, and he decided that
    the feast could not be canceled,[1]

so he took the body home and dried it.

All but one of the messengers returned and guests started arriving.

The feast was held and when all was gathered within the community house, the hunter brought in the dried body of the inviter.

The people were alarmed but the hunter said nothing.

Songs and dances were performed, but without enthusiasm because of the presence of the corpse.

The songs were sung hurriedly and the dancing was confused.

The first dance came to an end.

When it was over, the three comrades of the dead man decided to kill the hunter, but the hunter killed them before they could kill him. The story ends with the statement that

"Merrymaking and war succeeded each other.

It could not be otherwise.

Merrymaking and gaiety warm the mind;

it is but a step from wild exuberance to rash behavior.

But it is probably better so for humanity.

For who would exchange the joy of festivity for the intolerable monotony which made life so empty before the eagle's gift" (Rasmussen 1932:17–33; 1952:255–59).

Lucy Tanaqiq Koyuk's version, 1997, Nome, Alaska

Tiulana told us he wants to try the Wolf Dance.
In the old hall, while the old folks are still alive.

Some of us were looking at it,
Listening to it.
Ellanna, Koyuk, Pikonganna.

We start to practice.
Tiulana wants to do that.
King Islanders try to do it like they used to do before.
Practicing it from fall time until February.
We practiced it.

A lot of work.

A lot of work.
Ellanna says we're going to work.
A lot of work.

We were told how to do it.
We listened to the song, to the drum.
Stand up, sit down, whatever.

If they [dancers] have a husband,
they have to be a husband.[2]

There are only four holes.
That person got a wife.
She dance above him.

Five of us after all.
Frances and Gabe [Muktoyuk];
Marie and Mike [Saclamana];
Clara and Paul [Tiulana];
Me and Earl [Mayac];
And, Edna and Francis Alvanna.
Then, there's four guys that hold the curtains.
They put them up.
They put them down.
Henry Koyuk,
John Pullock,
Paul Omiak,
John Penatac.

When they get ready to come out of the hole,
the wolf;
Anili una—from the hole, he has to get out.

Tiulana,
he tells the younger ones.

Your grandma used to tell me,
when she first see [the Wolf Dance],
she was really scared.

Really scared.

She start to cry.
They stop her.
Everyone is supposed to be quiet.

She was really scared when she saw that wolf face when she was small.
Scary!

When they try to get ready [to hold a Wolf Dance], it happened.
They were hunting, long ago that time.
(Even Qawiaraġmiut [people from Kawerak] did Wolf Dance long ago.
I think they [Kawerak people] must be around here.)
Hunting, they [two men] were hunting on either side of a hill.
One man shoot *tuttu* [caribou] under their legs.
He hit the other man on the other side.

It took a long time because one person always dies.
That's what they tell me.
My aunt,
I hear her tell that story.

They try to get ready for the Wolf Dance.
[For the] Polar Bear Dance, they gave more things.
That hunter, hunting for a big bird for its feathers.
Their [the eagles'] son, that guy hit it and it died.
That father [of the dead eagle] took him far away.
He bring him in to his wife there, that big bird.
She said,
"Listen to my heart. We've been crying for the son that you killed.
We want you to *aġġi* [Eskimo dance].

He listen to those eagles.
The father took him back, flying around.
After that, he try to make all the preparations:
to make a drum,
but nothing sounds like her [the mother's] heart.
(He find a walrus stomach—
you got to split it—

blow it first, then make it tight and split it.

That's how you make a drum.

Very hard work, those Eskimos.)

So, they make a dance for the other drum [*kalukaq* or box drum].

That's the start of the drum—

before they can dance, you make the drum first.

That started the dancing.

So, they used these eagle feathers for those headdresses.

And, when they hold a Wolf Dance,

they hold the wands—one each with their hands.

It started since that time.

It happen that way.

Those dancers try to be like a wolf.

They use the head of a wolf.

From sitting, they try to go out.

I was only fourteen years old when your grandma-to-be told me this,

"They don't do it all the time.

Only once in awhile they do it.

Only once in awhile are they willing to do it."

Aqpataksraq—partner-to-be.

That guy has to be a partner to do the Wolf Dance.

Partners then get ready for the Wolf Dance.

Those partners like to be on the Wolf Dance,

to be Wolf Dancers,

to go into that hole.

My auntie used to say that those two guys used to be like this [crossing her
   fingers in the gesture that signifies that the men had a close relationship].

They had to be close, to be like a wolf.

That's why they don't do it right away [often].

They're partners-to-be on the Wolf Dance.

One of them dies.

He kills his partner-to-be when they do it.

I think the [Wolf] Dance is hard for them.

They didn't do it when I was growing up.

Earl Aisana Mayac's version, 1997, Nome, Alaska

Our grandfathers said it came from Kawerak.
We had to do it right.
No mistakes!
Leona's grandma said,
"That dance is no play thing to do."
It's a real dance.
It came from the eagles.

A hunter was hunting caribou by the Sawtooth Mountains, Kiglawiit.
He was hunting there.
A big eagle try to grab him and
he shot it with a bow and arrow in the stomach.

So many years later, the brother of the eagle took the hunter,
up, up there into space.
They go swirl up in a circle, five times [gesturing upward in a spiral].
The earth was this big [like a tennis ball].
Somewhere up in the stars.

Pretty soon, they hear, "Boom,
Boom,
Boom."
The eagle tell the man,
"That's my mother's heart.
She got hurt when you kill my brother.
When I take you back home, try to find wood that is like my mother's heart."

He tried everything, wood is the closest sound.
So, he made a drum out of it.
They practice [the dance] and his messenger went away [to invite another
     village to the dance].

They didn't know it was him.
The hunter snuck up on a caribou.
On the other side, his messenger was also sneaking up on the caribou.
And, they didn't see each other.
the other man shot at the caribou.

The arrow goes right through that caribou
and he kills that other man.

Even though he's dead, they perform that dance.
They had to perform it right.

My father tell me that story.
They never really tell that story very much, though.

King Island and Kawerak are good friends,
what they call trading partners.
Good partners.
They had a good relationship,
visit each other.

When someone try to make war with Kawerak,
King Islanders help them.

When some villagers want to make war with King Islanders,
Kawerak help them.

Kawerak people go to King Island and live there.
They [the King Islanders] probably do the Wolf Dance with Kawerak.

They only do the Wolf Dance once in awhile.
It's not a play thing to do.
Yeah, after that hunter kill that messenger,
messengers always die after that,
by sickness or accident.

I was a messenger.
I didn't die.
Tiulana let me be a messenger when they did it in Nome.
When Ellanna was still alive.
I was the only messenger.
Long ago,
it might've been different.
They call it *aqpataq* when you're the messenger.

Mayac [Earl's father] was a messenger,
along with Ellanna [a long time ago].

Introduction
King Island Inupiaq Stories

Told by Frank Ellanna

Transcribed and translated by

Bernadette Alvanna-Stimpfle and Lawrence D. Kaplan

Bernadette Yaayuk Alvanna-Stimpfle recorded the following stories on tape when she was a student at the University of Alaska Fairbanks in 1974. Working with Edna MacLean and Lawrence Kaplan, she learned Inupiaq writing and grammar. On a visit to Nome, she taped several stories by Frank Ellanna, a King Island elder who was respected for his knowledge of his people's culture and history. He was an active member of the King Island Dancers and a major contributor of stories and oral history to *Ugiuvangmiut Quliapyuit / King Island Tales.* The stories were transcribed and translated by Bernadette Alvanna-Stimpfle and Lawrence Kaplan.

King Island is located southeast of Bering Strait. It is about 2½ miles long by one mile wide. It is steep and rocky, with the village found on a rock slide along a stream called *Kuuk,* which is the primary source of water. The King Islanders are known for their rugged lifestyle, which depended on hunting of marine mammals and gathering of eggs and edible plants, as well as for their village perched on a steep slope, made up of houses supported by stilts. Their songs and Iñupiaq dancing are highly regarded in Alaska, and the King Islanders have performed nationally and even abroad. By the mid-1960s the King Islanders had all moved to the mainland and occupation of the island was limited to seasonal subsistence hunting and food gathering.

King Island Inupiaq is a distinct variety of the Bering Strait dialect, which differs significantly from North Alaskan dialects such as Minnie Gray's Kobuk Iñupiaq. The stories presented here are of different types: "The Oldsquaw and Her Ducklings" is found in different versions among a number of Inupiaq groups and is typical of stories that personify animals. "My Great Grandmother the Shaman" is a short piece of oral history demonstrating the power of shamans. When Ellanna talks about "up above" and "down below," it is a direct reference to locations within King Island village on its very steep slope. "The Little Girl Who Was Stolen" contains an exchange of formulaic expressions between the bear and the brothers, perhaps a sort of magical language.

—LDK

Iilan Amauga Aŋatkuq

Told by Frank Ellanna of King Island and Nome

UAŊA UNIPKAAQTUAŊA. IILANA UGIUVAŊMIU.

Uumaguuq, amauga, aanaŋma aakaaga, aŋatkuq. Qagrimi ittuaq, Attaaġmiuni, atiqa.tuamik Attaaġmiumik. Unnuami taimana aġnaq kanna itiqtuq. Itiq'ami piaa uini samna naŋitpalaŋniblugu sayaaqtuġaqublugu. Ugunaŋa uvvaa agilatuġaa. (Attausataagit agilatuqtaaganik piraġigait aŋatkut.)

Agilatuġaa iwalunik, iwaluluatanik. Iwalut taapkua nannimi, nanipiam, inupiaqtam nannim ataanun sanianun iligait. Malikłuu 'aa atqa.tuk taganuŋa. Uvvaa uyaġagvaum ataanun itiqtuk. Aŋun una naŋitpaktuq, atnanaqpaktuq, aŋuviaqsimaruaq imma, tuiġam aŋuviaqsimakaaga. Tavra taamna aŋuviaq piiġaa.

Taatnami tamauŋa qagrimun nayuqtaaminun. Siniktuq. (Uŋasigvaktuaguŋilaq, uaŋa aanaŋma aakaigaa.) Sinikłuni tuvak'ami iqqatuq, "Akkaa samma unnuaġnin agilatuusiatka." Nannimin ataanin tavraŋa izakait. Sagriit taapkua. Iwaluugaluaqturuuq tavra unnuaġnin qaitqaaqmiat sagriuqsimaruruuq. Nuŋuruq.

My Great-Grandmother, the Shaman

IT IS I, TELLING A STORY, ELLANNA, THE KING ISLANDER.

My great-grandmother, my grandmother's mother, was a shaman. She was in a *qagri* [community house], which was called *Attaaġmiut.* One night, a woman came in there [through the doorway in the floor]. When she entered, she said that her husband was in great pain and asked that the shaman help him. From her house down lower in the village, she would get something as payment. (*Attausataat* is what the shamans called the payment for their services.)

The woman paid her with sinew, with good sinew. Those pieces of sinew she placed under and alongside the Iñupiaq lamp, the old-style stone lamp. She went along with the woman, down to another house in the village. They entered a place under a large rock. There was a man suffering and in great pain. He had a lance in him, someone had speared him with a lance. She [my great-grandmother] removed the lance.

She went back to the *qagri* where she lived. She slept. (It wasn't far away... she was my grandmother's mother.) She slept and then woke up. She remembered, "Oh! Those things I was paid with last night are down below there." She reached and got them from underneath the stone lamp. They had turned into grass. The sinew she had been given the night before had turned into grass. That is the end of the story.

Niaqsaaġruk Tigliktaq

Told by Frank Ellanna of King Island and Nome

Niaqsaaġruuraġuuq una aniiqtuaq. Akłaġruuramguuq uuma tig-ligaa. Tigligmani, tamma.tuq imna niaqsaaġruk. Tigliglugu tamma.titkaa niaqsaaġruk. Iwaġaat ilainaq, paġisuitkaat nanitaima.

Tavra uguak iligaaġruuraak aŋayuuraagik aniiqtuak. Akłunaamik uuma naviqłuu aniiqtigaa silatimini niaqsaaġruuraq akłam.

Tavra uuma aŋayuuŋni natkiigaik. Natkiaŋamigik atuutiyaik taunuŋa, "Yuuwutkuu, yuuwutkuu. Aipaaga panalik. Aipaaga pitiksiaŋaulauranik pan-aliik." Akłaġruuram aviġiaa, "Tutiiŋ, tutiiŋ, tutiiŋ, sunatani piliuġataqpiuŋ?" Kiuġmaa niaqsaaġruuram, "Utkuaŋa quvanuaŋa, puyuqtuk, puyuqtuk." Atuusraigaik aŋayuuŋni, "Yuuwutkuu, yuuwutkuu. Aipaaga panalik, aipaaga pitiksiaŋaulauranik panaliik."

"Tutiiŋ, tutiiŋ, tutiiŋ, sunatani piliuġataqpiuŋ?" "Utkuaŋa quvanuaŋa, puyuqtuk, puyuqtuk." Natkiiruk uvvaa iligaaġruuraak nayaktik natkiigaak.

Utiqłutik aŋutit quliutiait samma nalaunivlugu nugaqtik. Immaguuq uviłuu. Akłaq taamna tuġuapagaat. Nuŋuruq.

The Little Girl Who Was Stolen

A LITTLE GIRL, IT IS TOLD, was playing outside. A bad brown bear stole her. When he stole her, the girl became lost. He stole her, and she was lost, that girl. They searched for her in vain but could not find her anywhere.

Then one time, two boys, her two older brothers, were playing outside. The bear tied her up outside where he lived. Then she spotted her brothers. When she saw them, she sang out, "yuuwutkuu, yuuwutkuu, one with a spear point, the other with a little drill bow and arrow!"

The brown bear asked her, "Grandchild, grandchild, grandchild, what are you saying again?" The little girl answered, "The ones down by the shore, the snow geese, are smoking, are steaming." And she kept on singing to her brothers, "Yuuwutkuu, yuuwutkuu, one with a spear point, the other with a little drill bow and arrow!"

(And the bear said), "Grandchild, grandchild, grandchild, what are you saying again?" (The little girl answered), "The ones down by the shore, the snow geese, are smoking, are steaming." Those two boys saw their little sister, they spotted her.

The two returned home and told the men that they found their little sister. Then they went to kill that brown bear. That's the end of the story.

Aa'aaŋilu Piayaaŋilu

Told by Frank Ellanna of King Island and Nome

AA'AAŊIURARUUQ TAAPKUA, aakait piayaaqa.tuaq una aa'aaŋiuraq, navrami ugiaksrautiait. Ugiaksraa taimana. Ayaguliqtut. Uvvaa ugua qituġnait miksruuraupmiut.

Uvvaa ayaguliq'ami qayaqtuutialuaqłuit navrami, akpituq aakaagat, "Miminaahaaŋaa, miminaahaaŋaa, ayayuuqsi, yayayuuqsi tapqaq manna, Ugiuvak qiniqhapku. Tapqaq manna, Ugiuvak qiniqhapku. Aa sauyuġyuq, nasipkuu sauyuġyuq ayaasalauqhii kasitaa ŋiq, ŋiq, ŋiq, ŋiq." Agluaġa.tut. Satamuuna iglatut.

Iglialuaqłutik aviqsruait, "Ipyaŋulavisii?" ipyaŋuliami kiziani. Nugaqłiuraat taamna ipyaŋulaman puira.tut ałłagun navragun. Nuna atautqataqłuu.

Tavrani ipyaŋuiqsiuraġaaqłuit akpitaqtut, "Miminaahaaŋaa, miminaahaaŋaa, ayayuuqsi, yayayuuqsi tapqaq manna, Ugiuvak qiniqhapku. Tapqaq manna Ugiuvak qiniqhapku. Aa sauyuġyuq, nasipkuu sauyuġyuq ayaasalauqhii kasitaa ŋiq, ŋiq, ŋiq, ŋiq." Agluaġa.tut.

Taimanaguuq tavra iliuqłutik ałłagun navragun puirainalutit. Kiitaimaguuq ununa imaanun pitaġa.tut. Imma ayaguŋnaqtut. Nuŋuruq.

The Oldsquaw and Her Ducklings

THERE WAS A FAMILY OF OLDSQUAW DUCKS, a mother with young, and they all spent the fall in a lake. They stayed there through the early fall. They made ready to go on a journey, but her young ones were still very small.

When the mother oldsquaw was all ready to leave, she floated her young around like a kayak in the lake and then began to sing, "Miminaahaaŋaa, miminaahaaŋaa, ayayuuqsi, yayayuuqsi, when I see the shoreline of King Island, when I see King Island's shore...." And then they dived and swam down under the water.

After they had traveled for a while, their mother asked them, "Are you out of breath?" when she herself was short of breath. When the youngest one had gotten out of breath, they all surfaced in another lake. They had traveled underground.

Then, when they had caught their breath again, they all began to sing, "Miminaahaaŋaa, miminaahaaŋaa, ayayuuqsi, yayayuuqsi, when I see the shoreline of King Island, when I see King Island's shore...." And then they would dive again.

They continued on like that and surfaced again in another lake, until finally, they reached the ocean. They must have traveled a long way. That is the end of the story.

Introduction
An Unwritten Law of the Sea

By Herbert O. Anungazuk

In his work for the National Park Service, Herbert Anungazuk has provided invaluable assistance to anthropologists and other researchers working in and around the Bering Land Bridge National Preserve, an area which is a remnant of the ancient land connection between North America and Asia. Anungazuk's native village of Wales sits on the westernmost point of the North American continent at Cape Prince of Wales, on the shores of Bering Strait across from the Diomede Islands and East Cape, Siberia in Asia. A fluent speaker of the Inupiaq language, Anungazuk's writings and talks often present his Inupiaq culture. The essay that appears here, "An Unwritten Law of the Sea," delves deeply into essential aspects of life and worldview that distinguish the Inupiat, particularly from non-Native peoples. The text begins with the relationship between all people and the earth, which sustains and nourishes them. Clearly, this relationship differs from one group to another, and Anungazuk points out how special the relationship is in the case of hunters and gatherers like the Inupiat, who depend on animals and must treat their prey with respect in order to achieve success in hunting. He tells us how traditions essential to physical and cultural survival are passed on by Inupiaq elders, and how this fundamental role makes elders the primary storytellers and pillars of the society. Unfortunately, Inupiaq beliefs and ceremonies have not been well understood by Western people, who often disparage them, failing to recognize concepts that have long since disappeared from agriculture-based and urban societies. Anungazuk tells us that these traditions are not lost or discarded but have gone underground, because culture does not go away easily, particularly where the underpinnings of an entire people are concerned. In the essay, some words and names are spelled in the standard Inupiaq orthography, some in the author's own system, and others in the author's spelling, followed by standard orthography in brackets, e.g., *aqlu* [*aaġlu*].

—LDK

An Unwritten Law of the Sea

By Herbert O. Anungazuk of Wales and Anchorage

WE HAVE AN ALLIANCE WITH THE EARTH. Each one of us does, and some of us as a people have continued to grasp this alliance and have anchored it into our hearts, our minds, and our souls. We have an alliance with the mammals, birds, and fish because through them we have gained a lasting balance as their flesh provides the nutrients which have, since dawn immemorial, continued to nourish our bodies. From this alliance our being probes into the world of our prey and learns their ways so we can increase our chances for a successful harvest. The implements used by our ancestors that continue to be found in ancient house pits commemorate the mammals, birds, and fish that provide for our survival. The jawbones of the mighty whale, skulls of the polar bear, and skin boats or kayaks adorn the graves of noble hunters. In my society, even in death a hunter lies according to his stature while he was among the living: his grave and those of his family lie high upon the mountain. His status as an *umialik* grants him the privilege of lying in state above many others on the mountain, and in time, the remains become naturally absorbed by the earth.

The lifeways of a people cover an entire spectrum, a spectrum so wide and profound that it continues to astound the Western mind as non-Inupiat learn more about us. Indigenous people are certainly a profound people but we too are astounded as we learn more about what was related to us by our elders. The flame of wonder about our culture and heritage may have been lit long, long ago by the story of an elder, but the flame may not mature with each one of us until decades later. You must share what you have heard, what you have learned. Sharing is how the people have endured up to this very day. You must never become obsessive because it is our way to share. It is known that if you do not share your harvest with others, you will meet with ill fortune in your effort to continue as a provider for your family and the community. No hunter would ever want to fall victim to that prophecy. Sharing knowledge with others has been the way of the people, because through knowledge we survive.

Our land is not only known as Wales, Alaska. It is a place of a multitude of names. Place names are a part of the voice of the land. Place names take us into our own geographical world, since the names relate directly to the land. The names show our union, our total existence, and our uniform standing with our universe. The names ring out: Ugalaturuaq, the place of many Arctic hares; Mapsaturuaq, an area of extreme danger where the land is prone to avalanches in the winter; Izraqit, a rocky slope resembling diced foods prepared for the table. The language of the Kingikmiut [Kiŋikmiut] has been reverberating over the land through countless ages. Although the language may have been temporarily silenced from the land when the people left ages ago for unknown reasons, the language returned with us when we found that our new land could not support our need for sea mammal oil. One voice may be just a whisper, but to speak the language shows an act of respect for the land because from the land came the language. When Kingigin [Kiŋigin] was first settled is no longer in the memory of the oldest elders. Whether occupation of our land occurred as stated in a context not of the people, one can only assume when the greatest event of my people's history took place, that of the settlement of our community, Kingigin. We are certain that we have long been on the land despite the fact that we moved away from Kingigin on one occasion. From that point forward, the people came to call themselves Kingikmiut, because we are "people of Kingigin."

The ways and methods of teaching by the elders are similar in indigenous societies. One elder will not know everything about the culture, but he will know many different elements. Our way of life revolves in a continual circle that, in turn, revolves around the spectrum of reality. Even the mere task of gathering wood is a part of the intricate realities of survival because from wood come many things. Special types of wood are used to make the shaft of a harpoon, or the frame of an *umiaq*, or in making a drum. Most of our elders are authorities in several categories of knowledge specific to the culture, be it knowledge of species of wildlife, geography within its natural realm, or diplomacy between people. These things are learned and are among the many elements that fulfill the completeness of a culture or society. The creatures of the land and sea are teachers also, but you need to catch them while they are teaching. If the elders are uncertain about any information that is asked of them, they are very quick to relay your question to someone else. No one is ever denied an answer.

The elders are very forthright in offering help because it is their duty to pass on to the new generations what they learned from the elders before them. Both man and woman are entrusted to teach and they teach in the same way as the persons who taught them. There is only one way, but there can be alternatives in very rare instances. We have never stated to one another to stay away from the old ones, but we have been thrust into a new age. The new generations with a wish to learn are drawn to the elder. Other societies are now seeing the importance of the elder, because the elder, for generation after ancient generation, has always been in the forefront of our quest to survive. The elders are and always have been the pillar of our society. To hear the words of wisdom of the elder, their vision and encouragement is a loud voice even though it is expressed in quiet tones.

It is rare for a hunter to call an animal an animal. To us they are our prey, and each and every one of them has a name. In our belief, each one of them has a spirit regardless of how other societies have arranged them in classes. Some of the creatures of the sea have been gifted with multiple names because of their importance to us as a source of survival. A whale is a whale until you identify the species. A walrus is a walrus until it too identifies itself in terms of where the Iñupiat have placed this mammal within their society. For example, a bull walrus is a *nugaaġruk*, which quite literally, in a fond way, can mean your younger sibling. Multiple definitions of words do occur. An *izavgalik* is a mother with calf, while she can be identified as an *aġnazaluq*. *Aġnazaluq*, or *aġnaq*, meaning female or woman, can be applied to any species: man, mammal, bird, or fish. The walrus, like the whale, is a mammal of many uses. The skin is used to cover the *umiaq* that ply the waters in search of the mammals that provide our livelihood. The inner membrane of the stomach covers the drum whose sound reverberates over the land in ceremony, ritual, and song. The bones can be made into a variety of tools that are useful in the everyday lives of the Iñupiat. Where do the whale, walrus, and seal spend their winters? There can be so many of them that you wonder why others who travel the same waters and who have the potential of winter encounters say so little about them. The Iñupiat know when the mammals, birds, and fish return, yet they can only assume where the animals go in winter.

When others come to the elders, they say, "I know where the animals are, I know when the animals will come to me." We know, for we have been anticipating the return of the sea mammal since the dawn of time. This thought continues in the hearts and minds of the new generations of hunters, because the glories of a successful harvest rest in every hunter. In this new age, the young continue to learn and to fulfill their duties as hunters, but the winds of change have taken over.

Hunters are maritime people. We are Imaaġmiut, people of the sea; we are Taġiuġmiut, people of the salt water. We are Tapqaamiut, coastal people, because the sea is our doorstep to survival. The sea sustains us, yet the sea can claim us if we do not heed its warning, since the sea has a character all her own. We have a strong relationship with the sea that goes beyond what other societies can understand. We live in a world where we need to know what we are doing. In our world, every second of every day, a whale, a walrus, a seal comes up from the depths and takes a breath of the very air that fills our lungs. Although we do not share the same watery existence, we share the same environment with the life that is found on the land and in the sea. Our sea is the most productive part of the earth and that is why many of the villages in Alaska are situated on or near the coast. The sea supports an entire people. Very few of the life-forms of the sea are not eaten. Although most forms are edible, you cannot be sustained nutritionally for indefinite periods because your body needs a variety of nutrients to survive. Our fate is set if we have only one form of food to sustain our bodies. Meat, leaves, berries, and undersea life forms create a balance as they have since the first dawn. The seasons decide what will be placed upon the table.

The stories of our ancient past are very complex. Stories are immeasurable wealth to any people. Some stories require intense hours, days, weeks, and even months before the story is deemed complete by the one relating the story. In reality, the storyteller is saying, "Let me read you a story from my mind," and the stories elevate your interest if you can see what is being told in your mind. You can see places as they are being related to you in the story. You can actually see the faces and hear the voice of a person you are learning about, or the voice of the walrus as stories are being related about them. Storytelling is a special skill that cannot exist without someone going through a complex process of learning our ways. Some societies place words into special categories that restrict their use in normal speech. Some of these words are for prayer and are sacred; these words have long been used by indigenous people from the depths of their hearts. The deadly sins that occur in other societies are also recognized by indigenous beliefs. Customs and rituals were seen as sinful in the eyes of others, and the young were warned to stay away from the old, not realizing that the elder is the teacher of the people. Indigenous beliefs were treated in a very disrespectful manner at the time of the first encounters with other societies from the east.

As mentioned, the hunter has a profound alliance with the mammals of the sea, an alliance that involves the spiritual beliefs of many, many hunters. This belief is that the people cannot survive without a hunter/prey bond that was begun by our ancestors ages ago. This belief conforms with those of many hunting cultures in the northern hemisphere. One belief among many, that respect must be paid to the spirit of the mammals, birds, or fish, is no longer observed, but many hunters continue to respect animals in spirit. From the first moments of contact with people from the East, our societies and cultures clashed because what was put in place of others' proven ways was not a perfect match with our concepts. Fortunately, in many ways, parts of the culture important to ceremony and observances of special events were just put underground and not discarded, because culture is necessary to read the story of a people. Efforts were made to obliterate the culture, and this trend continues in many different forms today. Culture is a crucial part of a people's being. Our culture is not uniform with that of other societies because we have our own ways. Its compelling power is revealed by a person telling a story, and this story is absorbed by the listener, to be told again to eager ears.

The traditions of the people define our relationship with the land, the sea, and the creatures that reside therein. Each village is a society, a nation, distinct on its own, and each and every group has a story of their own that defines and describes this relationship. Let me relate a story told by my grandfather Sigiaqluq on his first encounter with the *aqlu* [*aaġlu*] as a child. To us, the killer whale or orca is *aqlu*. The name does not signify that the mammal is a wanton killer, but the *aqlu* is a supreme predator. The *aqlu* is a hunter and he has gained an extremely high status in the lore of the northern hunter, yet is not a mythical being, although to some who do not understand our ways, the *aqlu* may have the nature of a myth. In the ancient stories of the Iñupiat the *aqlu* is at its own level in the hierarchy of predator and prey, and the majestic mammal resides at the top of its own universe. His position is absolute. Elderly hunters, refined in the art form of hunting on the northern ice and seas, will say to their crews, "Someone is already hunting here," when the *aqlu* is encountered during hunts. The hunters leave in search of other hunting grounds immediately.

Every young boy is an aspiring hunter, and my grandfather was certainly no exception; before a boy is taken onto the ice, his father conditions him to the life of a hunter by taking him to the *qargi* at a very young age. This is the time of awareness. The child is now conscious and begins his life as a human being. Prior to that time, the society entrusts him to a woman, and she takes complete responsibility for his livelihood. My grandfather was very young when my great-grandfather Kiapiq began to take him along on walrus hunts as the icy winter weather was being replaced by the warmth of spring. The weather can still be extremely cold, but even so, a boy child must be conditioned. A hunter is not born to hunt; he has to be made.

Stories begin in the life of a hunter at a very tender age, and as an aspiring hunter begins his training in the month when the weather begins to warm, it is usually the encounters with walrus that are his first awareness. The most menial of jobs is handed the aspiring hunter, and it will be years before someone considers him able to lead a crew. He will have filled every position on a crew before he can become an *umialik*, or someone who is truly capable of providing for others besides himself. He is made to know that he has a responsibility that must be continually fulfilled. The life of any hunter fulfills the life of only one individual, but in all cases, many lives can be influenced by the actions of a single individual. Some hunters attain an elite rank in the society of hunters at an early period, but some may never attain a high status until late in life. Some, despite a lifetime of hunting, never attain a high rank. A hunter never retires. Although he may no longer accompany the crew, he serves the community of hunters by teaching them what he learned from the elders who taught him the ways of the ice. The life of a hunter is a unique story, best told in the *qargi* during specific times of day when the night begins to wane and the young become restless.

Our ancient relationship with the sea is a relationship that you will not see among other groups of people. The relationship extends to all creatures that the sea and ice harbor, and it is this relationship that has made us into a class of hunters unmatched among other societies. Yet even as we are unmatched, we are not invincible. We are mortal, and in the ways of mortal beings, we have learned to adjust as best as we can within our environment. In fulfilling the responsibilities of a hunter, my grandfather gained the status of an *umialik*, but this honor was not accomplished in a short period. He went through a lifetime of training, observing men who taught him what they had learned in a lifetime of learning. In my society, every man and woman is a teacher, and their credential in life is their knowledge of survival in what is considered one of the most inhospitable of regions on earth. My grandfather had two *umiaqs* and one kayak when death overtook him before his time during an influenza epidemic in the winter of 1944. My grandmother, Tuġutaq, of Cape Espenberg origin, followed in death three days later. My grandfather told a story to my mother and the rest of the family while she was a young girl, and I heard her relate the story to us when we were very young. I never knew my grandparents. I only know them through a photograph that I cherish.

I will attempt to tell a story in the way that my grandfather may have told the story of an encounter with the beings of the sea during his lifetime. He would have begun, "Do you know the *aqlu*?" and saying that, he would have gained the immediate attention of everyone, young and old. The entire *qargi* would have gathered around to hear him speak in his soft voice as he began to tell the story. He would continue by explaining that there was no more night, but the time was late as the walrus season was near its end. A spring storm had kept the hunters off the ice for many days, but the days were again prime to pursue their efforts to fatten winter stores. The horizon glowed white in the distance revealing an expanse of ice, but the ice dances high above the sea, as a mirage. The boat moved as fast as the gentle northeast wind toward the islands in the middle of the sea, and the crew knew that the ice could not be reached in a short time. The ice insures a successful hunt, and the boat plied effortlessly over the water. With a gentle wind, the sea was light, but the men were grateful for the wind since it kept them from their paddles.

Since my grandfather was in training, he occupied the stern of the boat. His position in the crew placed him under the guidance of the hunter who steered the craft, and in complete view of those who manned other positions. The *umialik* was a seasoned hunter, as were the other crew members. His father, Kiapiq, was young but already envisioned himself as an *umialik*, and his position was in the bow of the boat, a position you cannot attain without being assigned to it by a person in authority. His actions insured a kill, and he did not take his responsibility for granted, nor did he take any unjust action.

The boat crept closer to the ice under full sail from the gentle wind. The rays of an early morning sun put my grandfather into a near stupor, but he struggled to remain awake as he knew everyone was watching him. He had been told that he must be observant, since an observant hunter is a successful hunter. The crew, including my grandfather, whiled the time away by tending to their equipment or scanning the sea for any prey they might encounter, but their minds were on reaching the ice and the promise of success. There is an intense quiet in an *umiaq* carried by the wind, and only the swish of the water parted by the bow of the boat can be heard. All was quiet, but suddenly the men were startled by the loud sound of a large mammal expending its breath just out of sight of the bow. Some of the men stood and some craned their necks to see what had surfaced before them. On seeing that it was an *aqlu*, many of the men were afraid because bothering an *aqlu* in any form violated a strict rule that must never be broken. To do so was a fault punishable by death, and the *aqlu* does not rest until it deals with the wrongdoer. Many of the men sat down, resigned to what might happen when suddenly the sea around them exploded with scores of *aqlut* [*aaġlut*] in perfect formation alongside them. Immediately the men began to ask themselves, "What is happening to us?" "What have we done?" "Who among us has broken the rule of the *aqlu*?" My grandfather had heard many, many times that you must not bother the *aqlu* in any way, and he could see and sense the tension and uneasiness among the crew members.

The *umialik* and Kiapiq assessed their situation. The pair and every member of the crew realized that many *aqlut* had surrounded the boat in two V formations, diving and surfacing in unison. The closest consisted of adolescent *aqlut* with an older one leading them. The farthest consisted of large *aqlut* with a larger one leading the formation. Leading both formations was an extremely large *aqlu* whose *inuk* was taller than Kiapiq, and Kiapiq was a tall man. The Inupiat call the dorsal fin of the *aqlu* the *inuk* or "person," for this is where the *inua* or spirit of the *aqlu* resides. The *umialik* wondered what could be done as he realized they might now be in peril, being in the open sea far from the islands of the strait and also the mainland.

Among the crew was an aspiring *angatkuq* [*aŋatkuq*], a shaman who was an unseasoned, but determined man. He came forward to the bow of the boat, grasped both gunwales, and prepared for what he felt he must do. Some of the men felt there was no alternative but to meet their fate. The *umialik* and Kiapiq welcomed his coming forward because they did not know what could be done in a time like this. The *angatkuq* began by stating, "We are hunters, like you. We are hunting, as you are. We have families. We have families to feed, as you do. Please let us continue what we are doing and I will give you the tongues of our harvest today as a share of our success." The *aqlut* kept pace with the *umiaq*, swimming on the surface and occasionally diving, but never completely disappearing into the water. Surely a voice could not be heard over the commotion made by the water, but the *aqlut* dove in perfect unison after hearing the plea of the *angatkuq*. The boat was in the middle of the sea, and the crew searched the horizon around them, but the *aqlut* did not surface so they could be seen. The crew continued on despite their encounters, and in time the ice field was reached. Throughout the day, the men harvested seal and walrus, and each time a successful harvest occurred, the *angatkuq* removed the tongues and dropped them into the water after saying he had repaid a part of his debt to the *aqlut* during the hunt. After the hunt was over, the debt was no more. You can ask the *aqlut* for a share of their harvest when you see them hunting, and a share of their harvest will be given to you. We are told that even if the current is not likely to cast anything ashore, your share, as if cut by a sharp knife, will drift in. This is an unwritten law of the sea that many aspiring hunters learn early in life in the Bering Strait region. I am sure many other young hunters of other nations learn this commandment very early in life. In the *aqlu* resides a powerful spirit. This majestic mammal has the power to transform into a man or a wolf, but that is a story best told elsewhere and in other times reserved for learning.

In seeking to understand the ways of the people, you must probe into the ways of survival of the northern hunter. This is where you hear the song of subsistence, for subsistence is the song of survival. The chorus of this song contains many unique elements, and each of these elements tells a special story. We give thanks to the Creator before each meal, and our thanks are also a silent prayer before the hunt. Prayers are stated for favorable winds and safe seas so that we can replenish winter stores for another season of survival. The quest to survive stands in a class all its own. The way of life of the northern hunter is a life of sincerity with oneself and of personal union with one's family and people.

In closing let me read a previous note that was shared as an abstract in a paper entitled "The Indigenous Identity in Framework, Collaboration, and Compromise with the Alaska Native Informant." The abstract begins, "From a simple flake of stone or ivory arise many questions. Where, when, how, or why is a specific product obtained, if the resource is not available within an immediate region?" Who is responsible is usually known except in rare cases, and the scope and depth of the question can astound even the descendants, as they become knowledgeable of their ancient past. Survival is a universal quest, as the will to survive was decided eons ago by the Ancient Hunter. Indigenous man identifies himself with the Ancient Hunter very easily because it is his story that is related to him by his elders. Some Arctic research began over a century ago, but with decades of lapses in between, and only in the last three decades, also with lapses, has research been renewed by a new generation of researchers. Even if this is very welcoming, it is possibly occurring only in what may be the twilight period for many groups of people; fortunately for all, there has always been a sunrise that follows. There is no time to waste, but the lack of funding cripples the efforts of many people. Some of the elders may have been consulted for only short periods, but always, the information they contribute adds much to the story. Remember Ruth Milligrock of Little Diomede who stated that "Our land is getting old; like an old woman she is changing." So little of the story of our periods of time with eras such as *issaq* or *aipaani* are documented. *Issaq* and *aipaani* are time periods of unwritten history thousands of years old that are only supported by oral tradition, and so little of the elders' knowledge of this period has been presented. Ernest Oxereok of Wales, just months before his passing, stated that from the earth came our health, as he related information about the abundant plants that grow upon our land, as traditional uses of these plants continue today. Patrick Ongtowasruk, also of Wales, is young in comparison to other elders that we have talked with. He stated that when the crust of the earth was thin there were many spirits roaming the earth. The elders of the 1930 to 1935 era may be considered "young" by some researchers, but this is the generation that lived a life being entirely Inupiaq, before the society and its culture became wholly immersed into Western ways. They can surely share the wisdom, pride, and honor that are the ways of the Inupiat. We have only to ask if they would like to share their lifetime of learning with us. Quyaana.

Notes

1   After a death, both Yupiit and Iñupiat are supposed to refrain from many activities for a period of time, including singing and dancing. His determination to continue with his feast is seen as an act of hubris, for it puts the whole community in danger. Because the hunter continued with the feast even though the messenger died foreshadows the upcoming negative consequences of his actions.

2   In 1982, four of the five couples of male and female performers were married to each other.

Works Cited and Suggested Reading

Anderson, Wanni. 2005. *The Dall Sheep Dinner Guest: Inupiaq Narratives of Northwest Alaska.* Fairbanks: University of Alaska Press.

Burch, Ernest S., Jr. 2006. *Social Life in Northwest Alaska: The Structure of Iñupiaq Eskimo Nations.* Fairbanks: University of Alaska Press.
    1988. "The End of the Trail: The Work of the Fifth Thule Expedition in Alaska," *Etudes/Inuit/Studies* 12(1–2):151–170.

Cleveland, Robert. 1980. *Unipchaaŋich Imaġluktuġmiut / Stories of the Black River People.* Anchorage: National Bilingual Materials Development Center.

Eliade, Mircea. 1964. *Shamanism: Archaic Techniques of Ecstasy*, trans. Willard R. Trask. Princeton, NJ: Princeton University Press.

Fortescue, Michael, Steven Jacobson, and Lawrence D. Kaplan. 1994. *Comparative Eskimo Dictionary with Aleut Cognates.* Fairbanks: Alaska Native Language Center, University of Alaska Fairbanks.

Gray, Minnie. 1978a. *How Stories.* Anchorage: National Bilingual Materials Development Center.
    1978b. *More How Stories.* Anchorage: National Bilingual Materials Development Center.
    1981. *Old Beliefs / Taimakŋaqtat.* Anchorage: National Bilingual Materials Development Center.

Gray, Minnie, Nita Towarak, and Ruthie Ramoth. 1976. *Timimun Mamirrutit.* Kotzebue, AK: Mauneluk Association.

Gray, Minnie, Mary L. Pope, and Tupou L. Pulu. 1981. *Qiaġumik Aimmiñialiq / Birch Bark Basket Making.* Anchorage: National Bilingual Materials Development Center.

Hall, Edwin S. Jr. 1998. *The Eskimo Storyteller: Folktales from Noatak, Alaska.* Fairbanks: University of Alaska Press.

Jenness, Diamond. 1991. *Arctic Odyssey: The Diary of Diamond Jenness, Ethnologist with the Canadian Arctic Expedition in Northern Alaska and Canada, 1913–1916.* Hull, QC: Canadian Museum of Civilization.

Kakaruk, John A. and William Oquilluk. 1964. *The Eagle Wolf Dance.* Self-published pamphlet on file at Rasmuson Library, University of Alaska Fairbanks.

Kaplan, Lawrence, Tadataka Nagai, and Minnie Gray. 2004. "The Young Woman Who Disappeared," in *Voices from Four Directions.* Brian Swann, ed., pp. 42–50. Lincoln: University of Nebraska Press.
   ed. 1988. *Ugiuvangmiut Quliapyuit / King Island Tales.* Fairbanks: Alaska Native Language Center and University of Alaska Press.

Kingston, Deanna M. 1999. *Returning: Twentieth Century Performances of the King Island Wolf Dance.* Ph.D. dissertation, University of Alaska Fairbanks.

Lee, Linda, Ruthie Sampson, Ed Tennant, and Hannah Mendenhall, eds. 1990. *Lore of the Inupiat: The Elders Speak*, vol. 2. Kotzebue, AK: Northwest Arctic Borough School District.

Lee, Linda, Ruthie Sampson, and Edward Tennant, eds. 1992. *Lore of the Inupiat: The Elders Speak*, vol. 3. Kotzebue, AK: Northwest Arctic Borough School District.
   eds. 1991. *Qayaqtuaġiŋñaqtuaq / Qayaq the Magical Traveler.* Kotzebue, AK: Northwest Arctic Borough School District.

Lowenstein, Tom, ed. 1992. *The Things That Were Said of Them: Shaman Stories and Oral Histories of the Tikiġaq People.* Berkeley: University of California Press.
   1995. *Ancient Land, Sacred Whale: the Inuit Hunt and its Rituals.* New York: North Point Press.

MacLean, Edna. 1980. *Abridged Iñupiaq and English Dictionary.* Fairbanks: Alaska Native Language Center.

Mather, Elsie. 1995. "With a Vision Beyond Our Immediate Needs: Oral Traditions in an Age of Literacy," in *When Our Words Return: Writing, Hearing, and Remembering Oral Traditions of Alaska and the Yukon.* Phyllis Morrow and William Schneider, eds., pp. 12–26. Logan: Utah State University Press.

Mendenhall, Hannah, Ruthie Sampson, and Edward Tennant, eds. 1989. *Lore of the Inupiat: The Elders Speak*, vol. 1. Kotzebue, AK: Northwest Arctic Borough School District.

Oquilluk, William A. with Laurel Bland. 1973. *People of Kauwerak: Legends of the Northern Eskimo.* Anchorage: Alaska Methodist University Press.

Pulu, Tupou L. et al. 1981. *Kuvriñialiq / Net Making*. Anchorage: National Bilingual Materials Development Center.

Rainey, Froelich G. 1947. *The Whale Hunters of Tigara*. Anthropological Papers of the American Museum of Natural History, vol. 41, pt. 2. New York: American Museum of Natural History.

Rasmussen, Knud. 1929. *Festens Gave: Eskimoiske Alaska-Æventyr med Tegninger af Ernst Hansen*. Copenhagen: Gyldendal.
   1932. *The Eagle's Gift: Alaska Eskimo Tales*. Garden City, NJ and New York: Doubleday, Doran & Company, Inc.
   1952. *The Alaskan Eskimos: Report of the Fifth Thule Expedition 1921–24*, vol. 10(3). Copenhagen: Gyldendal.

Seiler, Wolf A. 2005. *Iñupiatun Eskimo Dictionary*. Kotzebue, AK: NANA Regional Corporation.

Sun, Susan (compiler). 1979. *Kaŋiqsisautit Uqayusraġnikun / Kobuk Iñupiat Junior Dictionary*. Anchorage: National Bilingual Materials Development Center.

Webster, Donald H. and Wilfried Zibell. 1970. *Iñupiat Eskimo Dictionary*. Fairbanks: Alaska Rural School Project, Department of Education, University of Alaska.

PART III

St. Lawrence Island /
Siberian Yupik Narratives

ST. LAWRENCE ISLAND IS LOCATED IN THE BERING SEA, within sight of the Asian continent but out of sight of the Alaska mainland. The connection to Siberia is more than geographical—cultural and kinship ties to the Yupiks (or Yupiget) of the Chukchi Peninsula have long been an important part of life to the Alaska Yupik people, in spite of the more than forty-year-long Cold War between the United States and the Soviet Union that made contact between the two groups all but impossible. The population of St. Lawrence Island originated in Siberia, moving in successive waves of immigration that continued into the twentieth century. Several families are known to be of recent Siberian origin. International visits between Alaskan and Russian Eskimos resumed in the early 1990s, allowing relatives to remain in touch. St. Lawrence Island is known for its system of clans, social groups not found among mainland Alaskan Eskimos (Hughes 1984a, 1984b).

St. Lawrence Island has two villages, the older Gambell and the newer Savoonga, which dates to about 1914. The Native population of the island is about 1,100, and over a hundred St. Lawrence Islanders live on the Alaska mainland, primarily in Nome. Earlier villages elsewhere on the island were wiped out by a widespread famine in 1878–1879. The islanders hunt large sea mammals and gather greens on the island, with seals and walrus forming an important part of the diet, as well as bowhead whales, which are taken primarily in spring and fall. Spring whaling camps and summer fishing camps

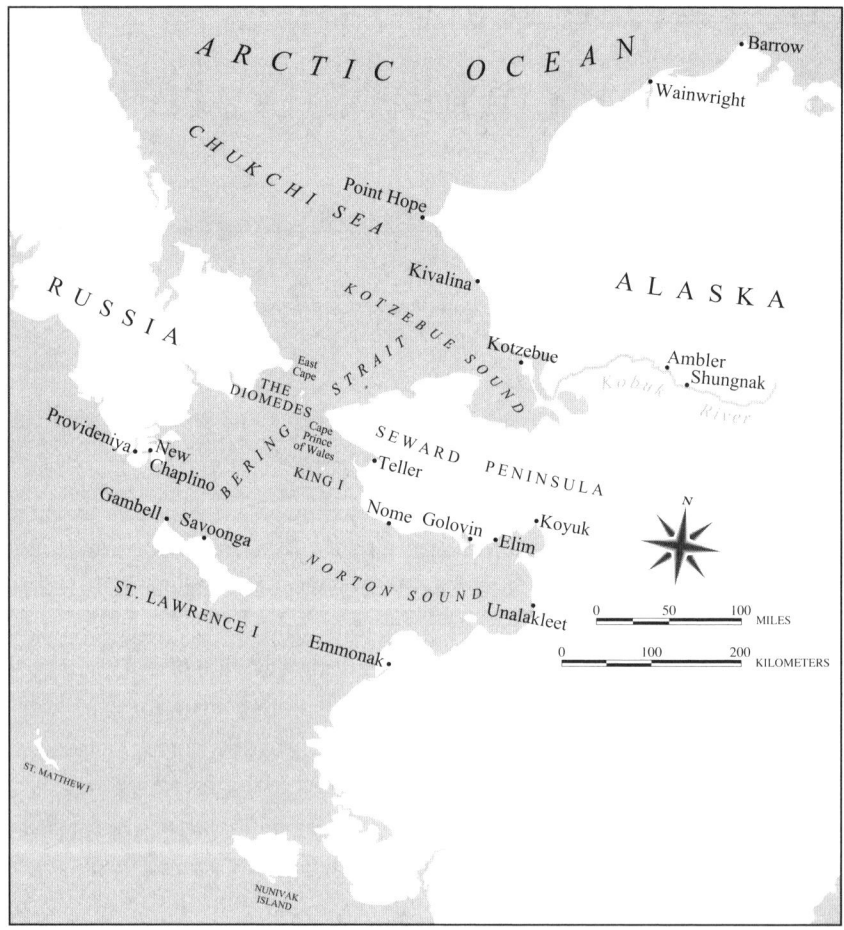

St. Lawrence Island relative to the Chukchi and Seward peninsulas.

Words of the Real People

are important locations for subsistence hunting. St. Lawrence Islanders are known as accomplished ivory carvers, making animals and other figures from walrus tusks.

The Native language of St. Lawrence Island is of the Yupik branch of Eskimo. The language is called Central Siberian Yupik by linguists, although local people prefer just "Yupik" or "Yupigestun" and some also call it "Akuzipik" meaning "original speech." The same language is found on the Chukchi Peninsula, primarily in the village of Novoe Chaplino, with minor dialectal differences. Two other Eskimo languages are also found on the Russian side: Naukanski is the language of the people who formerly lived at East Cape on the western shore of Bering Strait, and Sirenikski, now extinct, was spoken in the village of Sireniki. Books of stories and an interesting collection of schoolbooks have been produced for Yupik in Siberia, written in an adapted Cyrillic orthography. In Alaska a modern writing system was developed in the early 1970s by Michael Krauss and Adelinda Badten. A number of schoolbooks and story collections have been published that serve as teaching materials for school language programs in Gambell, Savoonga, and Nome. Siberian Yupik shows significant influence from non-Eskimo Siberian languages, primarily Chukchi, in the area of personal names and place names as well as other areas of the vocabulary (de Reuse 1994). Yupik is no longer being learned as a first language by most St. Lawrence Island children, who are primarily English-speaking. Similarly on the Asian side, Russian is the language of younger generations of Yupiks.

Storytelling is a primary part of oral tradition and a major means of cultural transmission for St. Lawrence Islanders. As for other Eskimo groups, a distinction is made between two types of stories. The ancient legend, known as *ungipaghaan*, tells of times no longer remembered by anyone living. A narrative or account, including oral history, is called *ungipamsuk* and typically tells of events of which the teller has had direct experience or of events which have been related to the teller by someone who has experienced them.

Della Waghiyi's story "Qati Hik" is an example of the first type of story, containing archetypal characters—orphan and grandmother—who possess magical powers. Vera Metcalf relates the *ungipaghaan* or legend "The Good Hunter" that she learned from her father and situates it within the context that it was told to her, giving an intimate picture of the role of storytelling in a

Yupik family. Susie Silook's essay tells of personal and family experiences, both on St. Lawrence Island and far away from Alaska in Chicago, where her family moved as part of the government relocation program for Alaska Natives. The storytellers all remind us of how stories are transmitted between generations within families and how the person who hears and receives the story has the responsibility to continue to transmit it accurately and respectfully.

—LDK

Yuuk Neqengyuqaq / The Good Hunter

Told by Vera Metcalf and Theodore Kingiikaq of Savoonga

I WANT TO SHARE A SHORT STORY, a tale my father told us called "Yuuk Neqengyuqaq," but I would like to point out that I am not a storyteller. I have heard many timeless tales when I was growing up in Savoonga, told by my parents: Kingiikaq, my father Theodore, and my mother Aghhaya, May. For some of you that don't know, we're organized into clans on St. Lawrence Island. My father's clan, the Qiwaaghmiit, originated from a point named Qiwaa on the Chukotka side, and my mother's clan that Susie [Silook] mentioned, Aymaramket, that's where she came from. My Eskimo name is Qaakaghlleq which comes from another clan. The name crossed over to my clan, which in those days was to maintain good relationships between clans.

My parents told many tales on many nights. They were the accomplished storytellers and I do have many personal memories of how they told these wonderful stories to us, mostly during long winter nights, on weekends in a bed made of reindeer hides with a long wooden log for a pillow. I remember that pillow, too. It wasn't very hard, but the reindeer hides would cushion it. My father and my mother would take turns telling these tales. At times my father, Kingiikaq, who was probably exhausted from the long day's work, would drift off to sleep and my mother, or one of us too involved in the story to let it end, would wake him up to continue. My father, not remembering what story he was telling, would start another one [laughter], but my mother would scold him and remind him of the correct one to continue. These tales were very intriguing and wonderful—similar to stories that some of you have heard, like *Treasure Island*, *Little Women*, or *The Arabian Nights* that you might have heard or read while growing up. There were, however, other times that we as children were excluded from the storytelling when only elders or men, especially, shared stories. It was not the appropriate time for us to listen to these types of stories. There were also shorter tales told by our parents in context with a place, name, or about a particular incident. And some stories like "Yuuk Neqengyuqaq" would continue for several evenings, enthralling us each evening and making us sorry when they ended.

To me my life was, and still is, truly enriched because of these stories, which are similar to great works of literature. They are our cultural literacy. Those of us who had parents or family elders who cared for us and told us these stories, even when they were exhausted, provided us with the knowledge to understand our world.

This story, "Yuuk Neqengyuqaq/The Good Hunter," was told by my father in 1985, and he told several stories that we recorded during that time at my house in Savoonga. And it begins:

> There once was a man who was wealthy and a very good hunter, *except* that he would hang his catch on a pole for all to see before celebrating [or giving thanks]. These catches would hang in direct sunlight until becoming bleach dried and worthless. This good hunter and successful whaler had a son. One day something happened! The hunter's son, a very kind-hearted young man, took a walk for exercise onto the tundra, then disappeared and never returned. The good hunter, desperate to find his missing son, gathered all his neighbors, including those capable of incantation and those with shamanic powers, and paid them to find his son. But to no avail—they couldn't find him. He then said to his wife, "Oh no, this is most unfortunate, my only precious son is lost forever. Maybe I should try to find him myself and do something—as hopeless as it is." His wife replied in despair, "Well, go try, if you can. Truly now we both have no son...maybe."

This tale continues with the hunter trying desperately to find his son by chanting songs using his special hunting drum. There are certain words used by my father to add suspense to the tale, words that I no longer hear of or don't know their literal translations. So it is one of my goals to find out the real definition of some of the words expressed to capture the true meaning behind the lessons presented.

This beginning, like all good stories, immediately captures our attention. It identifies the main characters and creates suspense with unresolved tension—the good hunter who disrespects nature. My father would use different voices and inflections, then pause, to help bring the story to life in a very meaningful way. The images came alive in our imagination. No matter how many times I've heard the story, listening to it being told in this way, it would take on a life of its own.

The story continues with the good hunter who, after trying many different ways to find his son, finally chanted a certain song, transporting himself upwards to enter the realm of the Great Grandfather, the Great God, who greeted him, saying: "Ahow, a visitor, come in—you must need something."

> The visitor replied, "Not at all. I'm only looking for my son." "Ah-ha! He's over there if you want to see him." Looking beyond, he saw a special box the size of a human body with edges lined with flames. The Great God now in a commanding voice said, "If you want to see him, he's over there!" [almost demanding and perhaps permitting the visitor suddenly to see]. The visitor peered in and saw a person with barely one eye open inside the box lined with flames. He saw something close to a skeletal-like person, squeezed in tightly, practically lifeless. He fell back humbly, saying, "You have made me grateful. You let me see my son—you let me see my son." The Great God replied, "Yes, it is because my gifts to you have only been made useless—the food and the whale." The visitor answered, "Yes, you let me see my son who is no longer one of us. Now I will no longer look for him. I am nothing. From now on, I'm going to give all your gifts away." The Great God replied, "That's the way we are—your life and mine!"

The richness and profound nature of the dialogue are very captivating, still today and even in English. But they also point to the difficulty in translating these stories. The descriptions of the son's condition and situation are practically impossible to translate with full effect. The precise imagery and the fundamental nature of the dialogue between man and the Creator give this story an authority and depth that keep it alive in the listener.

The cultural context of the story defines its philosophy and beliefs as positively Yupigestun. This is ours, from our ancestors and not from a people far away or a place I've never been to or don't truly understand. This story has been told many, many times—from one person to another. My father probably heard and learned it from his parents who remembered it from someone else who told it many, many years ago. Consequently, I don't know who the real owner of the story is, and it's really not my decision to have it written and published at this point. There is probably no one in Savoonga or Gambell who remembers the true owner of this particular story.

But I want to thank you all for listening and I apologize for a written text. It took me a couple days to prepare this for the conference. But I really appreciate you all for listening. It's been wonderful to be part of this and have the opportunity to share and give honor to my ancestors and their stories because I am very proud of them. These stories were passed from person to person—from the community to each new child of every generation. There was no great teacher who held all the knowledge. The elders of each generation possessed it and so each member would inherit the society's culture, history and traditions individually. In these societies, there is no individual who isn't linked to the past. Whether it's provable or not, I believe that because of our oral traditions and communal aspects of Native Alaskan upbringing, the ethical and spiritual lessons are held deeper and more precious. The story "Yuuk Neqengyuqaq" is a cultural treasure and with the others, a cultural inheritance.

At the end, my father would conclude his stories singing, "This is the end of the story because it's as far as I can remember." To me this implies that there was more to the story the next time it was told. Finally, all of our stories that I remembered would end with an expression saying, "Tefaay, aliinghakun, amsanakuun"—an expression saying, "This is all, but to wish for good and clear weather tomorrow."

That is the end of the story. My father passed away some years ago, and it's taken me this long to resolve that he is no longer with us. He may be gone forever, but even though he has left us, his legacy is still with us in these stories. I am fortunate that this volume allows me to get started transcribing the story into Siberian Yupik and then English. English is very difficult for some of us because our Siberian Yupik words are not easy to translate into English. When translated they lose their true meaning. So I hope eventually to translate this story into English, close to the way my father and others who were great storytellers told it, because there is a message in every story that was given to us.

Introduction
Three Generations of St. Lawrence Island Writers: The Work of Paul Silook, Roger Silook, and Susie Silook

By Susie Silook

Like Herbert Anungazuk's essay, the contributions by three generations of Silooks were written in English rather than spoken in an Alaska Native language. As Susie Silook explains below in her presentation to the American Folklore Society in Anchorage in 2001, each contribution is uniquely Yupik. Paul Silook's story is a traditional Yupik tale that Paul and many of his generation knew well. Paul had no formal education and learned English through reading the Bible and speaking with the teachers, missionaries, and anthropologists who visited St. Lawrence Island in the early 1900s. The wording of his English rendition of this traditional story reflects his eclectic and informal education. The story is unique in this volume, as it is the only example of the storyteller and translator being one and the same.

Roger Silook's essay and Susie Silook's poem are also noteworthy because, along with Herbert Anungazuk, they reflect the development of an Alaska Native literature—writings not only about Alaska Natives but by them. Storytelling continues, not as tales told primarily to kinsmen within a small community but as "talking on the page" to a diverse, global audience.

—AFR

Three Generations of St. Lawrence Island Writers: The Work of Paul Silook, Roger Silook, and Susie Silook

By Susie Silook of Anchorage

I AM NOT A LINGUIST, A HISTORIAN, NONE OF THE ABOVE. I'm an artist, and I'm here because my grandfather, Silook, did a lot of writing.

My name is Paallengetaq, and my father [Roger Silook] is Saavla. He's from St. Lawrence Island and is Silook's son. My mother is Norma Imanyuk Silook, who was an orphan. She was sent out [to St. Lawrence Island] in the 1930s during a diphtheria epidemic, and she's Irish and Inupiaq, originally from the Kotzebue area. I'm very proud of that part of my heritage, even though I don't know that much about it.

I grew up Siberian Yupik, and I'm the daughter of Saavla. Everything [on St. Lawrence Island] is traced through your father, and Saavla was the son of Silook and Silook was the son of Uwitelen. Paul Silook's Yupik name was just plain Siluk, so my last name comes from my grandfather. It shows how recently we were colonized. He had two brothers, and their father was Uwitelen. But when they were handing out surnames, they didn't take Uwitelen, though there's a branch of the family that has that last name. My grandfather, Paul Silook, took Silook as his last name, and my great uncle took Apangalook as his last name. So the same family split into three different last names, although we are the same clan.

Silook died long before I was born so Apanglook was actually my *apa*—he took that role for my grandfather. He used to come into Nome—we moved to Nome when I was six—and he'd come to Nome and we'd fight over who got to sleep with him 'cause we always wanted to hear his stories [laughter]. So I grew up with Yupik as my first language. But from moving back and forth, I lost it as my first language, and I'm more comfortable and a little bit more intelligent-sounding in English.

My grandfather in his day was a writer. The earliest writings we found are at the Alaska State Museum [Juneau]. As a young man he actually recorded a lot of stories for a medical doctor. When an article was published on Silook [*Anchorage Daily News*, 1999], the Alaska State Museum said, "Hey, we just got a box of this material from somebody's granddaughter." She donated it to the Alaska State Museum, so that's the earliest we know of Silook's writing. These are all collections of St. Lawrence Island stories and Siberian stories. Most of his writing concerns my clan specifically, but those stories actually belong to all the people. I'd like to see them eventually put into a separate volume with community input and illustrations. I'd like to see that turn into a community project because that is where it legitimately belongs. Those are not Silook's stories, those are our stories collectively as a people.

Silook was unusual in that he was bilingual and literate at a time when very few people were, so that was his distinction. Many people refer to him as the first Native American ethnographer. I have trouble with that because I think all elders in my culture are ethnographers, and the only difference was that Silook wrote in English. But every elder back home had the same degree of knowledge—or maybe more—than he did. Each of them is a bearer of wisdom of their own experience and their own people, so what he shares is specifically from his life and from my people.

Silook also worked extensively with the archaeologists who came out to St. Lawrence Island. St. Lawrence Island is considered the Rome of Inuit civilization. It's between Siberia and Alaska so the artifacts on St. Lawrence Island go back at least two thousand years and we think much longer. It's a specific style called Old Bering Sea, and it is found in Siberia and on St. Lawrence Island and parts of the [Alaska] mainland, including Wales and Point Hope. I did a lot of research into these forms and symbolism for my work as a visual artist. And I studied not just my people's cosmology but circumpolar culture. It all fascinated me. I like the very thin veil between what is preternatural and what is real. That is fascinating for me. I'm really grateful to come from a culture that has so much beauty in it in so many different ways.

Anyway, Silook did work with the archaeologists, including Henry Collins and Otto Geist. His writings are now at the Smithsonian National Museum of Natural History in Washington, D.C., where he wrote for Henry Collins extensively and where letters were exchanged. He recorded the archaeological digs they were doing on a daily basis. He kept records of hunting tallies for that day, who died, who was born. So there's some history that he provided at the time.

When you think about it, he was writing from the light of a seal-oil lamp and recording how many lamps are burning in the house and how many people are sleeping in the house. It's very poetic in a sense.

He's also unusual in that in his time he did speak about the ceremonies and religious beliefs of my people. Many people were hesitant for one reason or another to do that. I think he read [Edward] Nelson's thick book on the Inuit [*Eskimos about Bering Strait*, 1899], and he understood what ethnography was, so he knew what people were looking for. He knew what the anthropologists wanted so he tried to supply that [information] as best he could. Reading these [papers] for myself, I wish that a system for writing our own language had been in place back then. I think he would have been able to go into much more detail on a lot of the things he talks about in his writing.

Still, these are his words. We're still working on whether we're going to change any of it [for publication] to make it more understandable. He uses the language that was given to him at the time by the missionaries, so you are reading about moon worship ceremonies and sacrifices and the devils and sorcerers. You realize what they're feeding him [this language]. But somehow, you don't get the impression that he had a negative attitude about his culture.

I heard about his writing when Bill Fitzhugh from the Smithsonian told me about it. He wanted me to go [to Washington, D.C.] on a research grant. So I went there, and I was expecting just a diary or two. I was dazed just looking at boxes and boxes of material from my grandfather. In my mind, this was like my pilgrimage to Mecca because I was learning a lot of cultural things that I didn't have access to at the time.

The very first piece of paper I came across was one in which [Silook] says, "This year I am not going to do as my father has done. I am going to follow the ways of the Bible." This meant that he wasn't going to do the moon worship ceremonies anymore. I was astounded.

So in his writing you also get a sense of the time period he's living in where people are changing from their old beliefs to Christianity. There's debate over this, there's discussion. I find it was a very reasoned approach, and I think it happened not long after a major famine and epidemic in the memories of peoples' minds. To me that was a contributing factor in their conversion. Paul did this voluntarily, and he looked at it very seriously before he did it. So I have to respect that.

My father did a lot more traveling than Silook did, and he was involved in politics. He was also a writer, he wrote a couple of books, and [the passage below] is from one of his books [*Stories the Old People Told on St. Lawrence Island*, 1976]. He came back from his trips with an expanded view of Native politics. He passed that on to me, and so my work is very contemporary. I do just a little bit of writing.

I'm just going to read to you, very briefly, from all three of us.

Without further ado, I'm going to read "Trading with the Siberian Men," by my grandfather, Silook, and I think this gives you an idea of the close ties between our people and the people of Siberia.

> The people on the island keep walrus skin, big seal skin, and rope to sell to the Siberian men. About in the middle of June the Siberian men came down in three or four boats. Sometimes eight boats filled with men, women, and children. When they came ashore, each man of the house on the island took their friends to their houses. When they came in, they'd eat with them. Sometimes the man brought in four or five friends. After awhile the young men of the island have to test them to see if they are strong or fast. So they had to run around a circle. They ran for several hours. When they [were] done, they wrestled with them. Every year the people on the island beat them. When they wrestled quite a deal they went home.
>
> The Siberians brought deerskin parkas, trousers, sinews, Russian tobacco, and red leathers. Also willow bark for dying leathers and deer leggings. So when we gave them a walrus skin, they paid us two summer skins or a pair of trousers and a deerskin. A mukluk [bearded seal] is worth, like a fine parka. The Siberians bought from us small skins, mukluk skins, intestines, raincoats, drums, wood, wooden trays, and sometimes canoe paddles and oars. This is because there was no wood at Indian Point, which is over in Siberia, and barks and deer leggings. They paid whatever they wanted. Some of them just came to beg around for something. They came just for fun or to eat. They are the filthiest people. They had very poor clothing which smelled so bad. Of course, they carried meat on their backs sometimes and sometimes they carried them on their back without clothing.

I think that's funny because one of the things I hear is that my family is referred to as the dirty people, and Silook writes this about the Siberians. I didn't know if I should read it, but I decided, what the heck, I'm going to read it.

Now I'm going to read you a little excerpt from my father Saavla's book. This is about trading, also—trading with the whalers.

> After the whaling ships came was the first time people of the island had guns for hunting. They did not use the guns until after they had a good idea how to handle them. Then they buy guns from the whalers or rather they traded for them with baleen and ivory. Guns were muzzle loaders and not shotguns. Often the ammunition they got doesn't last until the next boat comes. When they are out of lead shots, they use sand as big as #1 or #2 shots. They get a lot of birds with sand, but they really wear their gun barrels fast. They traded for scraps of iron, too, and treasured the scraps. It must have been the best time for traders to trade anything on board the ship that was to be thrown away. The most favorite thing they traded was pilot bread. If you don't know, pilot bread is [N]ative food, which came in huge cases about five feet tall and four feet across. A case of syrup or a case of cookies was inside each case, too. When the ship arrived in the village each spring, they gave a bucket of pilot bread to everyone who came aboard. It became a habit of the villagers after they started to learn English, each man or woman when they had first come aboard the ship said, "Give me pilot bread. Give me tobacco." They must have been taught by the whalers to say the words for fun. Every year those old-timers got wiser as they learned to use American things. Then the arguing began in trading and trying to cheat each other. But these old-timers say they always get even when the trading is heavy. No one notices who traded their baleen, and afterwards somebody else took some from the pile, which was already traded and traded it again [laughter]. One piece of baleen could go into the pile several times before the boat leaves. These old-timers learned to get enough ammunition for a whole year. Ammunition is the very first thing they traded for. Rifles and shotguns became their treasures, and the people hunted more than ever. After this the bird hunting gets a little easier. They get birds every day of the year, but the old ways of catching birds never stop, either, like using nets, and the rocks. Birds begin to get scarcer and wilder, but there were still billions of them—they got used to shot and airplanes.

So, that's my dad's writing. That was him, and I am his seventh child. He got his first whale when he was seventy-three. First whale, which says a lot about persistence [laughter]. In the past the men who got the whales and the polar bears were placed at the top of the mountain for burial; it was a place of honor, and now everyone is placed up there. But after my dad got his whale, it was for us a sigh of relief—he goes to the top of the mountain.

My grandfather started writing in the 1920s through the late 1940s. My father was writing all my life. Now I'm going to attempt to find for you my poem "Adventure in Chinatown." This is in the *Alaska Quarterly Review.*

My family went to Chicago in a relocation program when [the BIA] was trying to eliminate the whole concept of reservations and decided they had to find another way to deal with Native people. Relocation was one of those experiments, and my family was sent to Chicago. My parents today, you can't get either one of them to agree on who decided to go to Chicago [laughter]. But this is part of the history in my family and so to me, I'm writing it in English because I'm comfortable with that.

Adventure in Chinatown 1958

My father was a steel worker in Muskogee Illinois.
   He would leave before dawn and return long after the
      sun no one ever saw in Chicago went down.

My mother says the buildings were too tall and the air stank.
   The only place I went was church, she remembers.

My brother Barry was a month old, making me nothing
  but
  a nagging worry in my mother's mind.
  No more babies she thought
  after the third child
  after the fourth child
  after the fifth child
  after the sixth child.

My father's hunting fed his family
   and his mother's family
   and his brother's family.

People still wonder why he agreed to the
   government relocation program and
   without my mother's consent
   took his Yupik family to Chicago.

In those days they paid the expenses to move
   Native folk out of Native neighborhoods
   and into Asian ones.

It would save them from the mistake
   of the reservation
   would solve the problem
   of that persistent Native identity.

My sister used to take all her clothes off
   and run around naked –
   that's everyone's favorite Chicago story.

My other sister got lost and only spoke Yupik
   so they took her all over Chinatown
   looking for her non-existent Asian family.

Someone must have told them
   that child is not Asian for
   she remembers eating ice cream at the
   precinct and my father remembers
   how big her eyes were when he
   came to claim his
   relocated but not indigenous to
   Chinatown girl.

Mrs. Silook, why do you want to poison your children?
　　the psychiatrist asked my mother.

My father would repeat day in and day out
　　Sakuma paneghaallequsi
　　You will all starve if something happens to me.

Finally my Inupiaq-Irish mother who spoke only Yupik shouted
　　then we should buy poison and prepare ourselves!

My father wouldn't go to work unless
　　she stayed up all night to watch everyone.

The woman was *tired* you got that?

I didn't mean it, she told the lady,
　　I was tired of Saavla saying we were going to starve.

So Custer's Last Stand II
　　or infinity
　　lasted one month
　　in Chinatown.

Better to starve as a Yupik than as impossible immigrant
　　read the fortune cookie of my father
　　who says only that
　　Chicago is too big to remember.

So, that was my reality. You know, my reality is drastically different from
the day when my grandfather was deciding that he was not going to do as
his grandfather did. Today I quest for the knowledge of my ancestors, and
it's in here, too. He talks about his grandfather's knowledge, so this goes back
a long way. And I'm very grateful just to have been left this legacy. I live in
my own time and place, so it's continuity. I guess the love of writing came
from my grandfather, and hopefully, somebody else will pick it up after me.
So that's all I have. Thank you.

Introduction
Qati Hik
A St. Lawrence Island Yupik Tale

Told by Della Waghiyi

"Qati Hik" is a traditional St. Lawrence Island Yupik story or *ungipaghaan* (pl. *ungipaghaatet*) recorded from Della Waghiyi (henceforth DW, originally from Savoonga, Alaska) in Nome, Alaska on April 15th, 1985. It was transcribed and translated with the help of DW and her husband, John Waghiyi, Sr. (deceased 1993).

Whereas some *ungipaghaatet* appear to be full-fledged myths, this story is primarily for children, reminiscent of the fairy tales of Western culture. Its purpose is to amuse and to entertain—DW called it a bedtime story. There are motifs in this story, however, that are found in more complex myths. One such motif is that of the orphan—typically the most pitiable and unfortunate role in traditional Yupik society—who becomes strong and powerful through magic powers (Woodbury and Moses 1994:19). It was pointed out to me, for I had not realized this, that the orphan's song is actually a magic formula that causes the animals to wash up on shore. The direct causal connection between the boy walking along the beach singing and the animals washing up is nowhere made clear in the text.

This story was not given a Yupik title by DW and was referred to by her in English as the "story of the little orphan boy." Another elder, Nick Wongittilin, in a discussion of his own performance of this story, called it "Qati Hik," the name of the boy, apparently after the sounds he makes when swallowing. This is the possibility that I have adopted as the title of the story, since *ungipaghaatet* are sometimes given Yupik titles after the name of the most important character. Since *ungipaghaatet* can also be titled using the designation of the first character or characters introduced, other suggestions for titles accepted by native speakers are "Yaywaalingiighhaq" ("the little orphan") and "Yaywaalingiighhaq nenyuqutalghiik" ("the little orphan and his grandmother").

The format of this version, discussed below, is inspired by the claim of a number of scholars, including Hymes (1980, 1981, 1985, 1992) for North Pacific Coast texts and Woodbury (1985, 1987) for Central Alaskan Yup'ik texts, that the literary qualities of traditional Native American oral narrative are more apparent when it is organized in lines (or verses) and groups of lines (or stanzas). This organization is based upon a variety of linguistic features, including, prosodically and intonationally signaled phonological phrasing, syntactic constituency, and patterns of parallelism and repetition (Woodbury 1985:153).

The format and conventions used for the Yupik text below are outlined here. All obvious mistakes, false starts, and hesitations have been taken out.

By presenting a "polished" version, I assume the existence of an underlying "ideal" form of this text, which DW tries to approximate. I regard the issue of the existence of such a form as essentially an empirical question. In fact, DW made it sufficiently clear to me that there is such a form, but this does not imply that an underlying form necessarily exists for every piece of Yupik narrative. In fact, there might be more than one "ideal" form that can be approximated for one tale.

I have left untouched the original order and names of animals occurring in sections 2 and 5. Ideally, the lists occurring in both sections agree, but they do not agree in any of the other versions I collected.

The Yupik version is given facing an English translation in the same format. This translation is primarily an aid to the understanding of the Yupik text. Although it is more literary than literal, it makes no claim to a literary value comparable to the Yupik original.

I will now describe the phonological and syntactic features that I used for obtaining the line and verse format.

Two phonologically relevant features were used for this text. First, the places where DW takes a breath, which correspond to short pauses, and second, the devoicing of several syllables that characteristically occurs before a somewhat longer pause, which is also a place where a breath is taken. This devoicing of syllables does not always occur when an exclamatory or interrogative intonation is also present. Thus, *iteghlaaki* at the end of group 21 and *kangsughtungaay* at the end of group 26, do not contain devoiced vowels. More systematically, the exclamatory intonation marking an exasperated command in *iitghi* (in groups 22, 25, and 28), and in *mighyaa* (in groups 33, 34, and 37), and the very high exclamatory pitch of the final formula in group 40 apparently prevent the devoicing from occurring.

Thus, this text can be organized into stretches of a few words that are breath groups; at the end of one or more of the breath groups, from one to five syllables will be devoiced. Breath groups followed by such a finally devoiced breath group form a higher unit. This unit usually corresponds to a Yupik sentence. I would like to equate a breath group to a 'line' as defined by Woodbury (1985:156) and the higher unit to his 'group' (1985:157). My usage of these terms is then essentially based on the congruence of pause phrasing and prosodic phrasing.

For organization beyond the group, I have used the patterns of sentence adverb phrasing and patterns of parallelism and recurrence that are obvious in the text. I have used these patterns to divide the text into titled and numbered sections and subsections, which help emphasize their unity or distinctness. Needless to say, the section and subsection titles are not part of the story.

I now turn to the conventions of formatting and punctuation used in the text. These conventions should help the reader to perform the story with a prosody approaching that used in DW's performance.

The titles and numbers of sections and subsections are in English and aligned flush right. Each group is numbered sequentially for convenience on the left side of the page. Song lines and the onomatopoeic expression qati:: hik are ignored in the numbering.

The beginning line of a group is not indented; if a group consists of more than one line, the following lines are indented. Dialogue lines are marked with an en dash.

In lines that did not fit in one typographical line, the part of the line that does not fit is given under the typographical line, with a half inch indentation.

Song lines, the onomatopoeic expression qati:: hik, and items pronounced with a list intonation are indented.

The punctuation marks used in the text have the following meanings:

comma (,)   end of a line which is not the end of a group, and
            does not end in a lengthened phonologically short
            vowel

semicolon (;)	end of a line which is not the end of a group, and ends in a lengthened phonologically short vowel
period (.)	end of a line which is also the end of a group
two colons (::)	expressive overlength
exclamation mark (!)	exclamatory intonation, which can occur either in the middle of a line or at the end of a group
question mark (?)	interrogative intonation, occurring only at the end of a group

The punctuation of the facing-page English version is identical to that of the Yupik version, with a few commas added for legibility.

Two paralinguistic phenomena are marked with square brackets: [h] at the end of the particles kaa, kii, and qa is not part of Yupik orthography, but indicates a strong aspiration of their initial stops and a breathy quality of the vowels. The indication [swallowing] following qati:: hik stands for the storyteller's imitation of two swallows or gulps, which are an integral part of the performance.

The spelling system of Yupik used here is the standard one described by Krauss (1975) and used in the reference works on the language (Badten et al. 1987; de Reuse 1994; Jacobson 2001). Additional philological, linguistic, ethnographic, and literary commentary of this story is presented in de Reuse (1986).

Finally, I am grateful first and foremost to the storytellers—Della Waghiyi, Jimmie Toolie, and Nick Wongittilin—for their patience and kindness. I thank the following colleagues for their comments and insights on this text: Shobhana Chelliah, Paul Friedrich, Dell Hymes, Irene Reed, and Anthony Woodbury. I thank the following native speakers for helpful comments on the story: Christine Alowa, Anders Apassingok, Linda Badten, Elmer Campbell, Sr., Mabel Toolie, John Waghiyi, Sr., John Waghiyi, Jr., and Nancy and Willis Walunga. This paper is based upon work supported by the National Science Foundation (grant no. BNS 8418256).

—Willem J. de Reuse

Qati Hik:
A St. Lawrence Island Yupik Tale

Told by Della Waghiyi of Savoonga

Section 1   Aperture and Background

(1) Ungipaghaninguq imani;
   taawanguq yaywaalingiighhaq;
   nengyuqutalghiik kiyaghlleghhiik,
   neqangisagllagek paneghnaqeghllagek,
   tamaani ayumequlleghmi.

(2) Amalleqa elngaatall aghneghmi ataasimi;
   mekelghiighhhaq taana;
   nengyughhani pimakanga,
   Apaay! Esnighqwataghnaqunga;
   esnamun samavek.

(3) Aangghumakanga nengyughhaan.

Section 2   Orphan Boy Goes Beachcombing

2.1   Finds Hair Seal

(4) Amenam atghaghluni esnamun taagavek igleghsimalghii.
   Esnightunga ngaya haa-aa ngaa
   Esnightunga ngaya haa-aa ngaa

(5) Inganguq elngaatall nazighaghhaq,
   tepsaqminigu.

(6) Tazingavek ketanquvikumakanga kaatqaghlluku
   qukaakun kepaghesanghluku legan tuufqaghsimakanga.
   Qati:: hik [swallowing]

Section 1   Aperture and Background

(1)   In a story long ago;

there was a little orphan;

living with his grandmother,

they had no food and were starving,

in that time of the year.

(2)   And on one day;

that little boy;

told his grandmother,

Grandma! I am going beachcombing;

down to the shore.

(3)   His grandmother agreed.

Section 2   Orphan Boy Goes Beachcombing

2.1   Finds Hair Seal

(4)   Going down to the beach he was walking there.

I am bea—eachco—ombi—ing

I am bea—eachco—ombi—ing

(5)   Over there was a small hair seal,

that had drifted ashore.

(6)   He ran over there and when he arrived

he just cut it in half and swallowed it.

Qati:: hik [swallowing]

2.2   Finds Spotted Seal

(7)   Taagken alla igleghllaataamalghii taagavek amenam.

> Esnightunga ngaya haa-aa ngaa
> Esnightunga ngaya haa-aa ngaa

(8)   Taaganiqaaghaghnguq whaa,
> qazigyaghpawaaghhaq tepqaghllaataamakanga.

(9)   Kaa[h] legan kaalluku qukaakun kepaghesnaghluku
tuufqaghllaataamakanga.

> Qati:: hik [swallowing]

2.3   Finds Ring Seal

(10)   Tuufluku taagken igleghllaataamalghii.

> Esnightunga ngaya haa-aa ngaa
> Esnightunga ngaya haa-aa ngaa
> Esnightunga ngaya haa
> Esnightunga ngaya haa

(11)   Kii[h] weni maaten wataqaaghaq aangataghaghluni
tepqaghsalghiimi,
> neghsapiwaaghllak.

(12)   Legan tawaten qukaakun kepaghesnaghluku tuuflaataamakanga.
> Qati:: hik [swallowing]

2.4   Finds Young Bearded Seal

(13)   Tuufsamigu taagken alla igleghllaataamalghii.

> Esnightunga ngaya haa-aa ngaa
> Esnightunga ngaya haa-aa ngaa
> Esnightunga ngaya haa
> Esnightunga ngaya haa

(14)   Kii[h] maaten elngaatall,
tepqaghsaqminigunguq teghiglugllak.

(15)   Elngaatall legan kaataghesnaghluku qukaakun kepaghesnaghluku
legan tuuflaataamakanga.
> Qati:: hik [swallowing]

2.2 Finds Spotted Seal

(7) Then he went on again.

> I am bea–eachco–ombi–ing
>
> I am bea–eachco–ombi–ing

(8) Not too far away,

> a spotted seal had drifted ashore.

(9) Oh, he just got there, he cut it in half and swallowed it again.

> Qati:: hik [swallowing]

2.3 Finds Ring Seal

(10) After that he kept on walking.

> I am bea–eachco–ombi–ing
>
> I am bea–eachco–ombi–ing
>
> I am bea–eachco–ombing
>
> I am bea–eachco–ombing

(11) Oh, and now something much bigger had washed ashore,

> a rather big ring seal.

(12) Just like that he cut it in half and swallowed it.

> Qati:: hik [swallowing]

2.4 Finds Young Bearded Seal

(13) And then he continued walking again.

> I am bea–eachco–ombi–ing
>
> I am bea–eachco–ombi–ing
>
> I am bea–eachco–ombing
>
> I am bea–eachco—ombing

(14) Oh, now,

> a young bearded seal had drifted ashore.

(15) When he gets to it he just cuts it in half

> and swallows it.
>
> Qati:: hik [swallowing]

2.5 Finds Minke Whale

(16) Legan tuufsamigu taagaveqaaghaq wata igleghllaataamalghii.

> Esnightunga ngaya haa-aa ngaa
>
> Esnightunga ngaya haa-aa ngaa
>
> Esnightunga ngaya haa
>
> Esnightunga ngaya haa

(17) Kii[h] maaten kaasaqminigu inga legan tepqaghlleghhii, qungvughaq.

(18) Legan kaataghesnaghluku qukaakun kepqaghluku tuuflaataamakanga.

> Qati:: hik [swallowing]

2.n Summary of Other Animals Found

(19) Taawa[h] igleghsimalghii tawaten tuufqaghtaqluki,

> qungvughaat
>
> aghvepiget
>
> ayveghet,
>
> tamana teghikusaq neghumakanga,
>
> kaanneghminiki legan tawaten tuufqaghtaqluni.

Section 3 Wants to Enter House

3.0 Introduction

(20) Taagken taglaamalghii mekelghiighhaq yaywaalingiighhaq taana.

3.1 Tries Door

(21) Kaalluni nengyughhani qamavek pimakanga,

> – Enaangaay! Nakun iteghlaaki?

(22) – Qa[h] nagun iteghnaluten pizin,

> amigkun iitghi! nengyughhaan pimakanga tawavek.

(23) – Kangsughtungaay! Kangsughtungaay!

2.5   Finds Minke Whale

(16)   After that he kept on going farther.

> I am bea–eachco–ombi–ing
> I am bea–eachco–ombi–ing
> I am bea–eachco–ombing
> I am bea–eachco–ombing

(17)   Oh, now, when he gets over there, there is a
minke whale.

(18)   When he arrives there he cuts it in half and swallows it.

> Qati:: hik [swallowing]

2.n   Summary of Other Animals Found

(19)   Well, as he was traveling, he also swallowed,

> Minke whales
> bowhead whales
> walruses,

all these animals he ate,
just swallowing them as he found them.

Section 3   Wants to Enter House

3.0   Introduction

(20)   Then that little orphan boy came back up from the shore.

3.1   Tries Door

(21)   As he arrived, he said to his grandmother,

> –   Grandma-aa! How can I get in?

(22)   –   Ah, how do you expect to come in,
come in through the door! said his grandmother.

(23)   –   I couldn't get through! Couldn't get through!

3.2 Tries Air Vent

(24) Aaplaataamakanga mekelghiighhaam nengyughhani,
– Enaangaay, nakun iteghlaaki?

(25) – Qa[h] nagun iteghnaluten pizin,
iiyakun iitghi!

(26) – Kangsughtungaay! Kangsughtungaay!

3.3 Tries the Eye of a Needle and Succeeds

(27) – Qa[h] sullevneghhaghmeng mekelghiighhaq qakemna
nagun iteghnaluni pii.

(28) Sikuum iiyngakun iitghi!

(29) Sunanguq taana mekelghiighhaq iteghtuq.

Section 4 Wants to Vomit

4.1 Tries Wooden Bucket

(30) Taagken aaplaataamakanga nengyughhani,
– Enaangaay, sakun mighyaghlaaki?

(31) – Qa[h] sakun mighyaghnaluten pizin,
ghhutegnekun mighyaa!

(32) – Esleqelleqagka.

4.2 Tries Honeybucket

(33) Pilaataamakanga tawavek nengyughhani,
– Enaangaay, sakun mighyaghlaaki?

(34) – Qa[h] sakun mighyaghnaluten pizin,
qullugnekun mighyaa!

(35) – Esleqelleqagka.

4.3 Tries Corner Of The Floor And Succeeds

(36) – Enaangaay, sakun mighyaghlaaki?

(37) – Qa[h] sakun una mighyaghnaluni pii,
ugatangakun mighyaa!

3.2   Tries Air Vent

(24)   The little boy asked his grandmother again,

–   Grandma-aa! How can I get in?

(25)   –   Ah, how do you expect to come in,
come in through the air vent!

(26)   –   I couldn't get through! Couldn't get through!

3.3   Tries the Eye of a Needle and Succeeds

(27)   –   Ah, what a pain, that little boy, how does he expect to get
in.

(28)   Come in through the eye of a needle!

(29)   Sure enough that little boy came in.

Section 4   Wants to Vomit

4.1   Tries Wooden Bucket

(30)   Then he asked his grandmother again,

–   Grandma-aa, where can I vomit?

(31)   –   Ah, where do you expect to vomit,
vomit in the bucket!

(32)   –   I will fill it up to the brim.

4.2   Tries Honeybucket

(33)   Again he asked his grandmother,

–   Grandma-aa, where can I vomit?

(34)   –   Ah, where do you expect to vomit,
vomit in the honeybucket!

(35)   –   I will fill it up to the brim.

4.3   Tries Corner of the Floor and Succeeds

(36)   –   Grandma-aa, where can I vomit?

(37)   –   Ah, where does he expect to vomit,
vomit in the corner of the floor!

Section 5　　Denouement and Closure

(38)　Kii[h] mighyaghyalghiiminguq elngaatall,

nazighaq

qazigyaq

teghigluk

maklak

ayveq,

unkuvak

puugzaq

aghvepik,

neqeghllaghughllutek nengyuqutalghiik.

(39)　Neqmeng aklunanighwaaghlutek.

(40)　Tefaay! Aliinghaku::n amsanaku::n!

Section 5   Denouement and Closure

(38)   Oh, he vomited everything,

> the hair seal
>
> the spotted seal
>
> the young bearded seal
>
> the adult bearded seal
>
> the walrus,
>
> the year-old walrus
>
> the beluga
>
> the bowhead whale,

he and his grandmother had enough food now.

(39)   They were no longer in need of food.

(40)   *Tefaay*! Through this story, nice weather, clear and calm!

Works Cited and Suggested Reading

Apassingok, Anders (Iyaaka) et al. 1985. *Sivuqam Nangaghnegha, Siivanllemta Ungipaqellghat / Lore of St. Lawrence Island, Echoes of our Eskimo Elders*, vol. 1. Gambell, Unalakleet, AK: Bering Strait School District.
1987. *Sivuqam Nangaghnegha, Siivanllemta Ungipaqellghat / Lore of St. Lawrence Island, Echoes of Our Eskimo Elders*, vol. 2. Savoonga, Unalakleet, AK: Bering Strait School District.
1989. *Sivuqam Nangaghnegha, Siivanllemta Ungipaqellghat / Lore of St. Lawrence Island, Echoes of our Eskimo Elders*, vol. 3. Southwest Cape, Unalakleet, AK: Bering Strait School District.

Badten, Linda Womkon, et al. 1987. *A Dictionary of the St. Lawrence Island / Siberian Yupik Eskimo Language*. Fairbanks: Alaska Native Language Center, University of Alaska.

de Reuse, Willem J. 1986. "Using Ethnopoetics in Teaching Traditional Native Texts." Paper presented at the 13th annual meeting of the Alaska Anthropological Association, Fairbanks, Alaska.
1994. *Siberian Yupik Eskimo: The Language and Its Contacts with Chukchi*. Salt Lake City: University of Utah Press.

Dolitksy, Alexander B., ed. 2000. *Tales and Legends of the Yupik Eskimos of Siberia*. Juneau: Alaska-Siberia Research Center.

Hughes, Charles C. 1984a. "Siberian Eskimo," in *Handbook of North American Indians*, vol. 5, *Arctic*, David Damas, ed., pp. 247–261. Washington, D.C.: Smithsonian Institution Press.
1984b. "St. Lawrence Island Eskimo" in *Handbook of North American Indians*, vol. 5, *Arctic*, David Damas, ed., pp. 262–277. Washington, D.C.: Smithsonian Institution Press.

Hymes, Dell. 1980. "Particle, Pause and Pattern in American Indian Narrative Verse," *American Indian Culture and Research Journal* 4:7–51.
1981. *"In Vain I Tried to Tell You" : Essays in Native American Ethnopoetics*. Philadelphia: University of Pennsylvania Press.
1985. "Language, Memory, and Selective Performance: Cultee's 'Salmon's Myth' as Twice Told to Boas," *Journal of American Folklore* 98:391–434.
1992. "Use All There Is to Use," in *On the Translation of Native American Literatures*, Brian Swann, ed., pp. 83–124. Washington, D.C.: Smithsonian Institution Press.

Jacobson, Steven A. 2001. *A Practical Grammar of the St. Lawrence Island / Siberian Yupik Eskimo Language*, 2nd ed. Fairbanks: Alaska Native Language Center, University of Alaska.

Krauss, Michael. 1975. "St. Lawrence Island Eskimo Phonology and Orthography," *Linguistics: An International Review* 152:39–72.

Krupnik, Igor, Willis Walunga, and Vera Metcalf, eds. 2002. *Akuzilleput Igaqullghet / Our Words Put to Paper: Sourcebook in St. Lawrence Island Heritage and History*. Washington, D.C.: Arctic Studies Center, Smithsonian Institution.

Nelson, Edward William. 1899. *The Eskimo about Bering Strait*. Bureau of American Ethnology Annual Report for 1896–1897, Vol. 18, Pt. I. Washington, D.C.: Smithsonian Institution Press (reprinted 1983).

Silook, Susie. 1999. "Adventure in Chinatown 1958," in *Alaska Native Writers, Storytellers, and Orators*, special issue of *Alaska Quarterly Review* 4(3–4):252–253.

Silook, Roger S. 1976. *Seevookuk: Stories the Old People Told on St. Lawrence Island*. N.p.

Woodbury, Anthony C. 1985. "The Functions of Rhetorical Structure: A Study of Central Alaskan Yupik Eskimo Discourse," *Language in Society* 14:153–90. 1987. "Rhetorical Structure in a Central Alaskan Yupik Eskimo Traditional Narrative," in *Native American Discourse: Poetics and Rhetoric*, Joel Sherzer and Anthony C. Woodbury, eds., pp. 177–239. Cambridge: Cambridge University Press.

Woodbury, Anthony C. and Leo Moses. 1994. "Mary Kokrak: Five Brothers and Their Younger Sister," in *Coming to Light: Contemporary Translations of the Native Literatures of North America*, Brian Swann, ed., pp. 15–36. New York: Vintage Books.

PART IV

Alutiiq Narratives

THE TRADITIONAL HOMELAND of the Sugpiaq or Alutiiq people (the former means "real person"; the latter is the word "Aleut" spoken in the Sugtestun language) extends along the southcentral coast of Alaska from Prince William Sound, around the southern tip of the Kenai Peninsula to Kodiak Island, and across Shelikof Strait to the Alaska Peninsula. In this essay, the terms "Sugpiaq" and "Alutiiq" will be used interchangeably in recognition of different preferences among the people; some prefer to use one designation, some the other.

Archaeological records of human habitation in the region extend back ten thousand years and follow a complex trajectory of movement, contact, and technological change. The Sugpiaq people were connected by a common culture and language (with two dialects), as well as kinship relationships forged through centuries of trade, intermarriage, and warfare.

Sugtestun/Alutiiq is an Eskimo language traditionally spoken by the Sugpiat (plural of Sugpiaq). The language is closely related to Central Yup'ik, but in the public mind the people and their language are more closely associated with a distantly related group, the Unangas/Unangan of the Aleutian Islands. Both peoples are now commonly called Aleuts, and indeed, many call themselves by that name. This has resulted in confusion among outsiders who often mistake the two for the same people. Neither Unangan nor Sugpiat used the term "Aleut" in the days before contact with Europeans. The term is probably of Siberian origin and was introduced by eighteenth-century Russian traders who applied it to Unangan, Alaska Peninsula Sugpiat, and Kodiak Sugpiat alike. The name had become widespread and "Sugtestunized" by the early nineteenth century and is only now declining in use in preference for the original term.

Alutiiq is an endangered language spoken by few people under age sixty. Ignatius Kosbruk, whose bear story follows, was a fluent speaker who pre-

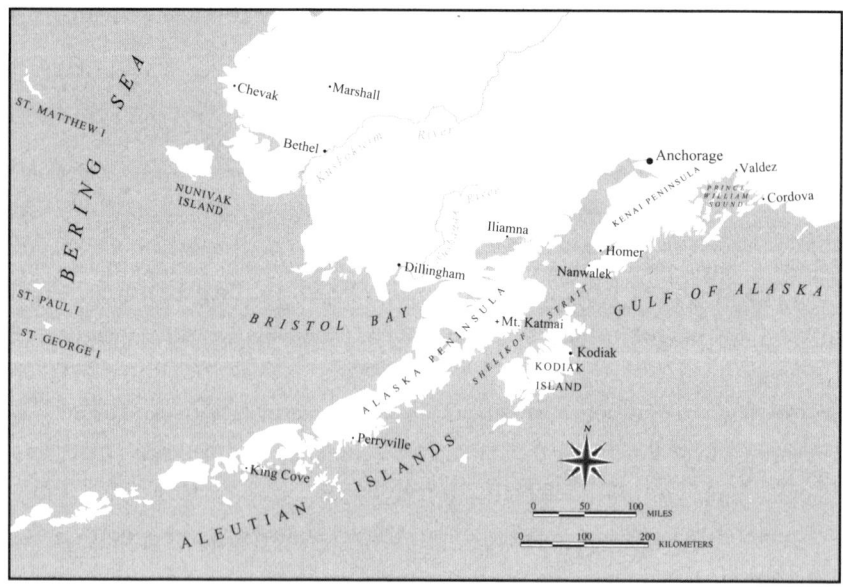

The Alaska Peninsula and Kodiak Island. The story "Arnaq Takukaraam Pillra" has been associated with Kodiak Island, the now-abandoned village of Katmai (near Mt. Katmai) and Perryville, where the Katmai residents established a new community.

Words of the Real People

ferred to tell the traditional narratives in his own language—but his example is rarely followed nowadays. Instead, most people recount and reminisce in English so their children and grandchildren can understand.

Recorded Sugpiaq history began a scant two hundred years ago when a handful of Russians built fur trading posts throughout the region. Through a combination of force, persuasion, and novelty, they quickly convinced the people to hunt and trap fur-bearing animals for the European fur trade; in exchange, they gave the hunters goods such as cloth, metal, sugar, and tea. By the middle of the 1800s, Russian priests were making regular visits to Alutiiq settlements, most of whose inhabitants had been baptized into the Russian Orthodox church. Today's Alutiit claim ancestry from Russian immigrants, and also from Yupiit, Unangan, Athabaskan Indians, and later voyagers born in Scandinavia, Italy, Greece, Japan, and points beyond.

Traditionally, Sugpiat located their villages in bays behind headlands. The perfect village site was protected from storms, near a freshwater salmon stream, and fronted by a smooth, wide beach where driftwood logs collected. A rocky promontory nearby provided an endless supply of sea urchins, mussels, octopus, and chitons; the plain behind the village was populated by caribou, fox, or bear, and a sea mammal rookery was within paddling distance. Lakes and ponds inshore provided nesting grounds for waterfowl. The ideal village was located near a lookout hill and was defensible against marauders coming by sea, while providing an escape route should defensive measures fail. Often a group inhabited two sites, one in the winter and one in the summer.

Each village consisted of several houses. In Kodiak and on the Alaska Peninsula these were semi-subterranean sod-covered houses, *ciqlluat* (singular *ciqlluaq*), which the Russians called *barabaras*. The size and shape of the family homes varied, depending on the number of inhabitants. Some *barabaras* were large enough to house twenty people and consisted of a large central kitchen and work area surrounded by attached private family rooms. Other side rooms were used for sweat baths. The dirt floor was covered with cut grass or grass mats. In Prince William Sound, the houses were rectangular structures made of wood with grass-covered roofs, similar to the dwellings of the Northwest Coast Indians.

In addition to individual *barabaras*, many villages had one or more larger, centrally located buildings called *qasgit* (singular *qasgiq*), similar in function to a community hall. Dances, ceremonies, and celebrations were held here, particularly during the winter. Because most Alutiit converted to Russian Orthodoxy within a generation of contact, the exact nature of the precontact ceremonies is not known. However, early Russian observers on Kodiak Island, such as Gavriil Davydov and Hieromonk Gideon, reported masking festivals, thanksgiving rituals, whaling ceremonies, memorial feasts for the dead, invitational feasts at trading time, rituals preceding battles, and the presentation of new village leaders.

Like Aleutian Islanders, Alutiit were known for their skill in building, maneuvering, and hunting from skin qayaqs. Their most common sea-based prey included seals, sea lions, sea otters, and whales. They developed a complex technology for hunting, harvesting, and processing food, each item ideally suited to a particular species, technique, and purpose. Men wore beautifully carved and painted wooden helmets, cone-shaped hats, and bentwood visors while on the hunt as a way of communicating honorable intentions to their prey (Black 1991). Salmon, halibut, and cod fishing were essential economic activities, and caribou and bear hunting were also important. Women sewed bear intestines into beautiful waterproof coats needed for sea mammal hunting on the open ocean. Children trapped ground squirrels for their skins, which their mothers then made into serviceable parkas. Men and boys hunted ducks, geese, and other birds for their skins and meat, and people of all ages gathered eggs. Women and children were expert shellfish gatherers, bringing in huge amounts of edible mollusks and sea urchins. Women and girls also picked and dug berries and roots, then preserved them in seal oil for the winter.

The oldest Alutiiq stories, which were commonly called *unigkuat* (singular *unigkuaq*), took place in the distant time when the world was different from today. In those long-gone days, animals and people could communicate with each other directly using the Sugtestun language. Animals could transform themselves into human-looking beings by taking off their animal skins and humans could reverse the process by putting on animal skins. This was when humans learned essential rules about the respectful treatment of animals, prohibitions against wasting game, and proper care of animal bones or skins. The elders say that the human-animal interactions that are described in *unigkuat* are rare nowadays but that in the past they happened to everyone. The animals have not lost their ability to understand humans, but few humans can now understand messages from the animals.

There are also more recent stories called *quliyanguat* (sing. *quliyanguaq*), which happened in the past, but are about people whom living Alutiit remember personally or remember hearing about when they were children. Ignatius Kosbruk characterized the following story as a *quliyanguaq*.

A tradition of oral scholarship within Alutiiq society has kept some stories alive through the centuries. In the 1930s Ignatius Kosbruk was chosen by his mentor to listen, recite, and pass down the *unigkuat* and *quliyanguat* he was told. But written versions of the stories are scarce. Two Russian visitors, one a soldier of fortune (Gavriil Davydov, who figures in the article that follows) and the other a Russian Orthodox priest, Gideon, transcribed versions of the tales they were told in the early nineteenth century. A Frenchman, Alphonse Pinart, visiting nearly three-quarters of a century later, reported summaries of a few traditional narratives. Frank Golder published traditional narratives from the Aleutians and Kodiak Island in the *Journal of American Folk-Lore* at the beginning of the twentieth century. Margaret Lantis examined the work of Golder and other collectors in an article about the mythology of Kodiak Island in 1938. The Danish ethnologist Kaj Birket-Smith, along with American anthropologist Frederica DeLaguna, recorded a number of *unigkuat* and *quliyanguat* from Prince William Sound in the 1930s. Father Harry Kaiakokonok, an Alutiiq elder from the village of Perryville, wrote a lengthy account of the 1912 Katmai eruption, which caused the evacuation of Katmai residents to Perryville, when he was in the hospital in 1956.

Jeff Leer began working with Alutiiq speakers in the late 1960s, encouraging them to transcribe traditional tales and compose original works, at the same time making electronic recordings for the Alaska Native Language Center's (University of Alaska Fairbanks) tape library. Independent researchers as well as those working for the National Park Service, University of Alaska Anchorage, and Bureau of Indian Affairs recorded life stories and environmental information for two decades beginning in the 1960s from informants such as Harry O. Kaiakonkonok and Spiridon Stepanoff. In the 1970s and 1980s, several high schools in the region undertook oral history projects that encouraged students to interview their elders and publish their stories. Kodiak's *Elwani* (see, for example, Nielson 1976) and English Bay's

Alexandrovsk are examples. Patricia Partnow worked on the Alaska Peninsula to record *unigkuat* and *quliyanguat* in the early 1990s. Several Sugpiaq scholars and writers have contributed their own works in recent years, notably Mary Jane Nielsen, whose nonfiction appears in several anthologies, and Gordon Pullar, scholar, university administrator, and co-editor of *Looking Both Ways: Heritage and Identity of the Alutiiq People*. Other individuals continue the tradition, both in oral performances and writing.

—Patricia Partnow

The Power of Story
Arnaq Taqukaraam Pillra /
The Woman Who Was Gotten by the Bear

Told by Ignatius Kosbruk of Perryville

Recording and commentary by Patricia Partnow
Transcribed and translated with notes
and commentary by Jeff Leer

I first heard "Arnaq Taqukaraam Pillra" on November 11, 1992, when Alutiiq elder Ignatius Kosbruk of Perryville, Alaska, agreed to record the story in his home. This *quliyanguq* (historical story) is about two brothers in search of a murderous bear. The narrative is a remarkable example of Alutiiq folklore by itself, but the story is rendered even more intriguing because a version was published in Russia two hundred years ago. As one of the few traditional stories that is still told today, it has survived the importation of a foreign culture, economy, and power structure, the immigration of thousands of strangers, and the geographic relocation of a large portion of the Alutiiq people.

As a boy during the late 1930s, young Ignatius Kosbruk had studied in trapping cabins and sod houses in Perryville with an elder who passed on *unigkuat* and *quliyanguat* to a cadre of boys—all potential tradition bearers, like their mentor. Ignatius showed an aptitude for storytelling and gradually assumed the role of community storyteller—a role that he retained until his death in 1998. While in training, Ignatius had been quizzed daily by his teacher to ensure that he had the details of his stories correct. Part of learning a traditional narrative from a mentor, for Ignatius as for other Alutiiq storytellers, was understanding the message it held for him and communicating that message to a living audience. This required a delicate balance, for he was not allowed to change the story to suit contemporary fashion or personal whim; instead, he had to study it until it flowed naturally and truly from his being. This process meant that each telling resulted in a version that was inspired by and responded to a specific situation while remaining true to the story as originally learned. In November 1992, Ignatius made clear that he was telling me the story to teach important lessons about the strength and vitality of the Alutiiq culture. He also requested that this and other narratives be recorded for the benefit of younger generations of Alutiit.

Context: Perryville 1992

In November 1992, as part of fieldwork for a doctorate in anthropology (Partnow 2001), I visited Perryville with Alaska Department of Fish and Game anthropologist Lisa Scarbrough, who was conducting a subsistence survey in the village. Between interviews we visited and chatted with our hosts. Bears are commonly hunted in the winter after the first snows, precisely the time of the visit, so the surveys brought to mind bear stories. One afternoon over tea and chewing tobacco Ignatius agreed to record one such tale in the Alutiiq language. He sat comfortably at his kitchen table, leaning toward the microphone, using what I would call a "broadcast voice"—that is, he spoke loudly and clearly, mindful that his recording would be a lasting legacy to his people. During the story's most intense sections, Ignatius's normal baritone dropped to a lower register and his volume decreased. He leaned even closer to the microphone, shaking his head or gesturing to illustrate the action. Although I could only understand a word here and there, the performance was mesmerizing.

The next day I returned with the tape and asked him to translate the story into English while I again recorded. Ignatius's daughter Vivian Kosbruk, a contemporary of mine, was present at the second session. Although she understands a great deal of Alutiiq, Vivian does not speak it, so her father's translation was as much for her benefit as mine.

Ignatius was only a couple of sentences into the interlinear translation of the previous day's recording when he became impatient with the exercise. He was an artist—a storyteller—not a linguist, and had little interest in the detailed work involved in translation. So he abandoned the task of interlinear translation and instead retold the rest of the story in English without listening to his Alutiiq recording from the previous day.

The English version sounded familiar to me and when I returned home I checked available literature on Alutiiq lore. The translation of Gavriil Davydov's book, *Two Voyages to Russian America, 1802–1807*, originally published in 1810, contained a story told by a Kodiak Islander that was identical in many

Ignatius Kosbruk in Perryville, 1992.

details to Ignatius's story, though told almost two centuries earlier. The time lapse between the two performances is remarkable, but the geographic distance is not. Kodiak Islanders and Alaska Peninsula Alutiit speak the same dialect of the Alutiiq language, the result of centuries of contact and intermarriage. Perryville, some two hundred miles from the closest part of Kodiak Island, is a recent settlement, established in 1912 by refugees from the Katmai coast who fled the devastating volcanic eruption in June of that year. Ignatius was therefore sharing an oral tradition that he derived from Katmai, which lies north, up the Pacific shore of the peninsula from Perryville. Katmai was just a day's trip in good weather by qayaq across Shelikof Strait from Kodiak Island.

Ignatius explained that his story was about bears and shamans. But were he alive today, he might also say that no story is about only one or two topics, for each listener will get out of it what his or her personal circumstances bring to it. In fact, most of his stories, including this one, contained a number of themes, each relevant to different people at different times of their lives. His favorite themes in stories told to me were:

The dual aspect of reality, at once natural and supernatural, human and non-human;

The physical and spiritual dangers posed by the Russian and American cultures to the Alutiiq people;

The ability of Alutiit to overcome the dangers inherent in living in the world both in the past and today through proper attitude, adequate knowledge, and careful behavior;

The importance of carrying on traditions so the young will learn the lessons acquired at great expense in the past.

The Stories

Four versions of the Alutiiq story "Arnaq Taqukaraam Pillra" follow. The first is a transcription in Ignatius's first language, Alutiiq, with an interlinear translation provided by linguist Jeff Leer, who had worked with the elder for more than a dozen years. The second is the free translation, in English, of the same version, again provided by Jeff. The third is the same story told by Ignatius the next day, this time in English. The final rendering is the English translation of the story from Gavriil Davydov's 1810 Russian publication of his visit to Kodiak Island.

Version 1

In the interlinear transcript and free translation that follow, numbers after nouns and pronouns clarify references to people. For instance, if two women are together, the first woman is called "she1" and the second "she2." Each referent is given its own number, followed throughout the translation. This practice is necessary because the clear difference in Alutiiq between reflexive and non-reflexive third person pronouns does not translate into English. This device is particularly important in understanding what the two brothers are doing during the bear-killing scene.

The characters and their numerical designations in the translation are:

she1	a berry picker
she2	the partner of she1; the woman who was killed and whose brothers sought her killer
they3	the dead woman's two brothers
he3a	the older brother
he3b	the younger brother
it4	the bear that killed the woman
he5 or they5	the shaman or shamans who controlled the killer bear
they6	people from the men's village
them7	the tools and means of training for the men's quest
it8 or they8	other bears encountered while the men searched for the killer bear

Una gguani gua'i quliyanguaq.

This | here | here is | a story.

Nallu'aqa ḵesiin nanirpiaq pillria,

I don't know | however | exactly where | it happened,

Katmaayami allrak,

at Katmai | perhaps,

gguall'u-qaa aagani nani, Nunamiuni;

or maybe | over there | somewhere | at Nunamiut;[1]

gguall'u Nunamiu'ak.

maybe | they were two Nunamiut people.

Mall'uk arnak[2] unatarsaumuuk uksuarmi.

Two | women | must have gone berry picking | in the fall.

Unatarlutek tawaten[3]

They were picking berries like that

cangami-gguq taima angayuni tamaraa.

at some point she1, they say, | suddenly | her partner2 | she1 lost her2.

Awa piciinani.

Now | she didn't know what to do.

Cali angicami quli'arluku

Back | when she arrived | she told of her2

nutaan angayuni tamarniluku.

just now | her partner2 | saying that she lost her2.

Nutaan kangircingamek taugkuk anngak,

just now | when they3 understood | those two | her two older brothers3,

taug'um arnaunertek tamarluku,

that one1 | their sister2 | she had lost her,

kangirciluku taquka'armen picaa.

they understood | a bear | the fact that it did it to her2.

Cali nallugkunaku taugna pistii,[4]

Also | they knew | that [bear] | the one that killed her2,

kallagalegnun piyuklluku.

a shaman5 | they3 thought they5 had instigated it4.

Nutaan tawaken suu'ut niu'ulluki

Now | after that | people6 | they3 talked to them6

iwaraaciqniluku taugna taquka'aq pistii,

saying that they3 would search for it4 | that | bear | the one that killed her2,

arnaunertek tamaqengartek.

their3 sister | the one they3 had lost.

Nutaan tawaken aularnirlutek,

Now | after that | they started,

taangami, nunami,

in the water, | on the land,

caqait makut tukningcarsuutet tamaita aturluki,

things | these | means of training for strength | all | using them7,

taangami pingurllutek,[5]

in the water | they3 [?]-ed,

nunamen aglutek.

to the land | they went.

Awa'i cangamek taima-gguq anngaan pigaa,

Then | at some point they3 | suddenly, it is said, | his3b older brother3a | he3a said to him [the younger brother],

"Kita, ugnerkarngan tamaana uksuq."[6]

"Come on, | because it is spring | that | winter."

Uksuq nangluku tawani tukningcarlutek.[7]

Winter | depleting it | there | they3 trained for strength.

Nallugkunaku kallagalegmen picaa taugna arnaunertek.

They3 knew | a shaman | the fact that he had done it to her | their sister,

Nutaan tawaken tukningcarlutek, uksuq nangpiarluku.

Now | after that | they trained for strength, | winter | completely depleting it.

Nutaan cangami anngaan piluku,

Now | at some point he3a | his3b older brother | he3a told him [the younger brother],

awa'i allrak taqnilutek.

now | perhaps | they3 were ready.

Caqait makut gguani egqaqlluki,

Things | these | here |they3 threw them one after another,

yaamasinat egqaqlluki.

big rocks | they3 threw them one after another.

Nutaan makut caa'itet amuursaurcamegtegneki

Just now | these | willows | then they3 started to pull them out [of the ground]

piluku anngaan,

he3a said to him3b | his older brother,

"Kita, awa'i ugnerkartuq."

"Come on, | now | it's spring."

Anngata taqukaraat qawaraarqelluki,[8]

When they8 went out | the bears | after they had been hibernating,

nutaan nunamen nangarllutek.

just now | to the land | they3 stood up [to go].

Tamarpiarpia'an taquka'aq man'a tekiskengartek cu'ukartestaarlutek,

Every single one8 | bear | this one8 |the one8 they3 arrived at | they provoked it to charge them,

cu'ukaqatek panaluku.

when it charged them | they speared it.

Tuqulluku tamarpiarpia'an nunamen ilaspiarluki[9] ilasaagluki.

They killed it | every single one | to the ground | mixing them in completely, | mangling them.

Nutaan cangamek agwa'anermegtegni[10]

Just now | at some point they3 | while they3 moved from place to place [?]

cali tawaten taqukaraat tuqulluki.

again | thus | the bears | they killed them.

Cangamek-gguq taima te̲kitaak taquka'aq,

At some point they3, it is said | finally | they came to it | the bear,

angegkunani-gguq.

it4 was not big, he said.

Nutaan tawaken anngarni piluku ayaqusqelluku uyaquikun.

Now | after that | his3b older brother3a | he3b told him3a | to spear it [the bear] | through its neck.

That tongs, they used to call [spoken in English].

They tong him on the head [spoken in English].

Put him down on the ground [spoken in English].

Nutaan anngaan taug'um qayagaluku,

Now | his3b older brother3a | that one3a | he3a kept yelling to him3b

atam ungu'atiikun niini̲luku.[11]

you see | through its heart [?] | saying that he3a heard it.

Tawaten pingnaquagaa-gguq.

Thus | he3b keeps trying to kill it, it is said.

Cangami-gguq taima aqumtaa.

At some point he3b, it is said | finally | he3b sat it4 down.

Aqumtengermiu anngaan taug'um pa̲nalarluku.

Even when he3b had sat it down | his3b older brother3a | that one3a | he3a kept on spearing it.

Ungu'atii-gguq ikugkunaku.

Its heart, he3a said, | he3a couldn't find it.

Nutaan cangami uyuraan piluku

Now | at some point he3b | his3a younger brother3b | he3b told him3a

itgain qalirni'itgun iqsuan tungiikun panasqelluku,

of its4 feet | through their tops | of the left of it | by way of the direction | he3b told him3a to spear it,

tawani-gguq allrak ungu'atii ec'imuuq.

there, he3b said | perhaps | its heart | must be there.

Nutaan tawaken pisqucaatun anngarmi panaluku itgat[12]

Now | after that | according to what he3b told him3a to do | his3b older brother | he3a speared it | feet.

on the left side, palm of his hand [spoken in English].[13]

Then he felt it, he found it [spoken in English],

that the heart was on the left hand side [spoken in English].

Nutaan tawaken ilasaagluku.

Now | after that | they3 mangled it4.

Nutaan tawa'ut killmaanun tekicamek

Now | there | to its4 stomach | when they arrived

killmaq quplluku.

the belly | they split it open.

Taugkut-gguq taima[14] piuqutet,

Those, it is said, | finally | the beads,

beads, what she was wearing, necklace [spoken in English],

they found them [spoken in English].

Nutaan tawaken ilasaagtuarluku nunamen ilaspiarpiarluku.[15]

Now | after that | they kept on mangling it4 | to the ground | mixing it4 in completely.

Nutaan angillutek.

Now | they returned.

Taugna taquka'aq pistellra ikugluku.

That | bear | the one that had killed her | they3 found it.

Cunang-gguq kallagalget pisaallrat.
In reality, they say | shamans5 | she2 was the unfortunate one killed by them5

It wasn't a human [spoken in English].

It was a shaman doing it [spoken in English].

They5 let him4 do it [spoken in English].[16]

Nutaan tawaken suu'ulutek tawani nunamegteni,
Now | after that | they3 lived | there | in their3 village,

tuknilliulutek.
they3 were strong men.

Cangamek-gguq taima angayuqaagken allrak,
At some point they, it is said, | finally | their3 boss | maybe,

after they get American food [spoken in English],

they feed them with corned beef [spoken in English],

and they died with it, poisoned themselves [spoken in English].

That was the end of the story [spoken in English].

Version 2

In free translation, the story reads as follows:

THIS IS A STORY. But I don't know exactly where it took place. Maybe it was at Katmai or maybe somewhere over in the Nunamiut area; maybe they were two Nunamiut women. These two women must have gone berry picking in the fall. As they were picking berries, after a while one of the women suddenly noticed that her partner was missing, they say. She didn't know what to do. When she got back, she told people that she had just lost her partner.

Now when her two older brothers learned that their sister was missing, they realized that it was a bear that had killed her. They also knew that the bear that had killed her was acting on behalf of a shaman.

After that, they told the people that they would search for the bear that had killed their sister whom they had lost.

Right then they started training themselves for strength, in the water and on land, using all these training techniques. They [?]-ed in the water and went back onto the land. After a while, the older brother suddenly said to his younger brother, "Let's get to it because spring is coming." They trained themselves there all winter long. They knew that a shaman had killed their sister. So they trained themselves all winter long. Then at one point the older brother said to his younger brother, "I guess we're ready now." They threw these huge rocks, rock after rock after rock. Then they pulled willows out of the ground. Then the older brother said to him, "Come on, let's go. It's spring now."

When the bears had come out of hibernation, they got up and started off into the country. Every single bear they came to, they provoked it into charging them, and when it charged them, they speared it. They killed every single one of them, mangling them and mixing their remains right into the ground. After a while they would move from place to place; every place they went they killed the bears in the same way.

Finally they came to a bear. It was not a big one, he said. Right away the older brother told the younger to spear it in the neck. Tongs is what they used to call them. They tonged him on the head, put him down on the ground. Then the older brother kept on yelling to him, "I can hear its heart." So the younger brother kept on trying to kill it. Finally the younger brother got it down on the ground. Even when it was on the ground, the older brother kept on spearing it. He said he couldn't find its heart. Then the younger brother told him to spear it on the top side of its feet, on the left-hand side. He said that was where its heart must be. So his older brother did as he said and speared it on the left side palm of his hand. Then he felt it, he found it, that the heart was on the left-hand side. Then they mangled it.

Then when they got to its stomach they split it open. Finally they found those beads, the ones she was wearing, the necklace. Then they kept mangling it and mixed its remains right into the ground.

Then they went back home. They had found the bear that killed her. But in fact, it was the shamans that made it do that. It wasn't a human; it was shamans doing it. They made him do it.

After that they lived there in their village; they were strong men.

Finally, maybe it was their boss's doing, after they got American food, they fed them corned beef, and they died from it, poisoned themselves. That was the end of the story.

Version 3

When Ignatius retold the story in English on the second day of recording, he entered a storytelling—as opposed to translating—mode at the point in the narrative when two boys have just learned that their sister has been eaten by the bear. Vivian and I were told that the killer was not a normal bear, but rather a shaman-controlled creature. We were not told the motivation for the murder. The following transcription of Ignatius's second recording session picks up the narrative when the boys have decided to wreak vengeance on the bear. Paragraph breaks represent long pauses in the narration.

BUT AFTER THAT, THEY [THE BROTHERS] went into the river and exercised themselves so they could be strong enough to fight the bear. They pull the trees down. The alders. That's how they were. They started to exercise in water and on the land. So they could attack the bear if they charged them. They were practicing for a whole year. Whole year! Exercising themselves so they could be strong enough. Finally when they thought they were strong enough, his brother, older brother, told him, "I think we're strong enough." And examined themselves when they start to pull the trees from the ground, roots and all. And he said, "That's enough. I think we're good. We could start now." They pulled the trees up right off from the ground. Roots and all. How strong they were.

So when the spring come, when the bears were out from hibernation, they started to look for the bear. And they attack every bear that they see and let the bear charge on them. So they kill every bear they see.

And finally they found one. It wasn't so big, he said. It wasn't so big a bear. And—and he hollered to his brother to use tongs to keep the bear down on his head. And he did. And he couldn't, he couldn't press him down to the ground. So he hollered to him that "Use a spear! If you can't find his heart, his heart must be on his left-hand side, on his top of his hand." On the top, yeah. They struggled for a long, long time. And his brother say that he got tired, he's getting tired. And his brother, older brother was spearing him for a long, long time. He couldn't find the heart. He kept on spearing him and spearing him and finally his brother hollered to him that his heart must be on the top of his hand, on the palm of his hand.[17] On the left hand side. To spear—put the spear on his left hand side. Soon as he put the spear on, fall dead.

So, it was made by the shaman.

And they tore that bear up all to pieces. And they finally found his stomach. They opened the stomach, and found her sister's beads.[18] And they tore him all to pieces. I don't know how small they were. Every bit of it.

And they brought the necklace back to their home. And keeped it for their souvenir. It was the end.

It wasn't the end. And they, when they first got this American food, I think they were poisoned by them food, corned beef.

Version 4

In contrast to Ignatius's frame relating the story to bears and shamans, Davydov's 1810 version is presented as neither a bear story nor a shaman story, but as scientific evidence of whether Alutiit love their families. He wrote,

> It is difficult to say for sure whether the islanders love their family or not; the latter would seem nearer the truth. There have been cases of vengeance being sought for them, but this can be found amongst other peoples. One case was very extraordinary; a bear killed and ate a little girl and her two brothers proposed to take vengeance on the bears for this; they would kill them all until in the stomach of one they found the earrings which had been in the girl's ears, or some other sign. Both of them were famous hunters, and they killed many bears on Kad'iak [Kodiak Island], and then crossed to the Aliaskan [Alaska] Peninsula where in one bear it is said they found the things the girl had been wearing. It is difficult to know how the bear, which ate the girl on Kad'iak, came to be in Aliaska, because the straits separating these two places are forty versts wide; but it could be that some unfortunate girl there, wearing the same things, was overcome by the same fate. I do not deny the veracity of this tale, but it is almost the only one which illustrates the love of the islanders for their relatives ([1810] 1977:167).

Davydov held firmly to his belief that the Koniags, as the Russians called the inhabitants of Kodiak Island, felt little love for their families in spite of this and other evidence to the contrary.

Discussion

The location of the bear's heart in his left hand is surely tied to ancient belief, albeit one that Ignatius could not explain. This detail suggests that for Alutiit, as for neighboring Yupiit, the hand was seen to be the site of power, source of bounty, and route between the natural and supernatural realms (cf. Fienup-Riordan 1996: 180–196). The bear's left-handedness is also significant. Native hunters from southwest to northern Alaska explain that all polar, brown, and black bears are left-handed. This presents a potentially dangerous situation for humans because it puts right-handed men, used to feinting to the right in a fistfight, at a disadvantage. But if a hunter knows this detail, he can duck at just the right moment and thrust the spear into the bear's chest.

The most interesting fact of the story, however, is that an ancient *quliyan-guaq*, ostensibly about bears, shamans, and vengeance, has retained both its essential plot elements and its relevance to the modern day. I think historical context offers an explanation.

By 1800, both Koniags and Alutiit on the Alaska Peninsula were heavily involved in the Russian fur trade, often against their will (Partnow 2001:64–65). At the same time, they continued to pursue traditional hunting activities when they were allowed breaks from company duties. Both in the service of Russians and in traditional hunting and warfare these people were accustomed to traveling immense distances by qayaq and knew much of the shoreline of southcentral Alaska. They had been familiar with trade goods such as beads from the late eighteenth century when trade with the Russians had begun. In 1802 when Davydov first visited the region, the Alutiiq people retained much of their precontact belief system, a type of animism brokered by shamanistic specialists called *kallagalget*. Today, vestiges of the old beliefs persist in spite of the fact that most Alutiit adopted the Russian Orthodox faith during the second third of the nineteenth century (Partnow 2001:87–89). The efficacy of these beliefs on the one hand, and their erosion, on the other, form a leitmotif in many of Ignatius's *unigkuat* and *quliyanguat*.

In 1992 Perryville, the Russian fur trade was a distant memory, but not as distant as the 1867 purchase of Alaska from Russia might suggest. In fact, the Russian fur trade had been supplanted by a nearly identical American one immediately after the sale. During the early years of the twentieth century the fur trade was overtaken by commercial fishing and government jobs as the basis of the economy of Kodiak Island and the Alaska Peninsula. Despite changes in industry, the relationship between fish canneries and Alutiit, many of whom fished and worked in processing plants, was until recent years one of owner and exploited laborer, just as had been the case during the fur trade era. Meanwhile, hunting, both for personal use and sale, continued, and with it, many traditional beliefs about the spiritual potency of animals (Crowell, Steffian, and Pullar 2001:172–175).

But Ignatius Kosbruk had seen a substantial weakening of these beliefs during his lifetime. The last acknowledged practicing shaman from Perryville died in the 1960s. Traditional beliefs continue to wane as some of today's young adults openly question the efficacy and validity of an ancient religion that has little relevance to their mechanized lives. The Alutiiq language is no longer spoken except among elders, and with its loss have gone many linguistically encoded understandings about the nature of the universe and the place of humans within it (Leer 2001:31). In Perryville, even Russian Orthodoxy is no longer supreme; many residents are now Christian fundamentalists.

The puzzling corned beef episode fits into this picture of economic subjugation and cultural colonialism. It alerts the listener to the fact that the dangers of modern living among the Americans are as deadly as those of the old days when people lived alongside bears and shamans. Jeff Leer suggests that the detail might also show that shamanism persists in the modern era as a force more powerful than ever, particularly in the absence of well-trained adversaries.

Corned beef does not appear in the Davydov text—in fact, canned corned beef did not exist in the Alutiiq world of the early 1800s. Nor does the Davydov version contain any reference to "bosses" or the colonial subtext that ended Ignatius's Alutiiq narration. It is doubtless true that the Koniag man who told the story to his Russian audience was acutely aware of the effects the fur trade had had on his people, but he either failed to include them in his narrative, or Davydov failed to record them. Similarly, the question of the bear's motivation for killing the girl—in the case of Ignatius's story the murder is part of the evil workings of a shaman—is missing from Davydov's rendering. Whether the original version of the 1802 story mentioned shamanism is a detail lost to time.

I believe that these two new aspects of the story—death by corned beef and shamanism—far from being irrelevant and anachronistic add-ons, are precisely what supply immediacy to a 1992 audience. The poisoned food episode tells us that the worst danger to the brothers, and by extension to any Alutiiq, does not lie in traditional hazards. Alutiiq lore and spirituality are adequate to deal with the age-old dangers. Rather, peril lurks in modern life in a seemingly benign item, the very sustenance that is supposed to keep one alive. Even the strongest hunter can be felled by it. I believe Ignatius also meant this to be a warning not to abandon subsistence hunting for the easy alternative of Western fast food.

Jeff suggests that shamanism plays an equally crucial role in the 1992 story. Perhaps Ignatius was implying that the forces of evil had the last laugh.

The shamans must have had a grudge against the dead girl's family—perhaps with the brothers themselves. The shamans killed the men's sister, and the brothers subsequently managed to take revenge on the bear, the agent of her death. Unfortunately, they never dealt with the shamans who had been the underlying cause of her demise. Perhaps the shamans bided their time to get their final victory over the brothers in the form of poisoned corned beef. This was a clever plan, because during the American period the belief in shamans became a taboo topic, ridiculed out of public existence, though not out of private belief. Thus when the two men died of "poisoned" corned beef, the official and public explanation given by priests, white entrepreneurs, and even Alutiiq elders would be that it was simply because the can had a leak and the contents were infected by botulism. But privately, people may have believed that the same cabal of shamans who had killed the sister had also poisoned the canned beef. The *kallagalget* successfully diverted blame from themselves to something else in two instances: in the first case, to the bear, and in the second, to the corned beef or the boss who had provided it to the hunters.

Perhaps, Jeff's interpretation continues, Ignatius was implying that the shamans got away with their ruse, largely because no one could publicly admit the possibility that shamans could do any such thing in the modern era. The erosion of traditional knowledge that explains how to deal with shamans meant that, even if people had been willing to admit their power, they would not have known how to counter it.

Whether Ignatius was communicating the dangers of modern society, or those inherent in forgetting spiritual knowledge of the past, or both, he was consistent in including this startling ending to the hunters' steadfast quest for vengeance.

Conclusion

For Ignatius Kosbruk, the world of 1992 mirrored the world that Alutiit had known since the days Gavriil Davydov visited—a world with both natural and supernatural dangers known to the people since time immemorial, augmented by new dangers brought about by colonial powers that called for spiritual abilities that were for a while beyond the capacity of even the strongest Alutiiq hunters. Though the two brothers died in the end, felled by an agent of foreign power, their fortitude in continuing what must have seemed like an impossible mission remains a model for today's Alutiiq youth. And like the hunters, Ignatius Kosbruk never gave up. He retained hope to the end that the abandonment of traditional beliefs could be reversed by spreading ancient wisdom through the old stories.

Notes

1   This seems to be either the name of a village in the interior of the Alaska Peninsula, or the general name for the interior Alaska Peninsula Alutiiq area.

2   He first says *aryagaak*, then corrects to *arnak*.

3   Here he says something I [Leer] can't decipher, perhaps a false start.

4   Here he says two words I can't make sense of, something like *sugluku, piyuklluku*. These may be false starts. The sentence reads fine without them.

5   I [Leer] am unable to make this word out; neither can Doris Lind, an elder and former Alutiiq bilingual teacher from Chignik Lake. It needs to be there, but I don't know what it is.

6   This sentence has something missing; it does not make sense as is.

7   This is followed by a false start: *Nallugkunaku augna…*

8   The word Ignatius says here sounds like *qawaraarqelluki*, but I do not know it and Doris Lind is not familiar with this exact form. Instead she suggested using *qawaliluki*, "hibernating."

9   I did not recognize the phrase *nunamen ilaspiarluki*. Doris Lind repeated it and translated it as "[killing them] right down to the ground," but said she does not use this construction. Literally, it seems to mean "mixing them completely into the ground," that is, mangling their bodies so that they were no longer recognizable as bears, but reduced to flesh mingled with earth.

10   I do not totally understand this word; neither did Doris Lind.

11   I am not sure I hear or interpret this phrase correctly. It sounds like *ungu'atiikun niiniluku*, which would mean "he said he heard it by/through its heart," but this does not seem to fit the narrative here. Maybe it should be corrected to *ungu'atii niiniluku* "he said he heard its heart."

12   Here he says *itgat*, "feet," a false start.

13   Note that in the preceding Alutiiq passage he refers to the "top side of its feet," but here he calls it "palm of his hand" in English. See note 1.

14 Here he says *piuqutai*, "her beads," a false start.

15 See note 9.

16 Here Ignatius says, "*Nutaan tawaken taugkuk awa* / this is the one, you made a mistake." This seems to be an irrelevant aside.

17 Ignatius uses both the "top of his hand" and the "palm of his hand," a confusion probably deriving from the fact that English is his second language. In the Alutiiq version it is clear that he meant the top of the hand.

18 There is no gender in Alutiiq possessives. Consequently, first-language Alutiiq speakers often use a possessive that agrees in gender with the item being possessed, rather than the individual doing the possessing.

Works Cited and Suggested Reading

Birket-Smith, Kaj. 1953. *The Chugach Eskimo*. Etnografisk Raekke 6. Copenhagen: Nationalmuseets.

Black, Lydia. 1991. *Glory Remembered: Wooden Headgear of Alaska Sea Hunters*. Juneau: Friends of the Alaska State Museum.

Crowell, Aron L., Amy F. Steffian, and Gordon L. Pullar, eds. 2001. *Looking Both Ways: Heritage and Identity of the Alutiiq People*. Fairbanks: University of Alaska Press.

Davydov, Gavriil. [1810] 1977. *Two Voyages to Russian America, 1802–1807*. Kingston, ON: Limestone Press.

English Bay Elementary and High School. 1980. *Alexandrovsk #1: English Bay and Its Traditional Ways*. Kenai, AK: Kenai Borough School District.
     1981. *Alexandrovsk #2*. Kenai, AK: Kenai Borough School District.

Fienup-Riordan, Ann. 1996. *The Living Tradition of Yup'ik Masks*. Seattle: University of Washington Press.

Gideon, Hieromonk. 1989. *The Round the World Voyage of Hieromonk Gideon 1803–1809*. Translated and with an introduction and notes by Lydia T. Black. Kingston, ON: Limestone Press.

Golder, Frank A. 1903. "Tales from Kodiak Island." *Journal of American Folk-Lore* 16(1):16–31, (2):85–103.

Johnson, John F. C., ed. 1984. *Chugach Legends: Stories and Photographs of the Chugach Region*. Anchorage: Chugach Alaska Corporation.

Lantis, Margaret. 1938. "The Mythology of Kodiak Island, Alaska." *Journal of American Folklore* 51(200):123–172.

Leer, Jeff. 2001. "The Alutiiq Language," in Aron L. Crowell, Amy F. Steffian, and Gordon L. Pullar (eds.), *Looking Both Ways: Heritage and Identity of the Alutiiq People*, p. 31. Fairbanks: University of Alaska Press.

Nielson, Helen. 1976. "It was a Simple Life I Led," *Elwani* I(1):108–116. Kodiak, AK: Kodiak Aleutian Regional High School.

Nielsen, Mary Jane. 1999. "What Hope Can Do," in Jeane Breinig and Patricia H. Partnow (eds.), in *Alaska Native Writers, Storytellers, and Orators*, special issue of *Alaska Quarterly Review* 4(3–4):228–231.

Partnow, Patricia H. 1995. "The Days of Yore: Alutiiq Mythical Time," in Phyllis Morrow and William Schneider (eds.), *When Our Words Return: Writing, Hearing, and Remembering Oral Traditions of Alaska and the Yukon*, pp. 138–183. Logan: Utah State University Press.
2001. *Making History: Alutiiq / Sugpiaq Life on the Alaska Peninsula*. Fairbanks: University of Alaska Press.

Pinart, Alphonse L. 1873. "Eskimaux et Koloches: Idées Religieuses et Traditions des Kaniagmioutes." *Revue d'Anthropologie* (Paris) II:673–680.
1874. *Voyage à la côte nord-ouest d'Amérique d'Ounalashka à Kadiak, Iles Aléoutiennes et péninsule d'Aliaska*. Paris: Librarie Ch. Delagrave.

Index

Page numbers in italics refer to illustrations.

A

Aġnazuŋaaq, 169–174
Aŋarraaq (Levi Cleveland), 141
aŋutauqan challenges Tikiġaq man, 156–157
Aaluk (Amelia Gray), 143
Aanaruaġiik, 140
abandonment theme, 41–63
abstinence practices, 65, 66
accuracy in storytelling, 131
adultery, 48, 59–60, 165
Afcan, Paschal, 4
Agayuliyararput (Meade and Fienup-Riordan), 5
Ager, Lynn, 4, 9
Agnus, Anna, 89
Agnus, Simeon, 89
Akaguagaankaaq, story about, 8
Akiachak, Alaska, 65, 68, 71
Akiak, Alaska, 68
Akuzipik language, 205
Alaska Native Claims Settlement Act (ANCSA), 3, 102
Alaska Native Language Center (ANLC), 103, 146, 241
Alaska oil boom, 3
Alaska Peninsula, *238*, 239
Alaska Rural Systemic Initiative, 144
Aleknagik, Alaska, 85
Aleutian Islanders, 237, 238
Aleutian Islands, 238, *238*
Alexandrovsk (oral history), 242
Alexie, Oscar, 5
Aliŋnaq, the Moon Spirit, 148
Alutiiq people (Alutiit), 237–242, 256
Alutiiq/Sugtestun language, 238, 246, 257

Alvanna, Edna, 175
Alvanna, Francis, 175
Alvanna-Stimpfle, Bernadette
    King Island Tales (Alvanna-Stimpfle and Kaplan), 180
    translator and/or transcriber
        "Aa'aaŋnilu Piayaaŋilu, The," 186
        "Little Girl Who Was Stolen, The," 186
        "My Great-Grandmother, the Shaman," 183
        "Niaqsaaġruk Tigliktaq," 184
        "Oldsquaw and Her Ducklings, The," 187
        "Unwritten Law of the Sea, An," 188–199
Ambler, 131, 135–145
American Folklore Society, 31, 211
Amos, Muriel, 5, 103
Amos, Nakaar Howard, 5, 103, 106–123
amulets (*iinruq*), 67, 81, 83, 123n11, 154, 164, 172
Amyag, the stone figure of, 119
Anchorage, 103
Andrew, Cecelia, 64
Andrew, Frank, 5, 64–83
Andrew, Noah, 64
Andrew, Virginia Ilutsik, 84–88
Angayiq, Anna, 30
anger, 38–39
Anglinarli, 81–82
animals
    dialog with, 11
    hats become, 61
    naming, 191
    respectful treatment of, 188–199, 240
    spirits of, 122n4, 129–130, 158, 191, 256
    spiritual potency of, 256

Anungazuk, Herbert O., 132, 188–199
Apangalook, 212
Aqalulik River, 147, 168
aaġlu (killer whales), 191, 193–197, 228–229
Arctic Odyssey (Jenness), 146
Asatchaq (Jimmie Killigivuk), 131–132,
    146–150, 151–168
Askin'at, 86–88
Askinat mountains, 109
Attaaġmiut community house, 183
avvuyutaq, 39
Aymaramket clan, 207
Ayuguta'arin's community house, 121

B

babies
    breast-feeding, 47–48, 50–51, 122n7
    crying at night, 72–73
    dead mothers of, 72–76
    killed by their mothers, 50–51
Badten, Adelinda, 205
Barnes, Sophie, 5
Barrow, 128, 143
bear. *See also* brown bear; polar bear
    brothers in search of, 185, 243–260
    shaman-controlled, 246–255, 258
    skin, 159, 160, 161
bearded seal (*ugruk*)
    eating, 226–227
    flag displayed when caught, 109
    hunting, 117, 156
    preparing, 111
    skin of, 80–81, 83, 215
    stomachs of, 44, 60
bed time stories, 84–85
Bering Land Bridge National Preserve, 188
Bering Sea and coast, 2, 71, 203
Bering Strait, 132, 188, 197
Berlin, Wassilie, *91*
berry bucket, dialog with, 11
berry picking, 8, 13–15, 247, 252
Bethel, 1, 3, 4, 7, 68
Bethel Regional High School, 4, 5
bilingual education programs, 8, 31
birchbark, 144–145
birds. *See also specific birds*
    feathers from, 176, 177
    how they got their markings, 11, 21, 25
    humans turning into, 11, 29
    hunting of, 216, 240

killed by Tikiġaq man's son, 163–164
    supernatural, 167
    wing used for shelter, 164, 167
Birket-Smith, Kaj, 241
Bitar, Joseph, 5
blackberries, 87
blackfish, 77
Black River (Imaġluktuq), 137
Bladder Festival (Nakciuryaraq), 57, 122n4
blueberries, 87
Bornite, Alaska, 141
bow and arrow, hunting with, 36–37, 80,
    172–173, 178–179, 185
bowhead whales, 204
bowl, wooden, 46, 49, 51–54, 58, 61–62
boy(s). *See also* son(s)
    becoming hunters, 194
    determining sex of in utero, 44–45
    teaching tradition bearers, 243
breast-feeding, 47–48, 50–51, 74, 122n7
breathing holes, killing at, 167
Brewster, Karen, 169
Bristol Bay, 1, *2*, 85
brothers
    in search of a bear, 185, 243–260
    sibling, 106–121
brown bear, 162, 185
brown bear people, 158–160
Burch, Ernest S., 169
Bureau of Indian Affairs schools, 137
Bureau of Land Management, 144
burials. *See* graves

C

Calista Elders Council, 64, 89
Canada, Native language spoken in, 129
cannibalism, 64, 65, 68–71
Cape Corwin (Cing'ig), 115
Cape Espenberg, 195
Cape Manning (Englu²rarmiut), 111
Cape Mendenhall (Cingigglag), 115
Cape Prince of Wales, 188
Cape Thompson cliffs (Imna), 147
Cape Vancouver, 111
caribou (*tuttu*), 70, 72, 117, 178
    heart-sacks, 172–173
    skin, 153, 159, 172–173
Carpenter, Ina, 10
Cauyarnariuq (Mather), 5
Central Siberian Yupik, 205

Central Yup'ik. *See* Yup'ik language
  (Central Yup'ik)
"Cetugpak" ("Big Nails"), 9
Cev'armiut Qanemciit Qulirait-llu
  (Woodbury), 5
Cevv'arneq, Alaska, 30
Chanar, David, 5
Charlie, Andy, 5
Chefornak, 30, 41
Chicago, 217–219
childbirth, 68, 72, 80–81
child/children. *See also* babies
  adopting, 162
  bullies and bullying, 81, 123n12
  cannibalistic, 64, 65, 68–71
  deformed, 65, 68–71
  escaping supernatural beings, 7–8
  killing, 164
  orphaned, 93–101, 148, 162, 205
  as riches, 40
  of spouse-exchange partners, 80–82
  teaching, 84–85, 89
  tiny child, 79–80
  of tiny couple, 79–80
children's stories
  Akaguagaankaaq, story about, 8
  "Cetugpak" ("Big Nails"), 10
Christian fundamentalism, 257
Chukchi Peninsula, 203, 205
Ciuliamta Akluit (Meade and Fienup-
  Riordan), 5
Clark's Point, Alaska, 84
Cleveland, Johnny (Inuqtuaq), 139
Cleveland, Katherine (Tatqaviña), 142
Cleveland, Levi (Aŋarraaq), 141
Cleveland, Robert Nasruk, 131
Cleveland, Truman (Tilak), 142
clothing, Sugpiaq, 240
cloudberries, 87
Collins, Henry, 213
colonialism, 137, 217–219, 252, 253, 256,
  257–258
cooking, 151, 158
Cortes Island, Canada, 144
cranberries, 13, 87
cranes, 8, 10, 11, 21–25
creation stories, 149
Creator, 209
Crowell, Aron L., 242
Cung'ar, 119

Cup'ig Eskimo Dictionary (Amos and
  Amos), 103
Cup'ig language, 4, 5, 103–104
Cup'ig literature, 4, 5, 102–105
Cup'ik language, 103–104
Curtis, Edward S., 3

D

dancing, 3, 48, 122n1, 174, 176, 200n1, 240
daughter-mother relationship, 138, 139
daughters. *See* girl(s); sisters
David, Margie, 103
Davydov, Gavriil, 240, 241, 244, 246, 255,
  256
the dead
  given food, 75
  mentioning name of, 11, 27
  mist representing, 72–74
  mother comes for baby, 72–76
  returning to life, 163–164
death
  activities following, 200n1
  after childbirth, 72
  by American food, 252, 253, 257, 258
  lifespan and, 33
  of tiny child, 80
  wife lies about husband's, 34–38
defecation in stories, 21, 95, 167
DeLaguna, Frederica, 241
de Reuse, Willem J., 223, 224–232
Deschout, Father, 30
diet. *See also* eating
  sea mammals, 204, 224–229
  St. Lawrence Islanders, 204, 216
  of tundra, 2, 35, 37, 204
Dillingham, 1, 141
Diomede Islands, 188
dog(s)
  eats tiny child, 80
  polar bear and puppy, 155
  Sedna's marriage to, 10
  the sibling's puppy, 117, 121
  uses for (pulling boats/sleds), 138
drums
  listening to, 175
  making, 173, 177, 178, 190, 191
  sound of, 176, 191, 208
Duchikthluk Bay (Tacirrlag), 117
ducks, eider, 109–111
dwarf couple, 67, 79–81, 167

E

eagle mother, 172–173
eagles, 172, 176, 178
  feathers, 176, 177
earth-human relationship, 132, 188–199
East Cape, Siberia, 188, 205
eating. *See also* diet; food
  akutaq, 73–74
  feasting after marriage ceremony, 48
  kenitat, 73
  reindeer, 139
  sea mammals, 204, 224–229
  sparingly, 36, 54
  using circular bowl, 51–52
economic subjugation of Natives, 256, 257
economy, 237–255, 256
  Yup'ik, 2–3
education
  of Alaska Native children, 84–85
  bilingual, 41
  Bureau of Indian Affairs schools, 137
  on Nelson Island, 30
  in Shungnak, 137
  storytelling for, 30–31, 130, 190, 244
  Yupik schoolbooks, 205
Ekuk, Alaska, 84
elders, as teachers, 190–191, 193–195,
  198–199, 210
Ellangellemni (Orr et al.), 5
Ellanna, Frank, 180–181
  performing the Wolf Dance, 174–175,
  179
Elliraaraurluq, the orphan, 93–101
Elwani (oral history), 241
Englullrarmiut, 115
Eskimo about Bering Strait (Nelson), 3, 214
Eskimo language dialects, 205
Eskimo Language Workshop, 4
Eskimo Narratives and Tales from Chevak
  (Woodbury), 5
Etolin Strait (Akulurer), 111, 115

F

Fairbanks, 143, 144–145
falcon, peregrine, 160, 166
fall camping for fishing, 33
family relationships. *See also* brothers;
  sisters
  anutauqan (co-husband/lover), 156

brother-sister, 185, 246–255
daughter-mother, 138, 139
father-in-law makes kayak, 107–109
grandmother-grandchild, 9–10, 17, 113
Kodiak Islanders, 255
Silook family, 212, 217–219
vengeance in, 246–255, 257
family relationships, stories of
  "My Great-Grandmother, the Shaman,"
  132
  "Yaqutgiarcankut," 7–29
fathers
  polar bears as, 163–167
  pride in sons, 42, 46
  sons killing, 163
  on spirit quest with son, 163–168
  traditional abstinence patterns, 65
fetus, shamans and, 68
Fienup-Riordan, Ann, 5, 31
fighting
  the *anutauqan*, 156–157
  Anglinarli and the *nukalpiaq*, 82–83
  bears and, 159, 162
  fathers and sons, 163
  with giants, 152–154
  husbands and wives, 157, 160, 161
  using whale bones, 162
fire baths, 72, 76, 77
fish
  eating raw, 77
  slime, 154
  storehouses, 54–55, 74–75
fish camp, 2, 33, 64, 72, 74–75, 84, 138
fishing
  Ambler village, 137
  salmon, 72
  by Sugpiat, 240
  at summer camp, 137
  through an ice hole, 71, 72
  Yup'ik region, 2–3
Fitzhugh, Bill, 214
food. *See also* eating
  akutaq, 73–74, 76–77, 122n1
  American, 252, 253
  corned beef, 252, 253, 257, 258
  dead given a small amount of, 75
  grass pack basket for, 49
  hiding, 33–34
  non-Native, 30, 33
  pilot bread, 216

poisoning by, 252, 253, 258
preparation, 66, 77
preserving, 240
rationing, 33–38, 52
the sea as provider of, 192
serving in urine buckets, 66, 77
song of subsistence for, 197–198
stealing, 54–55
sufficient, 232–233
Foote, Don C., 146
fox, 159
fox-men, 172–173
Fredson, Alice, 5
fulmar (sea bird), Sedna and, 10–11
fur trade, 239, 256

G

gaff (*negcik*), 50, 51, 109
Gambell, Alaska, 204, 205, 210
gathering
    berries, 13–15, 240, 247, 252
    lichen, 35, 37
    reindeer food, 35
    shellfish, 240
    Yup'ik region, 2–3, 8
Geist, Henry, 213
genitals, 165
ghosts, 66, 72–76, 122n8
giants, 8, 151–152, 154
Gideon, Hieromonk, 240, 241
Gillham, Charles E., 85
girl(s). *See also* daughter-mother
        relationship; sisters
    brown bear steals, 185
    disobedient, 9, 13–29
    escaping old women, 9, 13–29
    mothers teaching daughters, 138, 139
    sent by grandmother, 157, 159, 161–162
    storyknife tales for, 8–9
    on walrus' head, 165
Gloosnap, 148
Golder, Frank, 241
grandmother-grandchild relationship,
        9–10, 17, 113, 157, 159, 161–162
grandmother(s)
    with magical powers, 157, 159, 161–
        162, 205
    of orphan boy, 228–229
    as shamans, 132, 180, 183
    warnings given by, 161–162

gratitude, story teaching, 207–210
graves, 9
    of hunters, 189, 217
    marking, 51, 73–74, 122n2
Gray, Amelia (Aaluk), 143
Gray, Arthur (Qatlu), 141–142
Gray, George (Tiriq), 145
Gray, Minnie, 131, 133, 180
Greenland, 129
guests. *See* hospitality
guillemot, 161
guns, trading for, 216

H

hair seal, 224–225
hand, 157, 255
harvesting activities, 2
hate, 38–39
hauntings, 66, 72–76
Hawaii, travel to, 144
hawk owls, 29
healing, 159, 161
heart sounds, 173, 178
Hendrickson, Kay, 107
heros, stories with, 147–168
hills, 9, 86–87
Himmelheber, Hans, 4
home, finding the way, 78, 163–168
homesickness, 57–62
hospitality, 60, 76, 111, 113–115, 122n8,
        122n9, 172–173
houses. *See also iglu*
    beds and bedding in, 35, 36, 46–47, 79,
        123n10, 207
    building, 72
    ceremonial (*qalgi*), 158
    empty, 55
    entry into, 229–231
    of giants, 151
    separated from village, 111–113
    of sod, 25, 30, 151, 239
    Sugpiaq, 239
    of wood with grass-covered roofs, 239
human-animal interactions, 11
    bear people, 155–160, 163–167
    cranes rescue girls, 21–25
    seals that turn into humans, 66, 76–78
    in Sugpiaq stories, 240–241
human-object interactions, 11, 15
human-sea relationship, 193–195

hunger, 33–40, 51–52, 54
hunter-earth relationship, 132, 188–189
hunter-prey relationship, 188–199, 240
hunters
    aqlu as, respect for, 193–194
    brothers as, 246–255
    creating, 47–48, 122n7, 194–195
    orphan and, 95, 101
    killed by Tikiġaq man, 167
    killing humans, 174, 176
    niulut, 168
    nukalpiaq (great hunter and provider),
        44, 49, 81, 82–83, 90, 93
    nukalpiartaq (accomplished hunter), 43
    spiritual beliefs, 193
    status of, 189, 217
    survival of, 197–198
hunters, stories of
    "Arnaq Taqukaraam Pillra," 246–255
    "Good Hunter, The," 207–210
    "Story of the King Island Wolf Dance,
       The," 172
    "Unwritten Law of the Sea, An," 132,
       188–189
hunting and trapping, 204–205
    Ambler village, 135–137
    bear, 128, 246–255
    birds, 240
    bow and arrow used for, 36–37, 80,
       172–173, 178–179, 185, 216
    caribou, 72, 117, 178, 240
    eagles, 178
    fur-bearing animals, 239
    guns used for, 216
    mice, 19, 35–36
    muskrat, 36–37, 138, 139
    seal, 117, 128, 156, 168, 204
    sea mammals, 72, 128, 240
    by sibling brothers, 117–119
    from qayaq, 107, 240
    squirrel, 240
    by Sugpiat, 240
    walrus, 128, 204
    whales, 128, 151
    while hungry, 33–34
    at winter camp, 137–138
    Yup'ik region, 2–3
husbands. *See also* men
    aŋutauqan (co-husband/lover), 156–157
    dead wife and, 72–74

killing wives, 157, 160, 161
kindness of, 56
leaving wives, 109, 113–115
qat'ngutek (dual, spouse-exchange
    partners), 67
responsibilities of, 40
unfaithful, 48, 59–60
wives leaving, 34–38, 49–52, 155–156
wives who ask too much of, 160
Hymes, Dell, 221

I

ice
    fishing, 71, 72
    hunting on the, 195–196
    pick, 50
iglu. See also houses
    escaping from, 162–163
    games and, 152–153
    hawk's feet seen in, 153, 166
    jellyfish, 166
    a monster, 165
    Tikiġaq man's son enters, 165, 166
Igwaryar'er settlement, 117
Ilutsik, Esther Arnaq, 84–85
Ilutsik, Lena Atkiq, 5, 84–88
Imaġluktuq (Black River), Alaska, 137
Imaaġmiut (people of the sea), 192
Imnat, 148
Indian Point, Siberia, 215
infertility, 68, 76, 79
Ingigut'et beach, 119
Inmat (Cape Thompson cliffs), 147
intestines of seals, 44
Inuit, Canadian, 2, 3
Inuit story of Sedna, 10–11
Inuktitut language, 3
Iñupiaq language, 129, 180
    grammatical structure of, 170, 171
    teaching, 142–145
Iñupiaq literature
    additional readings suggested, 200–202
    early documentation of, 3–4
    landscape element in, 149
    performance cues, 171
Iñupiat, 127–130
    culture of the, 188–189
    revival of Wolf Dance, 169–179
    spiritual world, 129–130
    storytelling tradition, 130–131

Inuqtuaq (Johnny Cleveland), 139
ivory, 167
Iyaġaaluk, 139
Izraqit, a rocky slope, 190

J

Jack, Happy, 135–137, 139, 140
Jack, Teddy (Ugiaġnaq), 135, 140
Jack family, 135–137, 139
Jacobson, Anna, 5
Jacobson, Steven, 4, 103
Jenness, Diamond, 146
John, Martina, 89
John, Paul (Kangrilnguq), 30–32, *90, 91*
 "Atkuut Tengaurturalriit," 89–101
 "One Who Didn't Think Much of a
  Man's Stomach," 33–40
 Qulirat Qanemcit-llu Kinguvarcimalriit
  (Shield and Fienup-Riordan), 5, 31
 the story as a gift to relatives, 5
 variation on "Aanakalli Ner'aqallii," 65

K

Kaaguagacungaq, story about, 7–8
Kaiakokonuk, Harry, 241
Kanagar'er, 119
Kangirnaarmiut, Alaska, 64
Kangrilnguq (Paul John). *See* John, Paul
 (Kangrilnguq)
Kanralak, Victor, 5
Kaplan, Lawrence D.
 King Island Tales (Alvanna-Stimpfle and
  Kaplan), 180
 translator and/or transcriber
  "Aa'aaṇṇilu Piayaaṇilu, The," 186
  "Little Girl Who Was Stolen, The," 186
  "My Great-Grandmother, the
   Shaman," 183
  "Niaqsaaġruk Tigliktaq," 184
  "Oldsquaw and Her Ducklings, The,"
   187
  "Unwritten Law of the Sea, An,"
   188–199
  "Uvaṇa Atiġa Aliitchak" (Gray),
   134–145
Karluk, 146
kass'aq (non-Native) food, 33
Katmai, *238*, 245, 247
Katmai eruption, 241, 245

Kawerak, 171, 176, 178
Kawerak people, 131, 179
kayak, 107–109
Kenai Peninsula, 237
Kiṇikmiut (Wales people), 127, 190
Kiapiq (Herbert Anungazuk's great-
 grandfather), 194, 196
Kilbuck, John, 3
killer whales (*aaġlu*), 191, 193–197, 228–229
Killigivuk, Jimmie (Asatchaq), 146–150
 "Long Unipkaaq, A," 131–132, 151–168
killing
 by bear, 246–255, 258
 birds, 164
 a bully, 81
 by children, 81
 eagles, 172, 176
 a falcon, 166
 hunters at breathing holes, 167
 of hunters by hunters, 174, 176
 iñuqaġnailaq (a man who is always
  killing people), 152, 154
 the jellyfish igloo, 166–167
 the sacred messenger, 173, 178–179
 by Tikiġaq man, 166–167
 by Tikiġaq man's son, 162, 163–165
 wives by husbands, 157, 160, 161
Kilvaġiaq (Happy Jack), 135–137, 139, 140
Kingigin (Kiṇigin), Settlement of, 190
Kingiikaq, Aghhaya May, 207
Kingiikaq, Theodore (Qaakaghlleq), 205,
 207–210
King Island, 180
King Island Dancers, 180
King Island Inupiaq dialect, 180
King Island Native Corporation, 171
King Island people (Ugiuvaṇmiut), 127,
 179, 180
King Island Tales (Alvanna-Stimpfle and
 Kaplan), 180
Kingston, Deanna Paniataaq, 131, 169–171
kin terms, 10
Kiokun, Dorothy, 103
Kitik (Bertha Sheldon), 144
knife
 left in *qasgi*, 69–71
 thrust in *utchuk*, 165
 women's (*uluaq*), 8
Kobuk, Alaska, 137, 147
Kobuk Iñupiaq dialect, 180

Kobuk Iñupiaq Junior Dictionary (Sun), 131
Kobuk River, 153
Kodiak Island (Kad'iak), 237, *238*, 239, 240, 245
Kodiak Islanders, 238, 245, 255
Kosbruk, Ignatius, 237–255, *245*
Kosbruk, Vivian, 244
Kotlik, 41
Kotzebue, 142, 212
Kotzebue Sound, 128, 129
Koyuk, Henry, 175
Koyuk, Lucy Tanaqiq (Quyuk), 131, 169–171, 174–177
Krauss, Michael, 4, 205, 223
Kuiga'ar stream, 117
Kuik Rover, 68
Kungurkaq, John, 30
Kuskokwim River, 4, 64, 65, 68
Kuuk stream, 180
Kuutchiaq, Alaska, 141
Kwigillingok, Alaska, 64
KYUK radio station, 4

L

lamps
    oil, 69, 151, 158, 159, 160, 161, 166, 214
    of stone, 183
landscape element in narrative, 105, 119–121, 149
language, magical, 181, 185, 220
Lantis, Margaret, 4, 65–66, 241
Lee, Clara (Paaniikaaluk), 138, 144
Leer, Jeff, 237–255, 257–258
left-handedness in bears, 157, 255
lice, 9, 10–11, 17–19
lichen as food source, 35, 37
Lind, Doris, 258n5, 258nn8–10
listening, teaching, 89
Little Diomede, Alaska, 198
little people, 67, 79–81, 167
loneliness of wives, 47, 48
Looking Both Ways (Crowell et al.), 242
Lowenstein, Tom, 151–168
Lower Kuskokwim School District, 31
Lurtussiikar, 107

M

MacLean, Edna, 180
MacManus, Barbara, 144

Malimiut dialect, Iñupiaq language, 129
Manibozo, 148
Mann, Mary Jane, 5
Mapsaturuaq, 190
marriage
    appropriate actions in, 38–39
    to brown bear woman, 158–160
    ingulaq (dance ceremony), 48
    jealousy in, 159
    to polar bear woman, 155–160
    spouse-exchange partners (*qat'ngutek*), 67, 80–81
    terminating a, 38–39
    the tiny couple, 79–81
    traditional arrangements, 140, 158
    to whale woman, 160–161
    without children, 68, 76, 79
marriage, stories of
    "Flying Parka, A," 93–101
    "Long Unipkaaq, A," 151–168
    "One Who Didn't Think Much of a Man's Stomach," 30–40
Masserculleq (Marshall), Alaska, 71
Mastuliaq, Alaska, 71
Mather, Elsie, 4, 5, 11–29, 170
Mayac, Earl Aisana, 169–171, 175, 178–179
Mayac, Earl's father, 179
McKinlay, William Laird, 146
Meade, Marie, 5, 7, 10, 67, *91*
    "Flying Parka, A," translator, 93–101
Medicine Men of Hooper Bay (Gillham), 85
Mekoryuk, 103
Mell'arpag's stone balls, 119
memory and accuracy in storytelling, 131
men. *See also* husbands
    granting wishes by old, 86–88
    middle-aged, 59
menstruation, 65, 113–115
Messenger Feast, 170, 172–174
Metcalf, Vera (Qaakaghlleg), 205, 207–210
mice, 19, 25, 35–36
Michel, Karen, 7, 8
Milligrock, Ruth, 198
mink as hats, 61
minke whale, 228–229
miscarriage, 66, 78
missionaries, 3, 30
mist, 72–74
monster child, 64, 65, 68–71
Morrow, Phyllis, 4, 11–29

Moses, Angalgaq, 41
Moses, Cathy, 41–63
Moses, Cyril, 41
Moses, Nalugaralria, 41
Moses, Philip, 41
Moses, Stella, 41
Moses, Teddy, 41
Moses, Theresa, 89
mosquito, 166
mother(s)
    devouring of, 64, 65, 68–71
    of ducklings, 187
    heart sounds of, 173, 176, 178
    killing their babies, 258nn8–10
    returning for baby after death, 72–76
    sleep deprived, 47–48, 51, 219
    teaching daughters, 138, 139
mourning, custom of, 67
mouth (human) on tundra, 166
Mt. Katmai, *238*, 245
mukluk (bearded seal), 215
mukluks, making, 138
Muktoyuk, Frances, 175
Muktoyuk, Gabe, 175
muskrat, 36, 136–137, 138, 139

N

Nagai, Tadataka, 134–145
nagoonberries, 73
Nakaciuryaraq (the Bladder Festival), 57
Nakalpiartaq, father of Uilingiataq, 97–101
Nanwarrlim Kuiga stream, 119
Napaskiak, Alaska, 4, 9
Napaskiak storyknife tales, 9
Narulkirnarmiut, Alaska, 103
National Endowment for the Arts, 7
Naukanski language, 205
Navajo language, 3
Neck, Joan, 7
Nelson, Edward, 3, 65, 67, 214
Nelson Island (Qaluyaaq), 30, 89, 109–
    111, 122n5
Nelson Island Oral History Project, 41
Niġuvana (Asatchaq's mother), 146
Nielsen, Mary Jane, 242
Nightmute, Alaska, 30, 41
Noatak, Nuratar Andrew, 102–105, *104*
nomadic lifestyle, 8, 30, 64, 84
Nome, 142–143, 180, 204, 205, 212
Noorvik, 141

Norton Sound, 1, 107, 129
Novoe Chaplino, Chukotka, 205
nukalpiaq, Anglinarli fights, 82–83
Nunamiut area, 247, 259n1
Nunapitchuk, Alaska, 7, 9
Nunaumirutet, 119
Nunivak Island, 3–4, 102, 103
Nunivak Island stories, 106–121
Nunivak people, 4
Nunivak Yup'ik dialect, 102–103
Nuniwarmiut traditional stories, 105
Nuratar. *See* Noatak, Nuratar Andrew
Nushagak drainage, 1
Nuurviuraq (Shungnak), Alaska, 137, 139
Nuvuk (Point Barrow), 147, 157–158, 163

O

objects, inanimate, 11
Old Bering Sea, 213
Olrun, Prudy, 103
Omiak, Paul, 175
Omnik, Carol Tukummiq, 151–168
One Must Arrive With a Story to Tell (Orr
    and Orr), 5
Ongtowasruk, Patrick, 198–199
Oquilluk (Ukalliq), 171
oral history projects, 4, 41, 241
oral tradition
    in Alutiiq society, 241
    foreshadowing of future states in, 170
    Iñupiaq, 131
    St. Lawrence Island, 205
orphans, stories of
    adopting, 162
    "A Flying Parka," 93–101
    "Qati Hik," 205
    shamanistic initiation and, 148
Orr, Ben, 5
Orr, Eliza, 5
Oswalt, Wendell, 4, 9
Our Way of Making Prayer (Meade and
    Fienup-Riordan), 5
Oxereok, Ernest, 198

P

Paaniikaaluk (Clara Lee), 138, 144
parents
    of *nukalpiaq*, 82–83
    who believe daughters are dead, 11, 29

parkas
    making, 138
    polar bear, 156, 157
    taking off to breast feed, 47–48, 51
Partnow, Patricia, 237–255
Paul, Mark, 30
Pauyuuraq (Asatchaq's friend), 146
Penatac, John, 175
Penatac, Margaret Iiŋaq, 169
Perryville, *238*, 241, 244–245
Petmigtalegmiut, Alaska, 65
Piiyuuk (Frances Usugan), 5, 6, 41–63
Pikonganna, 174
pilot bread, 216
Pinart, Alphonse, 241
Point Hope (Tikiġaq), 128, 146, 147–148, 213
polar bear
    father as, 163–168
    fighting, 162
    hunting (and trapping), 128
    people, 155–160, 163–167
    skin, 158, 159
Polar Bear Dance, 176
polygamy, 106–121
poverty, 40
Pratt, Ken, 102
prayer, 5, 198
pregnancy, 43–46, 68, 80
Prince William Sound, 237, 239, 241
ptarmigan, 11, 29, 137
Pullar, Gordon L., 242
Pullock, John, 175
Pulu, Tupou, 143

Q

Qaakaghlleq (Theodore Kingiikaq), 205, 207–210
Qageryalqurmiut, Alaska, 65, 69–70
qalgi (ceremonial house), 158
Qałhaqpak (Helen Roberts), 144
Qanemcikarluni Tekitnarqelartuq (Orr and Orr), 5
qargi. See qasgi
qasgi (men's community house; *qargi*)
    Ayuguta'arin's community house, 121
    building a, 71–72
    elders experience of, 3
    feeding men in, 99
    helping men of, 93–95

knife left in, 69–71
learning from elders in, 30, 64
mentioned, 152–153
mist flowing into, 76
muskrat found under, 36
refurbishing, 122n1
seating positions in, 59, 97–99
sleeping in, 75–76
storytelling in, 4, 5, 194
Sugpiaq, 239–240
Qatlu (Arthur Gray), 141–142
Qawiaraġmiut (people from Kawerak), 176
Qawiaraq dialect, Iñupiaq language, 129
Qayaq (epic story), 130, 149
Qayaqtuaġiŋñaqtuaq (epic story), 130, 149
Qemirrlag hill, 119
Qiawig'ar, 107
Qikiqtaġruŋmiut (Kotzebue people), 128
Qikiqtaġruk, 152
Qinaq, Alaska, 64
Qipuk, 143
Qiwaaghmiit clan, 207
qulirat (tales, long stories)
    elements of, 42, 54, 55
    endings, 63
Qulirat Qanemcit-llu Kinguvarcimalriit (Shield and Fienup-Riordan), 5, 31
quliyanguaq, example of, 241
qununit (seals that turn into humans), 66
Quyuk (Lucy Tanaqiq Koyuk), 131, 169–171, 174–177

R

rabbit/rabbit skins, 137
rain boots, making, 49
Rainey, Froelich, 146, 150
Rasmussen, Knud, 169, 170–171
Raven Man (Tuluŋigraq), 149
reality, dual. *See also* supernaturalism
    brown bear people, 158–160
    father as polar bear, 163–167
    fox-men, 172–173
    hand as route between, 255
    inanimate objects, talking, 11, 15
    polar bear people, 155–160
    seals that turn into humans, 66, 76–78
    whale people, 160–161
Rearden, Alice, 5, 64–83
Reed, Irene, 4, 31, 102

reindeer
  corralling, 139
  food, 35, 37
  skin, 49–50, 51, 207
relocation programs, 217–219
retribution theme, 41–63, 246–255, 257
ring seal, 44, 226–227
Roberts, Helen (Qałhaqpak), 144
Russians, 239, 256
Russian Orthodox church, 239, 240, 256, 257

S

Saclamana, Marie Aakauraq, 169, 175
Saclamana, Mike, 175
Sailaq (Sarah Tickett), 144, 145
Sakurai, Takashi, 131
saliva of children, 66, 77
salmonberries, 87
Samaruna (Asatchaq's uncle), 146
Savoonga, Alaska, 204, 205, 207, 208, 210
Sawtooth Mountains (Kiglawiit), 178
Scarbrough, Lisa, 244
seagull, 167
sea-human relationship, 193–195
seal. *See also specific seals*
  bladders, 122n4
  blubber, rendering, 111, 115
  eating, 224–227
  hunting, 117, 128, 156, 168, 204
  oil, 49, 111, 113, 240
  skin, 44–45, 80–81, 83
  stomachs, 44–45, 49, 60
  on Tacirrlag, 117
  that turn into humans (*qununit*), 66, 76–78
sea mammals. *See also specific sea mammals*
  eating, 224–229
  hunting, 72, 128, 204
  oil of, 190
  origin of, 10–11
  in Sedna's story, 10–11
Sedna, Inuit story of, 10–11
Selawik, Alaska, 141
Seward Peninsula, 1, 129, 149
sexual intercourse, 155, 158–159
shamanic initiation, stories of, 149–168
shamanism
  persistence of, 252, 256, 257–258

shamanistic experience vs., 149
shaman(s)
  advises about deformed child, 65, 68
  grandmothers as, 132, 180, 183
  initiatory experiences, 148–150
  kallagalet (animism brokered by), 256, 258
  killing using bear, 246–255
  neutralizing, 122n8
  payment for services, 183
  power of, 68, 122n8, 180
  speaks to whales, 197
  walks on air, 75
Sheldon, Bertha (Kitik), 144
Shelikof Strait, 245
shellfish gathering, 240
Shield, Sophie Manutuli, 5, 30–40, 102
Shungnak (Nuurviuraq), 137, 139, 141
Siberia, 203–204, 205, 213, 215
Siberian Yupik language, 205
Sigiaqluq (Herbert Anungazuk's grandfather), 193, 195–196
Silook, Norma Imanyuk, 212
Silook, Paul, 206, 212, 215
Silook, Roger (Saavla), 212, 216–217
Silook, son of Uwitelen, 212–215
Silook, Susie (Paallengetaq), 206, 217–219, 234–235, 237–255
sinews, animal, 56–57
singing, 122n1, 166, 174, 200n1
Sirenikski language, 205
sisters. *See also* daughters; girl(s)
  brothers hunt bear on behalf of their, 185, 246–255
  responsibilities of, 8, 13–29, 39–40
sisters, stories of
  "Five Sisters, The," 86–88
  "Yaqutgiarcankut," 8, 13–29
sleds, marking graves with, 51, 122n2
sleep deprivation, 47–48, 51, 219
Snake Lake Rover, 84
snow geese, 185
Social Culture of the Nunivak Eskimo (Lantis), 4
social hierarchy, 99
"Something about the Inuit" (Kilbuck), 3
son(s). *See also* boy(s)
  amulets for protecting, 80–81, 83, 123n11, 154
  firstborn, 42

son(s) (*continued*)
   of hunter goes missing, 208–209
   killing fathers, 163
   shown their mother's past, 57–59
   on spirit quest with fathers, 163–168
   of tiny couple, 80–81
Spirit of the Universe/Great Being (*siḷam
   iñua*), 130
spirit quest, 148, 163–168
spirit world
   hills association with, 9, 86–87
   "Long Unipkaaq, A," 151–168
   "Story of the King Island Wolf Dance,
     The," 131, 169–179
spotted seal, 226–227
spring camp, life at, 72, 139
Stefansson expedition of 1913, 146
Stepanoff, Spiridon, 241
St. Lawrence Island, 203–206, *204*, 213
St. Lawrence Islanders, 207
St. Lawrence Island Yupik language, 205
   See also Yup'ik language (Central
     Yup'ik)
St. Michael, Alaska, 3
stones, siblings turning into, 119
Stories for Future Generations (Shield and
   Fienup-Riordan), 5
Stories the Old People Told (Silook), 215
storyknife tales, 4, 9
storyteller culture, 170, 188, 209–210
storytelling, 5, 194
   elements of, good, 208–209;
     intertwined, 65; *qulirat* (tales, long
     stories), 42, 54, 55, 57
   endings, 63, 210
   gift of, 5
   learning, 243
   performance cues, 171
   skill of, 192–193
   sound effects, 9, 32
   teaching through, 30–31, 84–85, 130,
     190, 244
   themes in Iñupiaq, 130
   voice used for, 244
   by women, 4, 9
   written versions, 241
storytelling, traditional forms
   aipaani (time periods of unwritten
     history), 198

issaq (time periods of unwritten
   history), 198
qanemciq (historical narrative), 4
quliaqtuaq (historical narrative), 131
qulirat (tales, long stories), 4, 10, 42, 54,
   55, 57
ungipamsuk (historical narrative), 205
unigkuaq/unigkuat (stories from a
   distant time), 240
unipaghaan (legend, times no longer
   remembered), 205, 220
unipkaaq (old story, myth, legend), 130,
   146, 149
uqaluktuaq (historical narrative), 131
subsistence
   song of, 197–198
   teaching children traditional, 89
   See also hunting and trapping
Sugpiaq people (Sugpiat), 237–242, 256
Sugtestun/Alutiiq language, 238, 246, 257
Sukannana, 155
summer camp, 141, 239
supernatural beings (spirits)
   babies eating their mothers, 68–71
   escaping from, 7–8, 9, 151–168
   in storyknife tales, 9
supernaturalism. *See also* reality, dual
   hats become animals, 61
   in hero saga, 147–149, 151–168
   Kaaguagacungaq, story about, 7–8
   monster igloo, 165
   mouth on tundra, 166
   niulut hunters, 168
   in Sugpiaq stories, 240–241
swallows, 173

T

Taġiuġmiut (people of the salt water), 192
Taamituryag, 119
Tacirrarmiut, Alaska, 103
Tanqiulria, 78
Tapqaamiut (coastal people), 192
Tatqaviña (Katherine Cleveland), 142
teaching
   elders role in, 30–31, 190–191, 193–
     195, 198–199, 210
   Iñupiaq language, 142–145
   storytelling for, 30–31, 84–85, 130, 190,
     244
   traditional occupations, 89

traditions, 245
Yup'ik language, 8, 31
Teeluk, Martha, 4
Tegin'gaq, 84
Tennant, Edward, 5
Things of Our Ancestors (Meade and
Fienup-Riordan), 5
Thomas, Elsie, 141
Thomas, Hugh, 141
Tickett, Sarah (Saiḷaq), 144, 145
Tikiġaġmiut (Point Hope people), 129
Tikiġaq (Point Hope), 146, 147–158,
162–163, 167–168
story of, 151–168
Tikiġaq *nuna*, 149
Tikiġaq peninsula, 149
Tilak (Truman Cleveland), 142
Time for Drumming, A (Mather), 5
Timothy, Nancy, 147
Tiriq (George Gray), 145
Tiulana, Clara, 174, 175
Tiulana, Paul, 175
tobacco, 9
Tobeluk, Jeannie, 9
Togiak, Alaska, 84
Toksook Bay, 30, 31, 41, 89, 122n5
"Trading with the Siberian Man" (Silook),
215
trapping. *See* hunting and trapping
trickster figures, 148
Tuġutaq (Herbert Anungazuk's
grandmother), 195
tuberculosis, 141
Tuluŋigraq (Raven Man), 149
tundra
diet from, 2, 35, 37, 204
human mouth on, 166
markings on, 115
stories set on, 10–11
Tuntutuliak, Alaska, 31, 64
Tununak, Alaska, 4, 58, 122n5
tutgara'urluqellriik (grandchild-related
pair), 10
*Two Voyages to Russian America 1802–
1807* (Davydov), 244

U

Ugalaturuaq, 190
Ugiaġnaq (Teddy Jack), 135, 140

Ugiuvaŋmiut (King Island people), 127,
179, 180
Uilingiataq, 93–101
uivluar (wooden bowl), 46, 49, 51–54
Uivvaq (Cape Lisburne), 163, 165, 167
Ukalliq (Oquilluk), 171
Ukuŋniq, 148
Umkumiut, Alaska, 30, 89–90
Unangas/Unangan (Aleutian Islanders),
237, 238
Up'nerkillermiut, Alaska, 41
urination, 9, 19–21, 38, 69, 95
urine, 49, 66, 77, 122n8
Usugan, Frances (Piiyuuk), 41–42
the story as a gift to relatives, 5
Usugan, Martina, 30
Utqiaġviŋmiut (Barrow people), 129
Uwitelen, 212

V

Vancouver Island, Canada, 144
vanity, consequences of, 86–88
vengeance, 246–255, 257
voles, 17–19, 25
vomiting, 230–233

W

Waghiyi, Della, 205, 220–233
Waghiyi, John, 220
Wainwright, 128
Wales, 132, 188, 190, 198, 213
walking stick, 50
walrus, 191
bones, 191
hunting, 128, 204
skin, 153, 165, 191, 215
stomach, 176–177, 191
tusk, 167
Warbelow, Marvin, 140–141
Warbelow, Willi Lou, 140–141
waste, human, 87–88, 122n8
wealth, defined, 40
weasels as hats, 61
Whale Hunters of Tigara, The (Rainey), 146
whalers, trading with the, 216
whales. *See also specific whales*
giants who eat, 151–152
hunting, 128, 151
jaws, 153, 162

people, 160–161
skull, 152
When I Became Aware (Orr et al.), 5
whirlpool, 53–54
White, Natalia, 9, 12–29
White Mountain, 141
winter camp, 2, 139, 140, 239
wishes, granting, 86–88
wives. *See also* women
   hiding food from husbands, 33–34
   killed by husbands, 157, 160, 161
   leaving husbands behind, 34–38, 49–52,
     155–156
   left by husbands, 109, 113–115
   loneliness of, 47, 48
   qat'ngutek (spouse-exchange partners), 67
   responsibilities of, 39–40, 49
   unfaithful, 165
   who ask too much of husbands, 160
Wolf Dance, of King Island, 169–179
wolverine ears, 172–173
wolves, 173
women. *See also* wives
   as bears, 155–160
   berry picking, 247, 252
   preparing food for husbands, 33–34
   restricted substances from, 66
   unmarried, inaccessible, 93–101
women, old, 10. *See also* grandmother(s)
   determining pregnancy, 45
   jellyfish, 166
   Kaaguagacungaq, story about, 7–8
   as supernatural beings, 7–10, 17–25,
     161–162, 166
Wongittilin, Nick, 220
Woodbury, Anthony, 5, 221
Worm, Mary, 11

punctuation, 8
terracing, 42
verse format, 41
dialects, 102–103, 205
geographic region, 129
immersion, 41
orthography, 4, 103, 221–223
phonological features, 221–223
taped documentation of, 4–5
Yup'ik Language Center (YLC), 4, 7,
   258nn8–10
Yup'ik literature, 1–6
   bilingual publications of, 4
   chapter marks in, 65
   documenting, 3–4, 11
   illustrating, 4, 9
   landscape element in, 105
   sound effects, 9
   to teach values, 84–85
   traditional, 65
Yup'ik people and culture, 1–4
   death in, 11, 27–29, 38
   early documentation of, 3
   learning in, 89
   non-Native influence on, 2–3
Yup'ik Lore (Tennant and Bitar), 5
Yup'ik Words of Wisdom (Rearden et al.), 5

Y

Yupigestun culture, 209
Yupigestun language, 205
Yukon-Kuskokwim delta, 1–2, *2*
Yukon River, 71
Yupiit Qanruyutait (Rearden et al.), 5
Yupik (Yupiget) of Chukchi Peninsula, 203
Yup'ik language (Central Yup'ik), 3, 238
   compositional structure
     dashes used in translation, 42
     line-initial particles, 32
     lines and stanzas, 221